LET'S GET TO WORK!

THE FUTURE OF LABOUR IN EUROPE

VOL. 1

Let's Get to Work!

The Future of Labour in Europe

Vol. 1

Edited by

Miroslav Beblavý
Ilaria Maselli
Marcela Veselková

Contributors

László Andor
Miroslav Beblavý
Iain Begg
Baptiste Boitier
Verena Drabing
Marina Fischer-Kowalski
Willi Haas
Ferry Koster
János Mátyás Kovács
Nicolas Lancesseur
Ilaria Maselli
Nicole van der Gaag
Olaf van Vliet
Marcela Veselková
Paul Zagamé

Centre for European Policy Studies (CEPS)
Brussels

The Centre for European Policy Studies (CEPS) is an independent policy research institute in Brussels. Its mission is to produce sound policy research leading to constructive solutions to the challenges facing Europe. The views expressed in this book are entirely those of the authors and should not be attributed to CEPS, the European Union or to any other institution with which they are associated.

ISBN 978-94-6138-406-5

Centre for European Policy Studies
Place du Congrès 1, B-1000 Brussels
Tel: (32.2) 229.39.11 Fax: (32.2) 219.41.51
E-mail: info@ceps.eu
Internet: www.ceps.eu

TABLE OF CONTENTS (OVERVIEW)

TABLE OF CONTENTS (IN DETAIL)

List of Figures

LIST OF TABLES

FOREWORD

Europe's labour market has been caught up in the seven-year storm created by the financial and economic crises. Unemployment has grown to record-high levels in the EU and especially within the eurozone. At the same time, Europe has experienced unprecedented divergences in employment and social outcomes across the member states.

This long and complex crisis has deprived many people of meaningful economic and social opportunities, resulting in a waste of human capital. The 'margins' of Europe's labour market are quite large today, with many people experiencing precariousness and underemployment, if they can find jobs at all.

As the financial, economic and fiscal crises reinforced each other against the backdrop of an incomplete Economic and Monetary Union, investors as well as citizens started to lose confidence in the EU project. Some governments have lost their ability to promote economic recovery and to address longer-term structural challenges affecting Europe's labour markets.

Key among these challenges are the ageing and shrinking of our workforce, the polarisation of the labour market associated with the phasing out of routine jobs, growing resource scarcity and climate change, and increasing technological competition from other parts of the world. Tackling these challenges requires structural public policy responses and investments.

The sovereign debt crisis put pressure both on countercyclical public spending and on *social investment* through public services, human capital development and support for people's transitions into the labour market. The EU has striven to respond to the economic crisis, the social emergency and the longer-term structural challenges by developing a more robust repertoire of policy options as well as through stronger policy coordination.

The Europe 2020 Strategy, agreed in June 2010, established employment, social inclusion and environmental targets as core elements of Europe's socio-economic development model. However, due to the eurozone crisis, the EU employment rate for 20-64 year-olds has actually fallen to 68.3% in 2013 instead of rising towards the 2020 target of 75%, and the risk of poverty and social exclusion has grown rather than diminished.

In 2012, the European Commission put forward an Employment Package that articulated an ambitious policy agenda for a job-rich recovery. Expanding upon the European Employment Strategy, the package outlined measures to boost demand for labour, plans to harness the job creation potential of the green, white[*] and digital economy, as well as steps towards a genuine European labour market with easier and higher-quality labour mobility across countries.

A recommendation on establishing a Youth Guarantee was then agreed in 2013 as a major structural reform (and investment) focused on improving school-to-work transitions. The Social Investment Package of 2013 has shown ways of further modernising the welfare state, focusing on 'capacitating' expenditure and public services that enable people to maximise their participation in the labour market and society.

All these initiatives were guided by the concept of a *dynamic and inclusive labour market* and by an awareness of the need for proactive public policy in helping integrate the less productive workforce into employment. This is necessary in view of the Europe 2020 employment target, but also in order to combat social exclusion and increase productivity in the longer run.

Compared to the pre-crisis years, the European Semester now provides a much stronger and integrated framework for employment policy coordination than the original open method of coordination. There is growing acceptance of the need for convergence towards certain quality standards in employment and social policies, even if these may not be enshrined in hard law. That said, a lot of progress still remains to be made in properly taking into account the synergies and trade-offs between fiscal, monetary and structural policies, including employment and social policies, both at European and national levels.

---

[*] Health, care and related services.

The NEUJOBS project has been very helpful in providing analytical background in the development of stronger employment and social policies in the first half of the 2010s, particularly because of its longer-term perspective on demographic, environmental and technological developments affecting Europe's labour markets and the character of work.

Seminars discussing interim NEUJOBS findings facilitated direct exchanges between researchers and policy-makers, enabling the project to make an impact in real time. Many valuable synergies emerged between the various strands of NEUJOBS and the in-house analytical work of the European Commission, particularly the annual reviews of *Employment and Social Developments in Europe*.

As the NEUJOBS project approaches the final stages of its work programme and a new generation of policy-makers enters the European Parliament and Commission in 2014, the findings of NEUJOBS can certainly provide a lot of useful input in further adapting Europe's economic, employment and social policies to the objectives of smart, sustainable and inclusive growth. This growth will inevitably need to be based on more *dynamic* and more *inclusive* labour markets.

Lászlo Andor
European Commissioner
for Employment, Social Affairs and Inclusion

ACKNOWLEDGMENTS

The editors would like to thank the entire network of the NEUJOBS project for the strong commitment shown throughout the project as well as in the preparation of this book.

They are particularly grateful for the enormous assistance provided by Elisa Martellucci in all stages of the book preparation, from its conception to its dissemination and they also wish to acknowledge her valuable contribution to the CEPS Special Report "Workplace Innovation and Technological Change", on which chapter 6 in based. They would also like to thank CEPS Director Daniel Gros whose interventions are as valuable as they are infrequent and their former colleague Anna-Elisabeth Thum without whom much of this would not have happened.

The editors would also like to thank Amin Bahrami for diligent assistance in the last stages, Anil Shamdasani and Anne Harrington for patiently improving the text and Els Van den Broeck and John Hates for improving its appearance.

János Kovács thanks Christina Pössel and Manuel Tröster for the excellent coordination of the work package. Verena Dräbing thanks Anton Hemerijck, Barbara Vis, Franca van Hooren and Ilaria Maselli for their fruitful comments and support.

1. THE FUTURE OF LABOUR IN EUROPE: AN OVERVIEW[*]

Work is not only an essential part of our daily lives, but also one of the top policy concerns across Europe. Unfortunately, the public debate of labour issues is all too often driven by political rhetoric and short-term concerns. In this volume, researchers from seven European countries attempt to explain in easily accessible language what the findings from various social sciences mean for the future of labour in Europe. Their findings are addressed not only to policy-makers, business persons, fellow academics and journalists, but to any concerned individual who is interested in the shape, size and character of the labour markets of tomorrow and beyond.

Since February 2011, the Centre for European Policy Studies (CEPS) has been deeply engaged as the coordinator of a major research project funded by the European Commission called NEUJOBS. This volume presents the results and policy recommendations distilled from the research and discussions that have taken place among the 29 partner institutes in the first half of the NEUJOBS project. A second volume will follow with a particular focus on employment in specific sectors, such as transport, energy and housing, and for specific groups in the labour force, notably women, elderly and migrants.

Our objective has been to analyse possible future developments in European labour market(s) under the main assumption that European societies are now facing or preparing to face profound transitions, or what we call 'megatrends', that will have a major impact on employment, particularly for some groups in the labour force or sectors of the economy. These natural and societal megatrends will reshape the global conditions

---

[*] Chapter 1 was drafted by Ilaria Maselli and Miroslav Beblavý with the objective of providing a general overview of the book, writing in their capacity as Deputy Coordinator and Coordinator of the NEUJOBS project, respectively.

for Europe, posing numerous challenges to societies and policy-makers in the area of labour. 'Societal megatrends' take the form of demographic transition, the ongoing shifts in the economic and political centres of gravity worldwide, the growing use of information and communication technologies and the related new forms of knowledge-sharing. By 'natural megatrends', we mean the increasing volatility of climate change, the energy transition from fossil fuels to renewable energy sources and rising challenges to resource security, all of which can be expected to have far-reaching implications for production and consumption patterns of European societies.

Since expectations for the severity of the changes vary, we distinguish between 'friendly' and 'tough' variants of each megatrend in two distinct time frames: by 2025 and by 2050. We then use these predictions to model global scenarios for Europe.

In chapter 2, we sketch three strategies for European policy-makers to cope with changing global conditions. Policymakers will react to the changes by choosing from scenarios ranging from 'business-as-usual' to 'substantial transformation' to 'sustainability'. Not only the choice but also the success of the response strategies will largely depend on the global conditions that actually materialise in the future.

This introductory chapter presents an overview of the nine other chapters in this volume, which are themselves summaries of a multitude of research papers produced in the context of the NEUJOBS project. We have elected to highlight here only the most consequential and surprising of the findings, leaving the reader to discover the full story in the individual chapters. And, of course, all of the original research is freely accessible on the NEUJOBS website (www.neujobs.eu).

1.1 How many workers for how many jobs?

Among the major variables that are likely to transform European labour markets, demographic developments are expected to have the strongest impact. There is a consensus on three trends that will impact Europe's labour market in the coming decades:

- The aging European population is a major policy problem. Even under optimistic scenarios, most European countries will see their working-age population shrink. By 2030, the European labour force will number between 279 and 302 million workers (under a 'tough' and 'friendly' scenario, respectively).

- The decrease in the labour supply, combined with the upgrading of skills ('upskilling') of the population, will lead to wage increases. The projections in both the 'tough' and 'friendly' scenarios suggest that higher wages will provide relief for public finances and partially compensate for the increase in pension and healthcare bills.

- Overall employment will be determined not only by demographic dynamics, but also by the macroeconomic health of the continent.

Even under the assumptions implicit in the 'friendly' scenario – high fertility, extended life expectancy and increased immigration – most EU countries cannot escape the prospect in the short term of a declining working-age population, while improvements in life expectancy can have only a minor impact. Even though migration can bring about immediate changes in population growth, it is unlikely to be able to fully compensate for a decline in the working-age population due to aging (although different countries may have different opportunities to increase their labour supply).

Marcela Veselková et al. explain in chapter 3 the importance of recognising that increasing or decreasing working-age populations will not automatically lead to changes in the number of workers or in the total number of hours worked, as labour supply also depends on labour market participation. Two more factors need to be taken into account: the labour market participation of this older population and the number of hours per week each individual is willing to work. Based on these factors, policies aimed at counterbalancing aging need to be targeted by country; for instance, labour market participation is still low in Hungary and Italy, while efforts to increase the number of hours worked may prove more effective in the Netherlands, Germany and Denmark.

The authors found strong divergences in the evolution of skill levels in the labour supply projections for Europe. The evolution of the low-skilled labour supply is similar in both scenarios; the difference arises from the supply of high-skilled labour. In the 'friendly' scenario, the potential quantity of high-skilled workers reaches almost 105 million in 2030, but only 83 million in the 'tough' scenario (i.e. 20% lower). This decrease in the labour force in terms of both quantity and, in the 'tough' scenario, quality reduces long-term potential economic growth and makes the rebalancing of European public finances more painful.

However, employment in the next decade will depend not only on the demographic dynamics, but also on the macroeconomic conditions of the continent, as Marcela Veselková et al. report in the second part of chapter 3. European GDP is expected to grow at an annual rate of 1.2% in the 'tough' scenario and 1.8% in the 'friendly' one. This translates into a net job creation that varies from no rise in employment in the 'tough' scenario to an annual creation of 1.5 million jobs in the 'friendly' scenario.

There is lasting destruction of low-skilled employment in the tradable sectors in both scenarios. In the non-tradable sectors, low-skilled employment is more protected, but the projections are still pessimistic compared to past trends. High-skilled employment in the non-tradable sectors is growing fast and is the major contributor to employment creation in both scenarios.

In the 'friendly' scenario, employment growth is mainly driven by the creation of an additional 15 million jobs in the private services sector between 2010 and 2030. The construction sector also exhibits non-negligible job creation, with 3.9 million additional jobs over the same period. In the 'tough' scenario, the fall in employment is large in the non-market services, with 3.1 million fewer jobs in 2030 compared to 2010. In the private services sector, employment creation of only 3.5 million jobs is estimated, which is much lower than in the more optimistic scenario. In both scenarios, most jobs are destroyed in the agriculture and industry sectors.

Technological progress also has a major impact on the evolution of the employment structure. The development of ICT enables the opening of a growing range of services to international competition, and can result in the replacement of workers in a factory by machines, or of workers in an office by a computer programme. This rising phenomenon induces polarisation of labour markets.

The organisation of human labour will also be significantly transformed by the transition away from fossil fuels. We assume that both rising costs of energy generation and a declining energy return on investment (EROI) will make energy more costly and less abundant. Sooner or later, energy consumption will become quite expensive, particularly in rural areas. If scarcity should dominate the future of resource use, it might have two substantial impacts. First, the share of jobs in activities related to supplying society with material and energy would rise due to both lower energy returns on energy invested and the declining quality of ore. Second, if commodity prices remain high or rise even further, this trend could substantially alter business strategies. A decline in continuously available, low-cost energy could lead to reduced substitution of human labour by mechanical energy, and thus increase the proportion of physical work performed in our everyday life.

Rising fossil energy prices would also have an impact on sectoral employment; energy-intensive goods and services become less attractive as energy prices rise. For example, employment in the transport and equipment sector is reduced by 15% over the period. However, this price increase will stimulate demand in the energy renovation sub-sector, which is labour intensive, and thus boost employment in the construction sector.

As the authors of chapter 6, we argue that the nature of work has also been changing. Workplace innovation can be a driver for changes towards sustainable forms of productivity gains. What does this mean in practical terms? In everyday working life, workplace innovation is translated into a number of specific actions such as flexi-time, teleworking, alternative payment schemes, employee empowerment and autonomy, task rotation and multi-skilling, team work and team autonomy. Evidence supports the notion that workplace innovation is beneficial for the economy as a whole, as well as for employees and employers. Despite the economic potential and more accessible technologies, we observe in the data that innovative practices still concern a minority of workers in most European countries. Moreover, only limited development has occurred over the last decade in this area. The authors suggest various explanations for this resistance, ranging from cost-related obstacles to a reluctance to move first and uncertainty about the results. New modes of working generate doubts and fears, which result in an uneven spread both geographically and across different practices.

Flexi-time, teleworking and alternative payment schemes still concern a minority of workers, whereas more qualitative elements, such as teamwork, team autonomy and task rotation, are more widespread.

The Nordic countries are in the lead when it comes to workplace innovation: Denmark, Sweden and Finland (as well as the Netherlands) rank highest in the diffusion of new ways of working, which are much more widespread in these countries than in the Mediterranean countries like Spain, Portugal, Greece and Italy. In between are the Baltic countries – Latvia, Estonia and Lithuania – which occupy the middle rank, creating a model of 'post-communist, almost-Nordics'. The most interesting case is Slovenia, which ranks fifth – just after the Nordic countries and the Netherlands – and has the same widespread diffusion across all elements.

We offer one major policy recommendation in our chapter 6 to overcome the obstacles and ensure that workplace innovation takes place: the public sector should be mandated to lead by example. A successful change in an environment that is often considered less productive and hostile to change could send an important message to the wider corporate world that workplace innovation leads to increased productivity, efficiency and sustainability.

1.2   Skills, polarisation and inequality: The long-term pattern

In an economy with a shrinking labour force, the main source of growth becomes productivity, which is (among other factors) a function of human capital. Therefore, Miroslav Beblavý and Marcela Veselková aim in chapter 7 to extract and synthesise the findings in NEUJOBS research on the relationship between education and labour markets. Their analysis is driven by the following research questions: What can we expect as higher education is extended to the masses? Which university degrees are worth pursuing? Is later tracking of students an answer to educational inequality and how likely is it to be politically successful? How can low-skilled individuals improve their skills in later stages of their lives – going back to school or learning on the job? What does it even mean to be a low-skilled worker?

In order to understand how the universalisation of higher education might take place and to explore its consequences, the authors conduct an in-depth study of the experiences of the universalisation of upper-secondary education in six European countries. Their findings are very interesting. The enrolment rates in upper secondary education expanded rapidly in the post-World War II period, although the pace of expansion differed: it was slower in the leading countries, such as the United Kingdom or Sweden, and laggards were able to catch up relatively quickly once the limiting conditions were removed. As a result, education systems are less selective today than they were 60 years ago. Nevertheless, there are still significant differences between countries. The authors confirm that later tracking and early childhood education might enhance the equality of educational opportunities. Despite this finding, elite forms of education stubbornly survive, even in the mass and universal stages of education systems.

It is difficult to predict future trends in this field, as they will result from opposing forces. On the one hand, continuing advocacy of later tracking by international organisations – such as the OECD and UNESCO – will create incentives for governments to converge towards 'best practices'. On the other hand, the continuing privatisation of education systems will work as a counterforce to the above trend. As a result of the neo-liberal revolution, the monopoly of the state as provider of education has been eroded and we are witnessing an increasing privatisation of the public sphere. Free choice of school may undermine efforts to increase equality of educational opportunities, because freedom in the selection of schools by pupils and pupils by schools tends to lead to segmentation and segregation.

After finishing upper secondary education, those entering university tend to prefer the humanities and social sciences over the so-called 'STEM' (science, technology, engineering and mathematics) courses. The authors therefore examine whether it is more beneficial to study engineering or art. To answer this question, they calculate the net present value of university studies five years after graduation for five European countries: France, Italy, Hungary, Poland and Slovenia.

Surprisingly, it was not the STEM degrees that ensured the highest return on investment, but rather, the social science degrees. Graduates of art, the humanities and education obtained the lowest net present value. Based on this evidence, the expansion of enrolment in fields such as economics, business and law can be explained by rational choice. However, despite the different economic fortunes of university graduates, the authors found that with the exception of Italy, private investment in education largely repays itself after five years.

What about the prospects for the low-skilled? The 'low-skilled' label can hide a number of different situations: apart from dropping out of school early, it can also be caused by labour market detachment, migration, possession of obsolete skills, as well as macroeconomic structural changes. In other words, you can be 'low-skilled' after leaving school, but you can also become so during your working life. For this reason, the numbers of low-skilled workers in the labour force will fluctuate over time, depending on various circumstances.

However, the meaning of the term 'low-skilled' needs to be clarified. An analysis of job advertisements in three countries – the Czech Republic, Denmark and Ireland – showed that the set of skills demanded for low- and medium-skilled occupations varies widely from one country to another. For example, Slovak employers tend to be quite demanding even for jobs that are marked as 'elementary' in the International Classification of Occupation (ISCO). They require not only an upper secondary education, but also language abilities and soft skills, such as a strong work ethic, a positive attitude or flexibility. Overall, our research indicates that the term 'low-skilled jobs' might be a misnomer. Since not only the size, but also the structure and other characteristics of low-skilled unemployment differ widely from one country to another, these findings should sound a strong call to policy-makers, in both EU and national institutions, to take not only a differentiated view, but also a holistic and more sophisticated view of this phenomenon.

The likelihood of different societal groups acquiring skills and training differs in later stages of life. The results in chapter 7 imply that older cohorts are less likely to participate in training. Furthermore, lifelong learning is also determined by individual characteristics. Whereas men and immigrants are more likely to obtain an upper secondary education in their adult life, native-born citizens are more likely to achieve tertiary education. Contrary to the existing literature, results here imply that higher-educated individuals tend to participate less in training than those with other levels of education.

Overall, the different strands of work in the interplay between education and the labour market lead us to assess recent and future developments in terms of job polarisation based on skills. Rising demand at the upper and lower ends of the occupational skills distribution took place during the decade from 1998 to 2008. Job polarisation also occurred in 17 out of 25 EU countries between 2000 and 2010. The authors analysed labour demand and supply with respect to skills and tasks in an attempt to anticipate what types of skills mismatch EU countries will encounter over the next decade. The European Centre for the Development of Vocational Training (CEDEFOP) forecasts that this trend will continue until 2020; new jobs will be concentrated in higher and lower skill-level occupations, with slower growth in the mid-level ones. Simultaneously, it is expected that with the expanding education sector we will see a continuing replacement of low-skilled workers by medium-skilled workers. This means that the medium-skilled might temporarily assume positions for which they are overqualified. The call for policy-makers is therefore to tackle polarisation, as it is likely to increase socio-economic inequalities within societies along lines of ethnicity, gender, age and skill.

1.3   What exactly do we mean by 'work'?

Human society – willingly or not, slowly or quickly – is in a transition away from the use of fossil fuels. This transition is expected to have implications that are as numerous and as far-reaching for human labour as those resulting from the transition towards the fossil fuel-based industrial society. Understanding the future of labour therefore implies more than simply looking at which sectors will be more or less successful and how many jobs will be created or destroyed. In chapter 4, Marina Fisher-Kowalski and Willi Haas question what work actually means, and what it is likely to mean under a different pattern of interaction between nature and society (the so-called 'socio-metabolic regime').

In quantitative terms, it is observed that the share of time humans spend on reproduction, the household and their community/economy changes with the socio-metabolic regime. In mature agrarian systems, not only were the number of working hours very high but a great majority of the population was preoccupied with producing sufficient food for most of their lives. In the coal-based industrial regime, the availability of energy facilitated the use of additional labour provided cheaply by the first demographic transition. A change was observed after World War II: as oil becomes dominant, a substitution was observed between labour and technical energy. This pattern may soon be reversed due to the increases in the price of raw materials, which could substantially alter business strategies. We can expect a shift in the dominant mode of cost reduction from labour to resources. In this case, it is not the increase of labour productivity that would be the key measure, but rather the saving of resources, possibly at the expense of more labour.

Their chapter also considers qualitative characterisations of human labour, with attention paid to three basic capacities: physical power, knowledge, and rationality and empathy. The prediction is that the long-term decrease in the use of physical labour will be reversed due to an increase of labour demand in sectors such as energy, agriculture, construction and repair/renovation, which are notably labour intensive. In view of an aging and increasingly culturally heterogeneous and demanding population, the authors also assume an increase in the type of work that is based on empathy. This is embedded in all those services, such as caretaking, that are very difficult to substitute by ICT and almost impossible to outsource to other countries because they involve face-to-face contact with recipients of the services.

1.4   What role for the state in the labour market?

What is, and what should be, the role of the state in a labour market comprised of older but more highly-skilled workers facing strong international competition and a potentially very different production environment? Currently, the competencies of the state fall mainly into two areas: the elaboration of institutions to enhance the labour market and the provision of services for workers through welfare systems to correct the negative consequences it may have (namely, reducing unemployment risks, preventing income loss and enhancing the transition of the labour market). National regulators still hold most of the competencies in this field, with European integration progressing in first steps over the last decades. Western, central and eastern European countries have converged, albeit slowly, in terms of their labour market institutions. However, we cannot speak of a single 'European social model'. The level of employment protection varies considerably across European countries, and some countries tend to put more emphasis on the protection of regular workers while others are more focused on protecting temporary workers. Furthermore, government spending on labour market policies varies considerably.

Labour market institutions also work differently, depending on the sector. Our research found that innovative sectors are much more sensitive to extensive protection of incumbents and labour market rigidity.

Another issue concerns the interplay between different institutions that protect income rather than employment and jobs. The results on this front are in line with the literature on 'flexicurity' in that employment protection legislation and unemployment benefits can be considered substitutes. The authors of chapter 9, Ferry Koster and Olaf van Vliet, also detected a general trend towards reduced employment protection legislation over the last decade, which may be the explanation for renewed calls from workers for job security.

As described by János Kovács in chapter 5, when workers were asked what mattered to them most with regard to the quality of their work, job security (in the sense of stable employment) dominated not only most of the 'post-materialist' values, but also the 'traditional materialist' quality features such as decent pay, appropriate physical working conditions (including health and safety at the workplace) and fixed working time. Moreover, the concept of the presumed 'north-south' cultural divide in employment discourses should be questioned. The case studies demonstrate the strength of global/transnational impacts, including those of the EU; they cut across national borders, homogenise the concept of job quality to a considerable extent, and turn large, cutting-edge firms into islands within which the employees order their preferences for good jobs quite independently of the dominant narratives of their countries' elites.

1.5 The state as a service provider: The call for a social-investment approach to social policies

An even more important role can be played by the welfare state. Our findings call for policy-makers to shift the functions of European welfare systems away from correcting the negative impacts of labour markets towards a social-investment perspective. As Verena Dräbing explains in chapter 8, the underlying assumption of social investment is that welfare spending on certain policies can contribute to economic development. Its core goals are to enable citizens to help themselves throughout their lives and to reduce their neediness. These policies are characterised by three areas of focus: societal development; human development and capacitating citizens; and the long-term reduction of neediness instead of short-term mitigation. The key areas of interest include education, quality childcare, training, job-search assistance and rehabilitation.

Although public perceptions may suggest otherwise, welfare states are not de facto immune to change. Following World War II, in an era of Keynesianism and predominantly male-breadwinner households, the focus of social policies was on the creation of jobs via public investment and on the increase in social expenditure on unemployment benefits, pension benefits, survivor and disability benefits, public healthcare and education. With the onset of the oil shocks in the 1970s, this model began to come under pressure. The rise of neo-liberalism as the dominant economic paradigm led to a series of privatisations, increased flexibility of the labour market and a retrenchment of public spending.

In the early 1990s, new social risks increased the pressure on European welfare states. Among these are risks related to changes in family structure and gender roles: a higher prevalence of single-parenthood, difficulties reconciling work and care, and the growth in the number of frail relatives. In addition, the shift from an industrial to a service economy rendered some skills obsolete, resulting in the dismissal of employees. In the same vein, the need for low-skilled workers decreased, creating a new risk group of workers with low and superfluous skills. Aside from the rise of new social risks, aging societies increased the pressure on the welfare state while at the same time prompting the question of how economic productivity levels can be maintained while the workforce shrinks. Specifically, social security needs to take care of single and well-educated mothers, as well as older workers dismissed from factories that have outsourced their production to China, while at the same time ensuring that the workforce as a whole is competitive. The resulting questions of how much welfare can be afforded and which productivity-increasing measures are available sparked the rise of the social investment debate. What are examples of social investment policies? And are they actually in place in European countries?

Social investment policies are also labelled 'capacitating' as they enhance labour market participation. Care services for the elderly and children are therefore included, as they facilitate female employment, along with leave policies. Expenditure on education and active labour market policies are included due to their strong focus on human capital development, as well as funding of public research. Data on public expenditure in this field suggest a tendency towards an increase in social investment expenditure on families, active labour market policies and education. However, a clear divide across countries is apparent: eastern and southern European welfare states continue to spend much less on social investment per capita. Nordic countries have been the forerunners of social investment, while Christian-democratic countries and, to some extent, Anglo-Saxon countries have been catching up. It is clear that investment in family policies is on the rise, especially in childcare services, but for the most part regime patterns still persist. A slow but general shift towards a stronger reconciliation of work and care is thus taking place, although overall levels of investment are still lower in southern and some eastern European welfare states.

1.6   What's next? And after that?

What are our recommendations for policy-makers at the EU level? Iain Begg suggests in chapter 10 a clear line of action: the reconciliation of the short-term goals dictated by the crisis afflicting Europe and the long-term goals driven by the societal, economic and ecological challenges. These transitions are a common concern, so it is vital to stress the collective costs and benefits of policy action and to recognise that collective long-term gains will often exceed short-term cost savings. An implication is that policy-makers should consider a collective discount rate for assessing such long-term gains. For example, in its governance processes (notably the annual cycle of the European semester and the country-specific recommendations), the European Commission and the Council should place more emphasis on medium- and long-run objectives for labour market institutions, including proposing milestones for their evolution.

Last but not least, a general line of conduct should follow the rationale that, since the relationship between labour market institutions and the behaviour of stakeholders is complex, simplistic policies (whether neo-liberal or social-democratic) are likely to be unhelpful. There is also a strong risk of either unintended consequences or of outcomes that satisfy one set of goals or normative considerations at the expense of another. The reform agenda therefore needs to be sensitive to such tensions.

The success of the socio-ecological transition, however, will depend not only on policies, but also on how natural resources and societies evolve. Megatrends in the evolution of climate change, resource scarcity, population and knowledge-sharing will result in a more or less 'friendly' world, for which different response strategies will be appropriate. In a 'tough' world, the sustainability transformation strategy might be the most suitable because it provides the vision and social cohesion required to overcome the hardships and challenges of a world shaped by ongoing and future transitions. This strategy is better suited to dealing with international volatility and supply shocks by focusing on inter-European activities and adaptation, thereby inducing changes towards a resilient and sustainable socio-metabolic regime with an emphasis on societal welfare rather than on increasing economic activity.

In a 'friendly' world, policy-makers should target an ecological modernisation strategy, given that market-based strategies work best under more stable and smooth conditions in which economic actors can adjust their expectations and implement investment activities accordingly. Structural change can then be brought about with relatively minimal distortions or negative side effects. Finally, irrespective of the state of the world, business-as-usual strategies need to be avoided, as they have proved incapable of coping with changing global conditions.

2. EMERGING MEGATRENDS AND SCENARIOS IN THE SOCIO-ECOLOGICAL TRANSITIONS*

This chapter will succinctly acquaint readers with the vision of the future on which the other chapters in this book are based. It is a vision of the future, or rather various possible futures, under the conditions of the socio-ecological transition and its consequences for employment overall, but also for key sectors and relevant groups. Specifically, the chapter describes the socio-ecological transition (SET) away from fossil fuels, which can be observed in two sets of megatrends. Megatrends in natural conditions include energy transition, rising challenges to resource security and increasing climate change impacts. Societal megatrends include demographic changes, shifting of economic and political centres of gravity, and growing use of information and communication technologies (ICT) and knowledge-sharing. The uncertainty and complexity associated with these megatrends are condensed into two alternative futures: a 'friendly' and a 'tough' world. These two alternatives delineate European policy options. Although Europe cannot influence the speed and the intensity of the unfolding of the socio-ecological transition, it must be ready to address the challenges it brings. Three European response strategies are proposed: i) no policy change, ii) ecological modernisation and eco-efficiency and iii)

---

* Chapter 2 was compiled by Marcela Veselková and Miroslav Beblavý based on the work of Marina Fischer-Kowalski, Willi Haas, Dominik Wiedenhofer, Ulli Weisz, Irene Pallua, Nikolaus Possanner and Ekke Weis (from the University of Klagenfurt) and Arno Behrens, Giulia Serio and Monica Alessi (from CEPS) in work package 1 (Socio-ecological transition and employment implications) of the NEUJOBS project.

sustainability transformation. The effectiveness of these strategies will depend on the respective alternative future.

The challenges associated with the socio-ecological transition away from fossil fuels can be expected to have far-reaching implications for production and consumption patterns, as well as for many other features of society. A change in an energy regime induces changes in society and other modifications in natural systems that occur either as an unintended consequence (such as resource exhaustion or pollution) or as intentional change induced by society (such as land use). These patterns of interaction between society and nature are known as 'socio-metabolic' regimes.[1]

What drives socio-metabolic regime transitions? On such a broad and long-term scale, one cannot easily talk about actors and their deliberate efforts. What one can mainly analyse is structural change of interlinked social and natural systems, across a broad range of variables. The socio-metabolic approach thus shares with complex systems theory the notion of 'emergence': one state cannot be deliberately transformed into another, and neither can the process be fully controlled. One is confronted with self-organising dynamics to which orderly governance or steering cannot be applied.[2] The socio-metabolic approach therefore focuses on a relatively narrow set describing the society-nature interface for which quantitative measurements can be reliably obtained in very different contexts. The advantage of this restraint is that it is possible to empirically demonstrate the interconnectedness of socio-economic changes and changes in natural systems (between population growth, diets, land use and species extinction, for example).

2.1 Introducing global scenarios

Historical socio-ecological transitions, such as the fossil fuel-based industrialisation of Europe and elsewhere, led to a new type of society with unprecedented levels of natural resource extraction and energy and material consumption for approximately 15% of the world's population. These were accompanied by an equally unprecedented growth in scientific and technical knowledge and democracy. These transitions led to a ten-fold increase in global material use and a seven-fold

The impact of human activity on natural systems has been accelerated by the ongoing industrialisation of emerging economies.

increase in domestic energy consumption (corresponding to an even larger 12-fold increase in total primary energy supply) in the period from 1900 to

2009.[3] During the same time, world GDP increased by a factor of 26 and the global population quadrupled.[4]

This transition is not only historical but is still ongoing. Economists use the term 'emerging economy' to refer to a country in the take-off or acceleration phase of the socio-ecological transition from an agrarian to an industrial regime, following pretty much the same pathway that mature industrial countries took in the centuries and decades before, based on the use of fossil fuels (increasingly, again, coal). Due to their much larger populations (comprising 60% of the world's population), the ecological impact of their transitions – in terms of climate; biodiversity; soil, air and water pollution; depletion of fish stocks in the oceans; and nutrient washout into the oceans – would be huge, much larger than the impact of the historical transitions of the mature industrial countries. From the point of view of resource scarcity, however, it remains questionable whether this process will indeed take place or whether it will be abruptly halted in the middle of its acceleration.

Between 1900 and 2009, industrialisation led to a ten-fold increase in global material use and a seven-fold increase in domestic energy consumption.

There is ample evidence provided by global change research that human activity caused, and continues to cause, major changes in the functioning of natural systems on every spatial scale – from local to global – and is transforming the earth's system at an increasingly rapid pace.[5] Such changes are now being accelerated by the ongoing process of industrialisation in the populous emerging economies. Thus, imagining 2025, or even more so 2050, the expansive continuation of the industrial socio-metabolic regime for a majority of the world seems biophysically infeasible and threatens to further erode humanity's natural base.

It is very hard to predict precisely *how fast* these changes will happen. What is not subject to debate, however, is that some of them *will* happen, such as the exhaustion of cheap fossil fuels and a number of other natural resources, and – to say the least – increasing volatility of the climate system. Indeed, some of these developments can already be observed. Fischer-Kowalski et al. refer to these developments as "global megatrends in natural conditions", the biophysical part of the on-going socio-ecological transition.[6] Still, these changes occur in response to, or as a consequence of, the continuing socio-ecological transition towards fossil fuel-based industrial societies and – sooner or later – will inevitably impose a new socio-ecological transition on societies away from fossil fuels. The global megatrends in natural conditions include energy transitions (towards and away from fossil fuels), rising challenges to resource security and increasing climate change impacts. Furthermore, it is possible to observe elements of the social part of the socio-ecological transition that are related to social and technical achievements generated by the last transition. Fischer-Kowalski et al. call these 'global societal megatrends', and they include the continuation of the global demographic transition, the ongoing shifts in the economic and political centres of gravity worldwide, and the growing use of ICT plus the related new forms of knowledge-sharing. These megatrends are fundamentally reshaping the global framework conditions for Europe. The speed of these megatrends and their magnitude are open to debate. Therefore, for each megatrend Fischer-Kowalski et al. distinguish between 'friendly' and 'tough' variants by 2025 and by 2050, and use these as global framework scenarios for the European policy option space.

Figure 2.1 The socio-economic reproduction of Europe in a global context shaped by the ongoing socio-ecological transitions

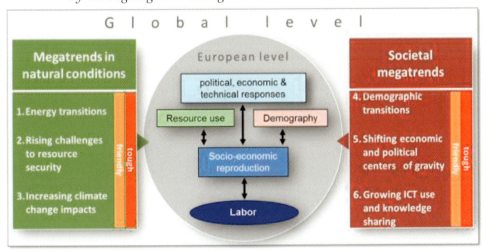

Source: Fischer-Kowalski et al. (2012, p. 77).

Figure 2.1 depicts the European option space in this (dynamic) global framework. At the centre of the figure is the socio-economic reproduction of the European population at a certain level of welfare. The population is subject to demographic change (depending on global and internal conditions). Its reproduction, depending on the mode of production and consumption, requires the use of natural resources, the supply of which is subject to global (and internal) conditions. It also requires a certain amount and quality of human labour, again depending on global and internal conditions. At the top of the figure is the European policy process – political, economic and technical response strategies in a changing world shaped by the ongoing as well as the beginning of the next socio-ecological transitions. As mentioned above, for each megatrend Fischer-Kowalski et al. distinguish between 'friendly' and 'tough' variants:

- A 'friendly' future entails moderate changes that pose fewer challenges for European policy-making. It entails incremental global changes in the lower ranges of change found in the literature.

- The sketch of a 'tough' global future is based on still quite likely, but rather severe changes that would be highly challenging for European policy-making, shifting into the higher ranges of change found in the literature, including possible abrupt changes.

2.2 Natural megatrends

The megatrends in natural conditions include increasing climate volatility, an energy transition from fossil fuels to renewable energy sources and rising challenges to resource security.

2.2.1 Energy transition

While fossil fuels enabled and still enable the transition away from agrarian regimes, high demand in mature economies, as well as rising demand in emerging economies will sooner or later be faced with peak oil, peak gas and peak coal. Various studies of peak oil have identified the peak as occurring between 2008 and 2037. This will fundamentally change the context for the ongoing fossil-fuelled socio-ecological transition, as well as for the next transition towards renewable energy sources.

In addition to future supply restrictions, climate change prompts global political responses, demanding mitigation policies that favour renewable energy sources and an overall reduction in fossil fuel consumption. Whether through climate mitigation policies or physical limits, a next energy transition is therefore inevitable and at least the take-off phase of such a new transition will be visible during the coming decades.

The energy transition will be accompanied by intensified global competition for scarce resources and, as a result, increasing and more volatile energy prices.

The transition away from fossil fuels will be accompanied by increasing and more volatile energy prices, as well as by higher energy investments to achieve the same amount of final energy supply, whether from renewables or from the remaining fossil fuel deposits (i.e. a declining energy return on investment, or EROI). While carbon capture and storage (CCS) technologies are seen as a glimmer of hope to mitigate these challenges, the feasibility of a large-scale rollout is under question and cannot safely be assumed in global scenarios. Finally, the bio-fuel demand of environmentally-oriented scenarios conflicts with food production, unless there is a major technological breakthrough.

2.2.2 Rising challenges to resource security

Enabled by increasing energy use, material consumption has increased tremendously in mature industrial countries and is currently stabilising at very high levels. As with energy, the overall global material demand will expand further, due to fast and rising growth in emerging economies. The overall rising global demand will encounter a deteriorating quality and a declining quantity of supply.

For the EU, several raw materials are considered critical since they are of high economic importance and pose high supply risks. Some of these critical raw materials are not produced within the EU, such as rare earth elements (REEs) and phosphorus, for which much of the world is dependent on a few mining countries such as China and Morocco. Intensified global competition for resources will lead to further price increases and could contribute to price shocks.

2.2.3 Stronger climate change impacts

Climate change is a product of the former transition from biomass-based to fossil fuel-based energy systems in the now mature industrial economies. Past emissions are already determining severe changes due to a strong time lag in the climate system between cause (emissions) and effect (warming). Greenhouse gas (GHG) emissions in the next decade will significantly determine the extent of future climate change, the risk of triggering irreversible damage to global ecosystems and their consequences for humankind.

If industrialised countries maintain their current levels of energy consumption and/or emerging countries increase their fossil fuel use to the level of mature countries (as they are currently projected to), this will greatly increase the risk of catastrophic climate change. It is reasonable to assume that unabated climate change will cause large-scale changes in the earth's system. In Europe, the Mediterranean countries will be hit the hardest with temperature increases, droughts, water scarcity, occasional flash floods and more forest fires leading to a loss of agricultural yields, with impacts on agriculture, tourism and health. Greece, Portugal and Spain, in particular, will be hot spots. A rise in sea levels is regarded as the greatest threat in the long term.

Climate change, regarded as a multiplier of existing environmental and social threats, is increasingly perceived as an international security risk. For example, intensified global competition for resources and the resulting price shocks might lead to armed conflicts over resources. Therefore in the long run, the severity of impacts depends highly on both effective mitigation at the global level and adaptive capacities.

2.3   Societal megatrends

Societal megatrends include demographic transition, the ongoing shifts in the economic and political centres of gravity worldwide, and the growing use of ICT plus the related new forms of knowledge-sharing.

2.3.1   Population dynamics

In mature industrial economies, the previous demographic transition was closely linked – via the increased availability of food and shelter and societal capacities to absorb a growing labour force – to the historical SET. This demographic transition has now been largely completed and led to a stagnating (or even declining) and ageing population. In emerging economies, present population growth is going hand in hand with growth in the use of fossil fuels and other resources, following a similar pattern – though fortunately not as steep – to that previously observed in today's mature industrial countries. The global population size and structure are crucial factors for environmental concerns, since environmental impacts are closely related to both population size and affluence. The observed slowdown of global population growth will probably lead to a stabilisation of world population within this century, but at a challengingly high level. Increasing short-term migration and relocation movements due to climate change impacts in Europe need to be considered.

2.3.2   Shifting economic and political centres of gravity

To date, the fifth of the world's population that is concentrated in the industrialised countries has been able to dominate the rest of the world. However, the transition of emerging economies into a fossil fuel-based energy system has allowed for an economic development that increasingly makes the other four-fifths of the world's population equal partners, if not the dominant players of the future. A shift of the political centres of gravity away from mature towards emerging economies will be a natural consequence of the faster growth of emerging economies. At the same time, global economic and political interconnectedness through trade, global production chains, international investments and media communications is steadily increasing. The next energy transition away from fossil fuels, issues of resource security, increasing climate change impacts and higher volatility of commodity prices will be important challenges for international collaboration. It remains an open question whether international relations will become more collaborative or more confrontational in the face of the challenges ahead.

2.3.3 *Growing use of ICT and knowledge-sharing*

This latest class of new technologies does not substitute – as most technologies before – for physical labour, but rather, it enhances and substitutes for intellectual labour and communications. It could provide crucial enabling tools for a next SET – enabling the handling of complex systems, speeding up the process of knowledge-sharing worldwide and across all areas, and creating a cheap communications space for the development of new world views and lifestyles. However, ICT tools are akin to a double-edged sword: analysing and managing complex systems are tasks performed by both democratic and dictatorial regimes. Transparency can help both enlightenment and surveillance, and social media may foster social innovation at the same time that it foments mass hysteria.

2.4 European response strategies

Considering the ongoing socio-ecological transitions and their global consequences, Europe has to be prepared for a more complex and challenging world than it has inhabited during the last few decades. Europe therefore must make its choices on how to adapt to higher energy, food and resource prices, more frequent extreme

Europe's educated population and ICT create an opportunity to actively shape the unfolding of the transition away from fossil fuels.

weather events challenging existing infrastructures, and possibly more international tensions over resources and mobility. Moreover, price increases will hit low-income people the hardest and further increase distributional tensions within Europe. On the other hand, Europe's population is better educated than ever before, ICT offers completely novel opportunities for democratic knowledge-sharing and for the smart regulation of complex systems, and Europe's immense wealth allows for investment in new infrastructure that, if implemented properly, will make Europeans less vulnerable to climate events, energy shortages and resource price booms.

Politically, rather than passively settling for more unfavourable conditions, there is the chance to play a pro-active role in moulding the unfolding of the next socio-ecological transitions of mature industrial economies into a more sustainable future. Will Europe be able to create conditions under which climate change can be kept within acceptable limits? Can market economies become less dependent on rising energy and materials inputs, possibly less dependent on growth altogether, and actively seek their margins in (input) cost reductions? Will Europe find ways to handle the distributional tensions that inevitably accompany low growth and rising prices in a peaceful and socially fair way? These are challenges that call for broad political visions that gradually need to emerge and be defended by authentic and plausible policy action and communication. The current financial crisis – not unlike what we saw with the oil crises in the early 1970s that were also preceded by a broad movement promoting cultural change – could provide a turning point for such a development. The current European policy priority of financial stability could be a first step in this direction.

Fischer-Kowalski et al. sketch three strategies for European policy-makers to cope with the changing global context of ongoing socio-ecological transitions. Two of these scenarios involve actively trying to shape the beginnings of the next socio-ecological transition away from fossil fuels.

2.4.1 Strategy 1: No policy change

First, no policy change assumes a business-as-usual approach without any additional policies to achieve sustainability. The overall aim is to defend the existing mode of production and consumption, as well as the vested business interests related to these consumption patterns, while trying to re-establish previous, more favourable conditions at the international level. As a result, existing sustainability policies are only partially implemented. There is a broad range of issues that are left unattended. For example, it is reasonable to assume that global megatrends will undermine the welfare of Europeans in the future. At the same time, there is a lack of shared political vision to prepare people for upcoming changes and to win support of voters. This further undermines national democratic systems and the common European vision, and may prompt a search for scapegoats (of foreigners, politicians, etc.). The halting of European political integration is a major impediment to any coherent common measures to address the global challenges outlined above.

2.4.2 Strategy 2: Ecological modernisation and eco-efficiency

In this second strategy, Europe attempts to actively deal with the challenges associated with the transition away from fossil fuels by achieving eco-efficient production systems through market-based instruments and the internalisation of externalities. Via increased eco-efficiency in Europe, levels of energy and resource consumption are stabilised or even reduced, while efforts continue to secure growth in income (i.e. relative or even absolute decoupling of growth and energy/material consumption).

This scenario assumes full use of the EU Emissions Trading System (ETS) to address climate change, support for investments in renewable energy sources, ecological tax reform reflecting energy and material intensity of products, removal of subsidies that promote wasteful use of energy and materials or using ICT for resource-optimised dealing with complex systems (smart grids, sustainable mobility satisfying present mobility needs, etc.) Although gains in the efficiency of energy consumption would result in an effective reduction in energy prices, the reduced prices would encourage an increase in the consumption of energy services.[7] This so-called 'rebound effect' is thus one of the main risks associated with the ecological modernisation and eco-efficiency strategy. The reliance on supply-side market instruments might also contribute to the growing inequality of access to resources.

2.4.3 Strategy 3: Sustainability transformation

This strategy recognises that there is bound to be a next socio-ecological transition and pro-actively tries to shape its take-off, while at the same time taking action to deal with fundamental changes in global conditions. This includes the recognition that a significant reduction in fossil fuel use is necessary and will have far-reaching social and economic consequences. Therefore, it requires a reconsideration of societal goals based on a thorough, informed public debate and entails changes in consumption (both patterns and levels) with a fundamental structural change in the economy.

In the 'sustainability transformation' strategy, substantial structural change is envisioned and pursued. Goals are set to achieve a smart, lean and fair societal metabolism with the aim of optimising European welfare. To be more specific, smart refers to measures taken in the ecological modernisation scenario. Fair refers to striving for a more equal welfare distribution in Europe and worldwide, which implies new definitions of work and time use priorities that better address age and gender differences and allow for improved work-life balances or high taxes on speculation. Lean implies a reduction in societal metabolism and therefore decreased demand for transport, a decoupling of labour from energy productivity, the avoidance of rebound effects and sustainability.

A number of measures should be taken to achieve these goals. For example, Diet change towards less meat/more vegetarian food would substantially reduce biomass metabolism and agricultural land use. Major investment in R&D could lead to a re-design of strategic products in a way that would save energy and resources in production and use. Similarly to the ecological modernisation scenario, ICT should be used to better understand and control complex systems. Additionally, ICT capacity may be used to shift consumption to less resource-intensive forms, e.g. virtual communications instead of travelling. A decisive ecological tax reform that is based on raw material equivalents (to include products' embedded energy for imports) could shift taxes from labour to resources, as implicit in a property tax and a financial transactions tax. Finally, the payoff from productivity gains should materialise in a reduction in working hours – not of income.

2.5 How to evaluate the European response

The success or failure of these response strategies will depend to a large extent on the global conditions, as described above. In terms of game theory, Fischer-Kowalski et al. created the general framework that allows for a straightforward evaluation and visualisation of the results for each scenario for a number of indicators of interest (environmental, social and economic) under different future global conditions (Table 2.1).

*Table 2.1 Speculative game-theoretical payoffs of three European response
strategies under two scenarios of global conditions*

Response scenario	Global scenario Rate of change induced by response strategy	'Friendly' world Gradual change	'Tough' world Rapid change
No policy change	Low	-	--
Ecological modernisation	Medium	++	-
Sustainability transformation	High	+	++

Source: Fischer-Kowalski et al. (2012, p. 95).

Fischer-Kowalski et al. argue that business-as-usual strategies will not be able to cope with the changing global conditions. An insistence on the stabilisation of the status quo will impede the necessary social and economic adjustments and structural changes, and therefore most likely lead to negative pay-offs under both sets of global conditions scenarios.

Under the ecological modernisation strategy, in contrast, outcomes will be the most satisfactory under the conditions of a 'friendly' world. This strategy, however, will fail under the conditions of a 'tough' world, in which the rebound effects could shake the new status quo. This assessment is mainly based on the judgement that market-based strategies work best under relatively stable and smooth conditions because the expectations of economic actors can adjust properly and implement investment activities accordingly. Structural change can be induced with relatively minimal distortions or negative side effects. The open questions are the magnitude of the negative feedback from this strategy and the speed with which the adjustments can happen.

The sustainability transformation strategy is expected to have a positive outcome under both scenarios of future conditions, but to be more valuable in a 'tough' world because it provides the vision and coherence required to overcome the hardships and challenges in a world shaped by ongoing and future SETs. This strategy is better suited to dealing with international volatility and supply shocks by focusing on inter-European activities and adaptation, thereby inducing changes towards a resilient and sustainable socio-metabolic regime with a focus on societal welfare rather than on increasing economic activity. This also includes numerous technical and social innovations, thereby strengthening the role of Europe as a leader in promoting and implementing sustainable development.

Bibliography

Fischer-Kowalski, M. and H. Haberl, (2007), *Socio-Ecological Transitions and Global Change: Trajectories of Social Metabolism and Land Use*, Cheltenham/Northampton: Edward Elgar.

Fischer-Kowalski, M., W. Haas, D. Wiedenhofer, U. Weisz, I. Pallua, N. Possanner, A. Behrens, G. Serio, M. Alessi and E. Weis (2012), "Socio-ecological transitions: definition, dynamics and related global scenarios", Institute for Social Ecology (AAU), Vienna, Austria; Centre for European Policy Studies, Brussels.

Greening, L., D. Greene and C. Difiglio (2000), "Energy efficiency and consumption – the rebound effect – a survey", *Energy Policy*, Vol. 28, No. 6–7, pp. 389–401.

IPCC (2007), "IPCC Fourth Assessment Report (AR4)", Intergovernmental Panel on Climate Change (IPCC), Geneva, Switzerland.

Karl, T. and K. Trenberth (2003), "Modern Global Climate Change", *Science*, Vol. 302, No. 5651, pp. 1719-1723.

Krausmann, F., S. Gingrich, N. Eisenmenger, K. Erb, H. Haberl and M. Fischer-Kowalski (2009), "Growth in global materials use, GDP and population during the 20th century", *Ecological Economics*, Vol. 68, No. 10, pp. 2696-2705.

Maddison, A. (2008), "Historical Statistics for the World Economy: 1-2006 AD" (http://www.ggdc.net/maddison/).

Maddison, A. (2010), "Statistics on world population, GDP and per capita GDP, 1-2008 AD", *Historical Statistics*.

Maturana, H.R. and F. Varela (1975), "Autopoietic systems: A Characterization of the Living Organization", *Biological Computer Laboratory (BCL Report 9.4)*, Urbana-Champaign, IL: University of Illinois Press.

Rockstrom, J., W. Steffen, K. Noone, A. Persson, F.S. Chapin, III, E. Lambin, T.M. Lenton, M. Scheffer, C. Folke, H. Schellnhuber, B. Nykvist, C.A. De Wit, T. Hughes, S. van der Leeuw, H. Rodhe, S. Sorlin, P.K. Snyder, R. Costanza, U. Svedin, M. Falkenmark, L. Karlberg, R.W. Corell, V.J. Fabry, J. Hansen, B. Walker, D. Liverman, K. Richardson, P. Crutzen and J. Foley (2009a), "A safe operating space for humanity", *Nature*, No. 461, pp. 472-475.

Rockstrom, J., W. Steffen, K. Noone, A. Persson, F.S. Chapin, III, E. Lambin, T.M. Lenton, M. Scheffer, C. Folke, H. Schellnhuber, B. Nykvist, C.A. De Wit, T. Hughes, S. van der Leeuw, H. Rodhe, S. Sorlin, P.K. Snyder, R. Costanza, U. Svedin, M. Falkenmark, L. Karlberg, R.W. Corell, V. J. Fabry, J. Hansen, B. Walker, D. Liverman, K. Richardson, P. Crutzen and J. Foley (2009b), "Planetary Boundaries: Exploring the Safe Operating Space for Humanity", *Ecology and Society*, Vol. 14, No. 2, Article 32.

Schellnhuber, H. (1999), "Earth system analysis and the second Copernican revolution", *Nature*, No. 402, C19-C23.

Sieferle, R.P. and V.D. Wissenschaftler (1982), "Der unterirdische Wald: Energiekrise und Industrielle Revolution", [eine Publikation der Vereinigung Deutscher Wissenschaftler (VDW)], München: C.H. Beck.

Turner, B. (ed.) (1990), *The Earth as Transformed by Human Action: Global and Regional Changes in the Biosphere Over the Past 300 Years*, Cambridge: Cambridge University Press.

UNEP (2007), *"Global Environmental Outlook 4: Environment for Development"*, United Nations Environment Programme (UNEP), New York.

Vörösmarty, C., D. Lettenmaier, C. Leveque, M. Meybeck, C. Pahl-Wostl, J. Alcamo, W. Cosgrove, H. Grassl, H. Hoff, P. Kabat, F. Lansigan, R. Lawford and R. Naiman (2004), "Humans Transforming the Global Water System", *Eos, Transactions American Geophysical Union*, Vol. 85, No. 48, pp. 509–513.

WBGU (2011), "World in Transition: A Social Contract for Sustainability Flagship Report 2011", German Advisory Council on Global Change (WBGU), Berlin.

Notes

[1] See Sieferle (1982, 2001); Fischer-Kowalski and Haberl (2007).

[2] Maturana and Varela (1975).

[3] Krausmann et al. (2009).

[4] Maddison (2008).

[5] IPCC (2007); Karl and Trenberth (2003); Rockström et al. (2009); Schellnhuber (1999); UNEP (2007); Turner et al. (1990); Vörösmarty et al. (2004); WBGU (2011).

[6] Fischer-Kowalski et al. (2012).

[7] Greening et al. (2000).

3. HOW MUCH WORK WILL THERE BE? WHERE IS IT GOING TO COME FROM?*

Demographic developments are expected to have a strong impact on European labour markets in the coming decade. As labour participation is a key determinant of the long-term economic growth and a source of government revenue, the ageing European population is a major policy problem. Employment in Europe will be strongly affected by aging, but also by other factors such as the upskilling of the population and the macroeconomic health status of the continent.

In this chapter a series of predictions are presented on labour force participation and on employment, the latter with details by sector. Projections show that total number of hours worked is expected to, at best, remain constant on average in Europe, but with strong variations across countries. This will translate into higher wages and higher revenues for public pockets. Job creation will occur exclusively in the service sector, although its size will be strongly influenced by fiscal policies. The time horizon considered is 2030, which is sufficiently close for forecasts to be considered trustworthy but also far enough out for change to be observed.

These forecasts are based on the scenarios described in chapter 2, where various possible visions of the future are described. Specifically, the

---

* Chapter 3 was written by a team of authors: Marcela Veselková based on research conducted by the team from the Institute for Labour Research (IZA), as well as Nicole van der Gaag (researcher at the Netherlands Interdisciplinary Demographic Institute), Baptiste Boitier (senior researcher at SEURECO - Société EURopéenne d'ECOnomie), Nicolas Lancesseur (SEURECO and Université Paris 1) and Paul Zagamé (scientific director at SEURECO and Professor Emeritus at Université Paris 1 Panthéon Sorbonne). It is based on findings from work packages 9 (Modelling economic and employment developments) and 10 (Modelling the evolution of the labour supply and labour demand) of the NEUJOBS project. The final version was compiled and edited by Marcela Veselková.

chapter describes the socio-ecological transition (SET) away from fossil fuels, which can be observed in two sets of megatrends. Megatrends in natural conditions include the energy transition, rising challenges to resource security and increasing climate change impacts. Societal megatrends include demographic changes, shifting of economic and political centres of gravity, and growing information and communication technologies (ICT) use and knowledge-sharing. The uncertainty and complexity associated with these megatrends are condensed into two alternative futures: a 'friendly' and a 'tough' world.

3.1 Changes in population and labour force: Theoretical considerations and 2000-10 dynamics

Since the start of this century, the average annual rate of population growth in the European Union has been below 0.5%, which is similar to other developed countries but modest in comparison to other world regions. Even with such a small rate of change, most European countries experienced population growth between 2000 and 2010, mostly thanks to migration. But in some – namely Germany and some eastern European countries – populations had already started to decline (Figure 3.1, left graph, yellow bars). With an average annual population decline of 0.8%, the drop was most severe in Bulgaria. Nonetheless, whether a more or less optimistic scenario is considered, the total population of the continent will be greater in 2020 than it is currently. The second most important fact about demographic development is that Europeans are, on average, getting older.[1] Does aging matter for economic growth? Surprisingly enough, the answer is only to a certain extent.

What really matters for economic growth is not the total population but the working-age population, which we define as the population aged 20 to 64. Despite the 'grey-looking' future, a large majority of the EU countries in the last decade saw the size of their working-age population increase (Figure 3.1, left graph). In the years to come, however, most countries will face a declining working-age population, even under the more optimistic scenario (Figure 3.1, right graph).

A larger working-age population is only foreseen for Austria, Belgium, Cyprus, Italy, Luxembourg, Sweden and the United Kingdom. However, with the exception of Luxembourg, the growth rate of the working-age population in these countries will still become smaller than the growth rate of the total population, and thus the pressure placed on the working-age population to take care of the young and the old will increase in almost all countries.

Table 3.1 Population (in thousands) and labour market participation factors contributing to labour supply

Country	2010				2030 'Friendly' scenario		2030 'Tough' scenario	
	POP[1]	WAP[1]	Emp[1]	Hours[2]	POP[3]	WAP[3]	POP[3]	WAP[3]
EU27	499,199.6	305,802.8	68.5	n.a.	536,289.5	301,620.9	488,329.3	278,919.0
Austria	8,375.3	5,153.3	74.9	n.a.	9,104.5	5,152.3	8,276.9	4,790.4
Belgium	10,839.9	6,496.9	67.6	1551	12,478.8	6,881.7	11,718.4	6,564.5
Bulgaria	7,563.7	4,795.2	65.4	n.a.	7,221.0	4,198.1	5,832.4	3,404.9
Cyprus	803.1	505.7	75.0	n.a.	994.9	576.8	886.9	511.9
Czech Republic	10,506.8	6,797.6	70.4	1811	11,185.3	6,554.1	10,109.2	6,038.9
Denmark	5,534.7	3,279.6	75.8	1546	5,974.7	3,292.8	5,670.5	3,183.7
Estonia	1,340.1	827.1	66.7	1879	1,419.5	808.2	1,133.2	635.2
Finland	5,351.4	3,218.0	73.0	1677	5,759.2	3,040.8	5,491.6	2,963.6
France	62,791.0	36,861.5	69.2	1480	69,458.1	36,791.4	66,195.2	35,565.4
Germany	81,802.3	49,560.8	74.9	1407	80,831.6	44,230.1	72,318.2	40,398.7
Greece	11,305.1	6,967.7	64.0	2016	11,797.1	6,799.8	10,851.2	6,399.1
Hungary	10,014.3	6,270.2	60.4	1959	9,740.6	5,788.2	9,182.9	5,680.3
Ireland	4,467.9	2,733.6	64.6	1542	5,269.9	2,969.0	4,654.1	2,545.8
Italy	60,340.3	36,688.6	61.1	1772	67,635.2	38,465.1	60,648.3	35,230.4
Latvia	2,248.4	1,405.3	65.0	n.a.	2,133.8	1,253.9	1,767.6	1,067.9
Lithuania	3,329.0	2,054.3	64.4	n.a.	3,133.4	1,780.0	2,824.1	1,632.5
Luxembourg	502.1	313.1	70.7	1636	654.8	387.1	609.4	366.6
Malta	413.0	259.8	60.1	n.a.	432.0	242.9	373.9	211.3
Netherlands	16,575.0	10,108.3	76.8	1381	18,065.8	9,866.4	17,002.6	9,442.9
Poland	38,167.3	24,694.0	64.6	1940	38,290.3	22,412.8	34,817.1	20,928.0
Portugal	10,637.7	6,553.2	70.5	1740	11,066.6	6,444.2	10,016.5	6,049.5
Romania	21,462.2	13,740.0	63.3	n.a.	21,881.2	13,451.3	18,032.3	11,128.2
Slovenia	2,047.0	1,315.7	70.3	1675	2,267.2	1,289.2	2,058.3	1,187.2
Slovakia	5,424.9	3,560.3	64.6	1807	5,706.0	3,426.1	5,254.0	3,234.0
Spain	45,989.0	29,131.0	62.5	1674	51,972.5	30,574.9	44,787.9	26,525.0
Sweden	9,340.7	5,461.9	78.1	1635	10,976.2	5,945.3	10,330.4	5,680.4
UK	62,027.3	37,050.2	73.6	1652	70,839.1	38,998.5	67,486.1	37,552.8

Notes: POP = Total population. WAP= Working age population (i.e. population aged 20-64). Emp = Employment rate of working age population. Hours = Average number of working hours per week on main job. n.a. = Not available.

[1] Data source: Eurostat; [2] Data source: OECD; [3] Data source: NEUJOBS.

Figure 3.1 Annual average change in working-age population (aged 20-64), 2000-20 and 2020-30 under 'friendly' and 'tough' scenarios

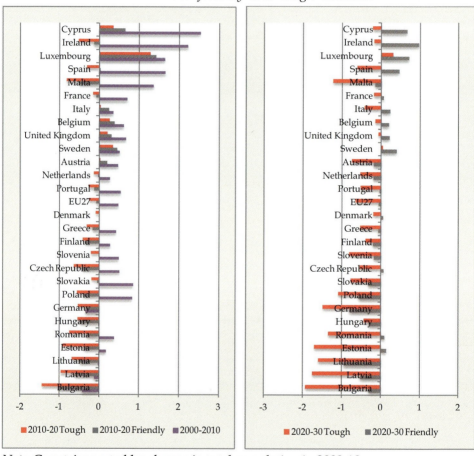

Note: Countries sorted by change in total population in 2000-10.

Data sources: Eurostat and NEUJOBS; calculations: Netherlands Interdisciplinary Demographic Institute (NIDI).

Even under the 'friendly' scenario – with rather high fertility, life expectancy and immigration assumptions – in the short term most EU countries cannot escape their aging fate. Given the relatively short projection

> *Most EU countries will face a declining working-age population under both scenarios.*

period, this is not surprising. In a time horizon of only 20 years, developments in fertility will not contribute to changes in the population aged 20-64 at all, as the first children born during this period only enter the working-age population after the projection period ends. Furthermore, in most countries, mortality rates for those aged 20-64 are already rather low, so improvements in life expectancy at these ages can have only minor impacts. Finally, even though migration can bring about immediate changes in population growth, it is most unlikely to fully compensate for declines in the working-age population.

The future is not altogether gloomy, however. Population aging will, in fact, be partially compensated for by behavioural changes linked to demographic developments and the characteristics of this new (but older) labour force. In other words, a 1% decrease in the population will not automatically translate into a 1% decrease in the labour force.

What matters for the health of the economy is the total number of hours worked, not the head count of workers. For this reason, to understand the evolution of the future labour supply it is important to decompose the average annual

A 1% decrease in the population will not automatically translate into a 1% decrease in the labour force.

change in total numbers of working hours into three components:

➢ changes in the working-age population,

➢ changes in employment rates and

➢ changes in the average weekly number of hours worked per employee.

Figure 3.2 shows how each item contributed to changes in the labour supply between 2000 and 2010. In all countries, one observes a decline in the average number of working hours per employee. In all countries, however – with the exception of Denmark, Estonia and Hungary – this decline in average working hours is more than offset by favourable demographic dynamics and increasing employment rates. In Germany, the working-age population in 2010 was lower than in 2000, but the resulting decline in labour supply due to demographic changes and falling working hours was less severe than the increase due to rising employment rates. Overall, therefore, labour supply in Germany grew slightly. Denmark, Estonia and Hungary, on the other hand, experienced an annual average decline in their labour supply of 0.5%, due to falls in both working hours and employment rates, with hardly any change in the working-age population.

*Figure 3.2 Annual average change in labour supply due to changes in working-age
         population, employment rate and annual average hours per week per
         employee, 2000-10*

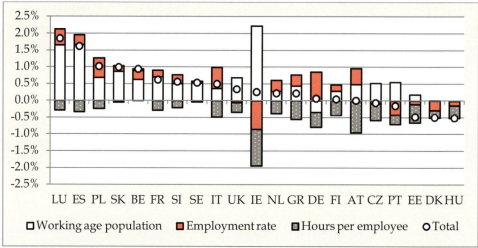

Note: Countries sorted by total change.

Data sources: Eurostat and OECD; calculations: Netherlands Interdisciplinary
Demographic Institute (NIDI).

In the years to come, the picture will change. Even under a rather
favourable population scenario, the working-age population will start to
decline in most countries. Increasing labour supply will therefore need to
come from changes in labour market participation and/or increasing
numbers of hours worked per employee. As has been the case for the past
decade, different countries will have to choose different strategies to
achieve this result.

3.2 Structural and behavioural aspects of labour supply: A look at the next two decades

As explained in detail in the previous section, the total labour supply is
affected not just by structural aspects, such as changes in the size and
composition (e.g. age, gender, skill-level or household type) of the
workforce. The behavioural dimension, i.e. the individual decision on
whether or not to work and how much, matters as well.[2] It is crucial to take
this behavioural dimension into account in predicting potential challenges
arising from the changing composition of working-age populations.

From a policy perspective, the distinction between the structural and behavioural aspects is crucial. Dolls et al. illustrate this distinction using the following example.[3] If the relative share of socio-demographic groups which prefer to work part-time or which have a high preference for leisure increases more than the relative share of groups which prefer to work more hours, the change in total labour supply (measured in hours worked) will not be equivalent to the change in the size of the working-age population. This has important policy implications, because the change in head counts and the change in hours worked might be more effectively addressed by different policies. A reduction in the size of the labour force could be tackled with targeted migration policies, while fewer total hours worked as a result of high

Individual decisions on whether to work or not influence labour participation, and hence the total labour supply.

numbers of people working part-time could be tackled with improvements in childcare services. Dolls et al. therefore provide projections of both the size and the composition of the labour force for the 'tough' and 'friendly' scenarios developed by Huisman et al.[4]

Figure 3.3 depicts the change in the size of the labour force in terms of the headcount. On average across all countries, the labour force shrinks by 9.2% in the 'tough' scenario and by 1% in the 'friendly' scenario.

Figure 3.3 Decline of labour force (headcount)

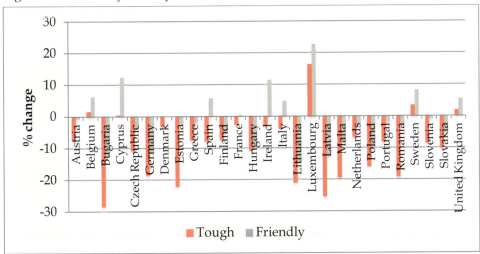

Source: Dolls et al. (2013, p. 5).

However, the projections imply divergent trends across countries. The demographic trends will be least favourable in Bulgaria, Germany, the Baltic states and Romania, which will experience the strongest decrease in labour supply. In these countries, the labour supply in terms of the headcount is projected to shrink by between 18% and 28% in the 'tough' scenario. In contrast, the labour force in Belgium, Cyprus, Luxembourg, Sweden and the UK is projected to grow under both scenarios.

Figure 3.4 shows the projected changes in total hours worked, which under the 'tough' scenario is expected to shrink by 8.9%, on average. In contrast, the 'friendly' scenario implies no aggregate change to hours worked. However, there is strong variation in the total hours worked across countries. The 'friendly' scenario projects an increase, or at least stagnation, in hours worked in about half of the EU countries. Large increases are expected in Belgium, Cyprus, Luxembourg and Sweden. Furthermore, these increases tend to be greater than the increase in headcount. In contrast, significant reductions in total hours worked are projected for Bulgaria, Germany, the Baltic states and Romania.

> *The total amount of hours worked is expected to shrink by 8.9% under the 'tough' scenario and to remain constant under the 'friendly' scenario.*

Figure 3.4 Change in total hours worked

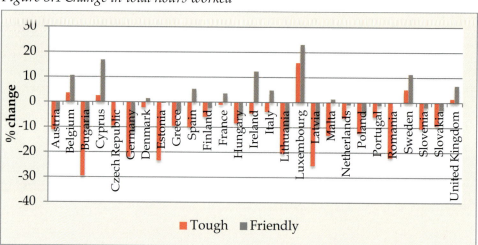

Source: Dolls et al. (2013, p. 11).

In order to fully capture the difference between the structural and behavioural dimensions of demographic change, it is important to examine the difference between the percentage change in hours and the percentage change in headcount, also known as the excess difference (ED). An ED of less than zero indicates that the structural tendencies are reinforced by individual behaviour patterns. This implies that, given projected demographic changes between now and 2030 (which are negative in most cases), the drop in total labour supply will be even stronger than the drop in headcount. This represents a future in which the share of older workers is growing and these older workers choose to work fewer hours. In contrast, an ED greater than a zero indicates a future in which the reduction in hours is less severe than the reduction in heads (due to fewer part-time workers, for example), thereby weakening the adverse effect on total labour supply. Figure 3.5 suggests that the demographic development is particularly worrying for continental Europe and the UK and Ireland, at least under the 'tough' scenario.

Figure 3.5 Between now and 2030: Reduction in hours is less severe than the reduction in headcount

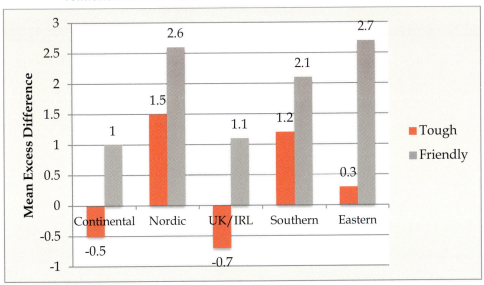

Notes: Continental = AT, BE, DE, FR, LU, NL; Nordic = DK, FI, SE; Southern = CY, EL, ES, IT, MT, PT; Eastern= BG, CZ, EE, HU, LT, LV, PL, RO, SI, SK.

Source: Dolls et al. (2013, p. 14).

3.3 Labour demand and wage adjustment: Fewer but better paid workers?

Disregarding the demand-side reaction to demographic changes may lead to an underestimation of employment rates. Figure 3.6 depicts the adjustment in the labour market that is likely to occur between now and 2030. Point A represents the equilibrium in 2010. A decrease in the labour force due to demographic trends (as will be observed in most EU countries

> *A decrease in the labour force will push wages up and higher wages will induce higher labour participation.*

between 2010 and 2030) shifts the aggregate supply curve to the left. As a result, the equilibrium moves from point A to point B. However, point B will not be the new equilibrium because the labour demand will respond to a shift in labour supply. At the old wage level, there is now an excess labour demand and the wage must rise. Wage increases yield both a higher participation rate and a higher level of hours worked. The shift in the labour supply curve thus raises the equilibrium from point B to point C, which is characterised by an increase in employment and an increase in wages.

Figure 3.6 Wage adjustments due to demographic change

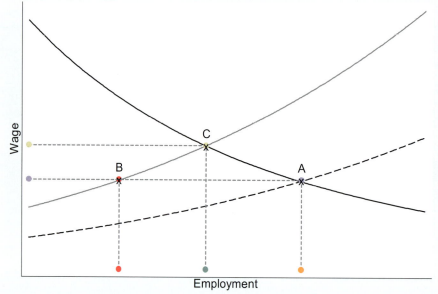

Source: Dolls et al. (2014, p. 6).

The wage adjustment to demographic change is composed of two distinct parts: 1) the change in average wages in response to demographic change between 2010 and 2030; and 2) the change in average wages caused by the labour market reaction to this demographic change (the shift from point A to point C in Figure 3.6). Figures 3.7 and 3.8 illustrate the relative magnitude of these effects. Under both the 'tough' and 'friendly' scenarios, the effect of demographics on average wages is positive. This reflects not only the well-known aging issue, but also the continuous upskilling of the population. Overall, future European workers will be not only older but also better skilled and more productive and, as a consequence, also better paid.

Under the 'friendly' scenario, average wage changes due to demographics exceed +20% for some countries – such as Greece, Malta, Poland, Portugal and Romania – which are expected to experience a large upskilling of their populations between 2010 and 2030. In others, the overall wage changes are modest because the positive demographic effect is counteracted by a negative labour market effect, notably an increase in headcount or an increase in hours worked. The largest average wage decreases induced by the labour market are found in Cyprus, Luxembourg and Sweden, countries that are expected to experience the largest increase in headcount under the 'friendly' scenario.

Under the 'tough' scenario, the effect of labour market adjustment on wages is positive. The largest increase in average wages in response to the labour market are found in countries expected to experience the largest decrease in headcount, such as Bulgaria, Germany, Estonia and Latvia. Germany represents an extreme example: under the 'tough' scenario, the total labour force is projected to fall by 18.7%, the share of 50-64 year olds is projected to increase by 5.8% and the level of upskilling is expected to remain constant. As a result, the hours worked (before wage adjustment) are expected to fall by 22%. In response to this scarcity of labour, the wages of those left in the labour force are projected to increase by 50%, on average. The labour supply will therefore increase in response to the higher wages, particularly at the farthest margin.

Figure 3.7 Average wage changes due to demographic changes and the labour market response, 'tough' scenario

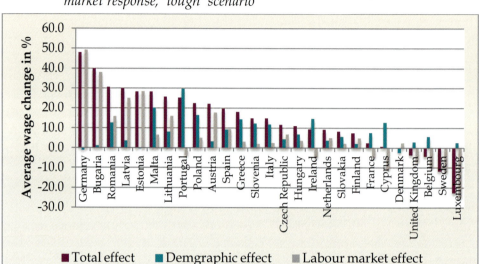

Source: Dolls et al. (2014, p. 10).

Figure 3.8 Average wage changes due to demographic changes and the labour market response, 'friendly' scenario

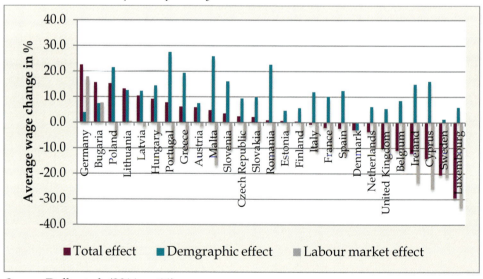

Source: Dolls et al. (2014, p. 11).

3.4 Fiscal effects of demographic change: Public finances likely to find relief despite ageing

The demographic shock is expected to have an impact well beyond the labour demand and supply dynamics, and to also affect government revenues. One question comes directly to mind: with fewer people paying taxes, will the predicted wage increase compensate for the shrinkage in labour supply with regard to tax revenues and social security contributions? Projections for the 'friendly' and 'tough' scenarios suggest that this might be the case. Table 3.2 lists percentage changes in income tax revenues and revenues from social security contributions.

Under the 'friendly' scenario, the percentage change in tax revenues in the EU-27 attributable to the wage increases reaches 30%. The positive development in income tax receipts is a result of two counteracting effects. First, the 'friendly' scenario assumes an increase in hours worked and employment rates. Average wages therefore decline in many of the EU-27. This drop leads to an additional small increase in employment rates, while overall hours worked remain constant. As a result, the tax base widens and tax revenues increase. Under the 'tough' scenario, the percentage change in tax revenues in the EU-27 attributable to the wage increases reaches 35.7%. This greater projected increase in income tax receipts is a result of a smaller projected labour force, and consequently higher wages. For example, the 50% average wage increase in Germany is largely responsible for the 69% increase in tax revenue projected for the country.

Social security contributions (SSCs) are projected to increase between 2010 and 2030 under both the 'tough' and 'friendly' scenarios. The wage changes implied by demographic change have two roles in increasing SSC projections. First, SSCs increase in response to wage increases. Second, the wage increase will be followed by increases in hours worked and employment rates, and subsequently an increase in SSC

Higher wages, and as a result higher tax and social revenues, may ease fiscal pressures associated with ageing populations.

revenue. Overall, the increase in income tax contributions is higher than the increase in SSCs because after an assessment threshold, these contributions are fixed. SSCs increase by 10.2% under the 'tough' scenario and by 11.7% under the 'friendly' scenario.

Table 3.2 Percentage change in public revenue between 2010 and 2030 with projected wage changes

	Taxes		Social contributions	
	'Tough'	'Friendly'	'Tough'	'Friendly'
AT	52.1	43.5	5.4	-0.1
BE	20	17.8	18	16.9
BG	-6.1	8	-9.4	2.8
CY	19.4	31	3.4	5.2
CZ	25.7	27.4	12.5	18.3
DE	68.6	29.1	7.3	5.3
DK	29.9	49.2	15	20.7
EE	3.2	8.1	-3.8	5
EL	40	41.2	4.6	5.1
ES	41.6	31.1	17.1	22.1
FI	17.8	20.7	11.8	13.2
FR	44.8	57.2	12.9	16.7
HU	6.2	8.1	4.9	9.4
IE	61.3	25	40.6	18.4
IT	39.6	35.8	11.5	10.2
LT	8.1	12.6	4.9	10
LU	-8.3	-7.4	3	5.5
LV	0.7	7.5	-1.7	5.7
MT	36.6	23.6	1.9	12.3
NL	46.1	40.4	6.3	7.2
PL	12.9	24.5	4.6	14.4
PT	45.9	28.3	25.2	20.8
RO	10.9	7.2	4	7
SE	13.3	20.8	8.2	5.1
SI	25.4	13.5	12.4	12.2
SK	19	22	7.5	13.3
UK	16.5	17.2	11.6	10.1
Unweighted avg.	25.6	23.8	8.9	10.8
Population weighted avg.	35.7	30.0	10.2	11.7

Source: Dolls et al. (2014, p. 11).

The large increase in projected fiscal income may help to ease the fiscal burden associated with the growing pension bill and the public healthcare needed due to population aging. However, the presented projections should be taken as an upper bound of future fiscal revenues because of strong modelling assumptions.[5] Despite some caveats, it is possible to derive policy conclusions from the above analysis. Of particular importance is the difference between the social security contributions and personal income taxes: whereas the former is proportional to the volume of labour, the latter is not. A progressive income tax system, as is present in most EU countries, may therefore be a measure to stabilise the fiscal consequences of demographic transitions on public budgets.

3.5   What jobs and for whom?

Whereas the previous section focused on the projections of overall labour supply and labour demand, this section examines the possible overall future of European employment up to 2030 with regard to how many jobs and which type will be created and destroyed in the coming decade. Computations produced using the NEMESIS model,[6] in combination with the assumptions of the 'friendly' and 'tough' scenarios, deliver two possible detailed pictures of the European economy up to 2030.[7] The resulting projections of employment by skill level and by sector enable specific challenges related to changes in the labour market to be identified and policies to be better targeted.

Table 3.3 Scenarios based on assumptions on the general context (situation in 2010 and 2030 or variations from 2010 to 2030)

		'Friendly'	'Tough'
Societal	Demography (millions)	+37M	-11M
	Old age dependency ratio (%)	26% to 38%	26% to 39%
	Working age population (millions)	-4.5M	-29M
	- High-skilled	+36M	+11M
	- Low-skilled	-40.5M	-40M
Energy prices	Oil price ($US'10/bbl)	$78 to $117	$78 to $195
	European gas price ($US'10/Mbtu)	$7.5 to $11.7	$7.5 to $12.6
	European coal price ($US'10/t)	$99.2 to $109.3	$99.2 to $115.9

Financial	World GDP growth (AAGR)	3.80%	2.5%
	European rate of interest (%)*	3.6 to 4.4	3.6 to 5.9
	€/$ exchange rate	1.3 to 1.3	1.3 to 1.4
	Public finance rule	Stabilisation of public debt	Stabilisation of public debt

* Average nominal government bond yields, 10 years' maturity.

Source: Boitier et al. (2013).

3.6 Labour supply projections: Strong divergence in the evolution of skill levels

3.6.1 *Two contrasting macroeconomic pathways leading to employment disparities*

European employment will be strongly affected by macroeconomic conditions. European economic growth takes two different pathways under the scenarios. Under the 'friendly' scenario, European *European GDP grows at 1.8% in the 'friendly' scenario and at 1.2% in the 'tough' scenario.*

economic growth is prompted by favourable international and financial conditions. In addition, the long-run potential growth of GDP is pushed up by significant growth in the quality of the labour supply. On the other hand, under the 'tough' scenario world demand does not help the European economy to recover from the crisis, as the shrinking labour supply reduces long-run potential GDP growth and makes rebalancing public finances more difficult. Thus, for the whole period, annual European real GDP growth is 1.8% on average under the 'friendly' scenario and 1.2% under the 'tough' scenario.

The contrast between the scenarios is also visible in European total employment, which stood at over 221 million workers in 2010. The total creation under the 'friendly' scenario is about 23 million by 2030, whereas under the 'tough' scenario, the European economy destroys almost 9 million jobs. Under the 'friendly' scenario, European employment growth goes back to pre-crisis trends, with an average annual creation of 1.5 million units between 2015 and 2030 (close to the 1.8 million average annual creation between 1995 and 2005).[8] The 'friendly' scenario is a post-crisis scenario assuming a return to the pre-crisis European development pathway, even if these pathways are not exactly of the same kind. At the opposite end, the 'tough' scenario entails a break with European pre-crisis economic development. The European Union recovers economic growth, but this growth is not high enough to increase employment.

Table 3.4 Average annual GDP growth rate (%)

	Friendly				Tough			
	2010-2015	2015-2020	2020-2025	2025-2030	2010-2015	2015-2020	2020-2025	2025-2030
Austria	1.5	2.0	2.1	2.2	1.4	1.3	1.4	1.5
Belgium	0.8	1.9	2.0	2.1	0.7	1.0	0.9	0.9
Bulgaria	1.2	2.9	2.6	2.3	1.1	2.0	2.1	2.1
Cyprus	-4.6	1.9	2.9	3.2	-4.8	0.9	1.4	1.5
Czech Republic	0.8	2.6	2.6	2.6	0.8	2.1	1.8	1.9
Denmark	1.1	1.9	1.9	2.0	1.0	1.8	1.4	1.6
Estonia	3.8	4.0	3.8	3.7	3.5	3.5	3.3	3.2
Finland	1.1	2.2	2.2	2.3	1.0	1.8	1.6	1.6
France	1.0	2.0	2.1	2.2	0.9	1.4	1.4	1.4
Germany	1.9	1.7	1.5	1.5	1.8	1.0	1.0	0.9
Greece	-3.7	1.9	2.5	2.5	-3.7	1.3	1.4	1.4
Hungary	0.4	1.5	1.8	2.1	0.4	1.0	1.2	1.6
Ireland	2.0	2.5	2.4	2.5	1.8	1.9	1.7	1.7
Italy	-0.2	1.9	1.9	1.9	-0.3	1.0	1.0	0.9
Latvia	4.9	4.4	3.6	3.5	4.7	3.9	3.2	3.2
Lithuania	4.6	4.0	3.8	3.6	4.3	3.5	3.3	3.3
Luxembourg	0.9	3.1	3.3	3.0	0.8	2.6	3.0	2.7
Malta	1.6	2.8	3.2	3.2	1.5	1.5	2.0	2.4
Poland	2.1	2.8	2.7	2.5	2.1	2.1	1.6	1.5
Portugal	-1.6	1.9	2.2	2.1	-1.7	1.2	1.0	0.9
Romania	2.1	4.0	4.1	4.1	1.8	3.0	3.3	3.7
Slovakia	2.7	2.9	2.6	2.6	2.6	2.1	1.7	1.7
Slovenia	-0.8	2.7	2.6	2.6	1.0	2.0	1.9	1.8
Spain	-0.7	2.3	2.7	2.5	-0.8	1.3	1.4	1.0
Sweden	2.1	3.0	2.7	2.4	2.0	2.7	2.2	2.2
The Netherlands	0.1	1.8	1.8	1.8	-0.2	0.8	0.8	0.7
The United-Kingdom	1.1	1.9	2.0	2.2	1.1	1.8	1.2	1.0
European Union (EU-27)	0.9	2.0	2.1	2.1	0.8	1.4	1.3	1.2

Source: Boitier et al. (2013).

At the national scale, the contrast between the scenarios is similar, with more employment for all countries in 2030 under the 'friendly' scenario than under the 'tough' scenario (Figure 3.9), but with strong differences across countries. In the four biggest economies of the European Union (excluding Germany), the evolution of total employment is relatively similar under each scenario. In the 'friendly' scenario, total employment grows by between 15% (in Italy) and 25% (in Spain), while under the 'tough' scenario it remains relatively stable, growing by between -2.5% (in Spain) and +5.4% (in the United Kingdom). Between 2010 and 2030, these four European countries represent more than 70% of the total European employment increase, with more than 16 million jobs created. Under the 'tough' scenario, these countries create 1.8 million jobs between 2010 and 2030, which alleviates the fall in total European employment (8.7 million by 2030 compared to 2010). In Germany, total employment is stable under the 'friendly' scenario but falls strongly under the 'tough' scenario, with a loss of 5.3 million jobs by 2030 compared to 2010, i.e. constituting two-thirds of the total European employment loss under this scenario.

Figure 3.9 EU-27* employment growth between 2010 and 2030 under the 'friendly' and 'tough' scenarios (%)

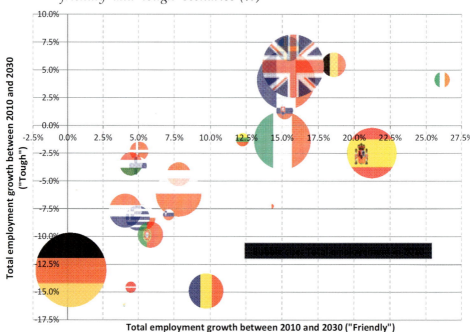

* *Luxembourg and Bulgaria's colours are not shown to enhance the clarity of the graph.*

Source: Boitier et al. (2013).

3.6.2 Sectoral mutations: The explosion of private services

An analysis of sectoral interactions allows a better understanding of the drivers of employment creation (or destruction) under both scenarios. Figure 3.10 depicts the change in sectoral European employment between the 'friendly' and 'tough' scenarios.

We start the analysis with the non-market services sector, which is an atypical sector as its evolution is strongly dependent on government fiscal policies. Therefore, European employment in these sectors, which represented almost 62 million persons in 2010, is the most sensitive to the variation in public expenditure between the 'tough' and the 'friendly' scenarios. In 2030, the number of people working in the sector is 15 million higher (i.e. one quarter of the 2010 level) under the 'friendly' scenario than under the 'tough' scenario. Indeed, public expenditure on social protection, education, economic affairs, education, defence or general public services is lowered significantly under the 'tough' scenario. In 2030, total public consumption is €3.2 trillion (constant € 2005) under the 'friendly' scenario and only €2.7 trillion under the 'tough' scenario.

This strong difference between the scenarios regarding public expenditure and employment in the non-market services has consequences for the financing of the welfare state. Thus, social investments, which have provided positive returns in the past,[9] will be weaker under the 'tough' scenario despite important needs, especially under the pressure of an aging population. As a consequence, the public finance constraint does not allow the development of these new services to the same extent, even if some are likely to be provided by the private sector. Instead, the smoother deleveraging under the 'friendly' scenario enables states to develop a wide range of new services in response to ageing populations.

Figure 3.10 Change in European total employment under the 'friendly' and 'tough' scenarios (millions)

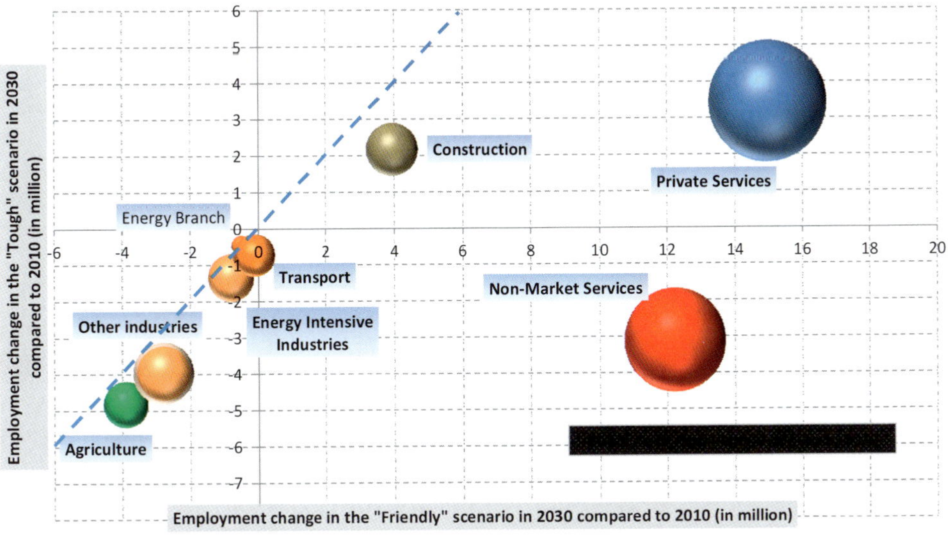

Source: Boitier et al. (2013).

Under the 'friendly' scenario, employment growth is mainly driven by job creation in the private services sector, with an increase of 8 million between 2010 and 2020 and of 7 million between 2020 and 2030, i.e. a total increase of 15 million between 2010 and 2030. The construction sector also exhibits non-negligible job creation, with 3.9 million additional jobs by 2030 compared to 2010, while in the European industry sector, employment falls by 4.1 million jobs (2.1 million in the first decade alone). Finally, agriculture loses about 3.9 million jobs between 2010 and 2030 (a 32% reduction).

Two-thirds of employment creation comes from private services under the 'friendly' scenario.

Under the 'tough' scenario, as previously explained, the fall in employment growth is large in the non-market services, with 3.1 million fewer jobs in 2030 compared to 2010. It is also very significant in the private services sector, in which employment in 2030 is 11.5 million lower under the 'tough' scenario than under the 'friendly' scenario, though it still rises by 3.5 million compared with 2010. For industry and construction, the differences between the scenarios are less accentuated – industry destroys 5.7 million jobs and construction creates only 3 million jobs. Finally, agriculture is the sector least impacted by the slowdown in economic growth, with a loss of 4.8 million jobs (i.e. only 900,000 fewer jobs than under the 'friendly' scenario).

The evolution of the sectoral employment structure depends on several factors. The main factor related to the socio-ecological transition is the increase in fossil fuel energy prices. The goods and services that are energy-intensive become less attractive as energy price rises. As an example, the share of transport in household consumption budgets decreases from 13% to 10% between 2010 and 2030 under the 'friendly' scenario. By the same token, the level of employment in the transport equipment sector is reduced by 15% over the period. However, this price increase will stimulate demand in the renovation sub-sector, which is labour intensive, and will then boost employment in the construction sector.

The most influential factor in the rise of employment in services is the improvement in the standard of living. When a household get richer, expenses for culture, recreation, communication, and so on are released, inducing a higher demand for the corresponding services and more employment potential in these sectors. In all European countries, the service sectors are the major contributors to employment creation. The global evolution of the sectoral structure fits within a historical context of transfer between industries and services.

Creative destruction (or 'Schumpeter's gale'), mostly in the form of employment destruction in industry and employment creation in services, takes place under the 'friendly' scenario but does not happen under the 'tough' one. As a result, under the 'tough' scenario the usual leading sector in the employment growth – the private services sector – does

Is the 'tough' scenario a 'sleeping policeman' on the road of employment mutations?

not develop as it does under the 'friendly' scenario. Worse still, after 2020 only the destruction process takes place in the private services sector, which loses almost 1.5 million jobs between 2020 and 2030 under the 'tough' scenario. Other sectors also face difficulties, but to a lesser extent than services. Thus, the 'tough' scenario can be viewed as a wasted opportunity for potential job-creating sectors, as the continuation of slow economic growth prevents the restart of private demand.

3.7 The rise of high-skilled workers...

The distribution of skills across sectors is obviously uneven; more workers with PhDs are needed for medical research than in the waste collection sector. An interesting way to understand this split is to consider the sectoral dichotomy between tradable and non-tradable sectors, where a tradable sector is defined as a sector with a ratio between import and production of below 15%. Broadly speaking, agriculture, energy industry, manufacturing sectors and sea and air transports are tradable sectors, whereas construction, private services and non-market services are non-tradable sectors.[10] The skill level is defined by the educational level attainment, with high-skilled corresponding to ISCED 5 and 6 graduates and low-skilled corresponding to ISCED 0 to 4 (it therefore includes the category of medium-skilled, which is usually defined as levels 3 and 4 of ISCED).

Table 3.5 European employment by skill level in the tradable and non-tradable sectors, difference in thousands

			'Friendly' scenario		'Tough' scenario	
		1997-2007	2010-2020	2020-2030	2010-2020	2020-2030
Tradable	High-skilled	3,054.1	3,791.3	3,092.2	2,533.8	1,042.3
	Low-skilled	-6,609.1	-5,042.6	-5,068.0	-4,876.2	-5,111.2
Non-Tradable	High-skilled	16,446.8	11,686.2	16,291.2	5,404.6	2,714.1
	Low-skilled	10,220.2	-3,434.1	1,585.6	-4,290.4	-6,191.6

Sources: Boitier et al. (2013) calculations based on Timmer (2012) and the NEMESIS model.

According to the results of our model, there is a lasting destruction of low-skilled employment in the tradable sectors under both scenarios. The pace of the destruction is similar to that of the previous decade. This result corroborates the fact that, in the tradable sectors, the lower the labour productivity, the higher the activity and so employment is vulnerable to international competition. In the non-tradable sector, low-skilled employment is more protected but the projections are pessimistic compared to past trends. Indeed, during the last decades, the creation of low-skilled employment was mainly due to public services. With the public finance constraints, this leeway cannot be used to the same extent. In the tradable sectors, highly-skilled workers are more resilient to international competition than the low-skilled, since there is an expansion of employment. Finally, highly-skilled employment in the non-tradable sectors is growing fast and is the major contributor to employment creation under both scenarios. From 2020, creation goes back to its previous trend.

Technological progress plays a major role in the evolution of the employment structure. The development of ICT enables the opening of a growing range of services to international competition. These technologies make the atomisation of the global supply chain easier, as multinational firms can subdivide the tasks of the production process more efficiently and choose the most competitive workforce from among different countries. Beyond this evolution, the most powerful impact of the technological progress is the replacement of jobs by machines or computers. This concerns a worker being replaced by a machine in a factory or a worker being replaced by a computer programme in an office. The more routine the task, the more the chance that the job will be replaced, a process already observed in the 2000s.[11] Workers endowed with a low stock of skills and specialised in manual non-routine tasks as well as workers endowed with a high stock of skills and specialised in conceptualisation and intellectual tasks, are relatively favoured by the impulse of technologies, implying the skill polarisation of labour market. The construction and the lodging and catering sectors can provide some good insights into this phenomenon. Indeed, on the one hand, the workers of these sectors have a very low endowment of skills, on the other their tasks entail very little routine and in fact they are almost the only sectors to create both low-skilled and high-skilled jobs in a context of an overall fall of the low-skilled employment.

3.8 …without forgetting unemployment!

Total unemployment depends on the macroeconomic path, since the relatively high growth rate under the 'friendly' scenario allows the global unemployment rate to return to its pre-crisis level by 2030, whereas the weak growth under the 'tough' scenario implies a rising unemployment rate until 2030, reaching 12.1%. For all the reasons underlined previously, low-skilled employment is highly vulnerable to the evolution of the European economic structure. Under the 'tough' scenario, the unemployment rate of these workers does indeed grow strongly. Nevertheless, under the 'friendly' scenario, the significant decrease in the low-skilled labour supply, coupled with robust economic growth, reduces the stress on the market and thus reduces the unemployment rate.

What may come as a surprise and seem to be a paradox is the rise in the high-skilled unemployment rate. Indeed, this rate grows even under the 'friendly' scenario. To explain this paradox, one should remember that in the model, the skill level is defined by the level of education attained. Thus, the rise of the unemployment rate under the 'friendly' scenario stems from a demand from firms for real high-skilled tasks that is not high enough to absorb the significant growth of the high-skilled labour force (in addition to wage rigidities delaying the return to the equilibrium of the labour market). Therefore, the increase in the high-skilled unemployment rate should be considered as an indicator of

Under the 'friendly' scenario, the over-qualified group will expand, and the under-qualified diminish.

a skills mismatch between the education of workers and the tasks needed by firms. A recent OECD study could support this result.[12] Its results suggest that in the OECD countries, one in four workers could be over-qualified and one in three under-qualified. The results for the 'friendly' scenario suggest that over-qualification would expand while under-qualification would decrease. Accordingly, fostering R&D and innovation by firms would provide an outlet for this labour supply by increasing the potential tasks for high-skilled workers.[13]

Table 3.6 European unemployment rate by skill level (%)

	2010	'Friendly' scenario 2030	'Tough' scenario 2030
Total	9.7%	7.6%	12.1%
High-skilled	5.1%	6.6%	10.2%
Low-skilled	11.4%	8.2%	13.2%

Source: Boitier et al. (2013).

In the long run, the best solution to offset the decrease in the workforce so as to support economic growth is to stimulate labour productivity by improving human capital

The decline in the European workforce puts economic growth at risk. To avoid this pitfall in the short run, the employment rate must be raised, bearing in mind that the greatest potential lies in women and older workers.[14] The mobility of European workers between European countries, as well as immigration of extra-EU workers, should also be fostered to facilitate the absorption of the shock. In the long run, the only solution to offset the decrease in the workforce so as to support economic growth is to stimulate labour productivity by improving human capital.

A rise in labour productivity would not only be an appropriate response to the economic growth challenge, but also to the employment issue. Indeed, there are two main threats to the evolution of employment. Although technical progress and international competition can provide new opportunities to develop high-skilled employment, they also weaken the situation of low-skilled workers in the labour market. As confirmed in the scenarios, large-scale destruction of low-skilled jobs will occur up to 2030. Once again, implementing an efficient system of skills upgrading aimed at improving labour productivity seems to be the best employment policy. Under the 'friendly' scenario, the strong growth in the high-skilled labour supply enables the compensation of the destruction of low-skilled jobs. This proves that the potential of firms' demand for high-skilled labour is sufficient to reduce global unemployment and to give rise to lasting economic growth. In contrast, the weak increase in the high-skilled workforce under the 'tough' scenario constrains economic growth, which implies a rise in total unemployment.

Despite the favourable global evolution of high-skilled employment, the 'friendly' scenario shows that some bottleneck effects and skills mismatches could appear in the labour market. The increase in firms' demand for high-skilled tasks is not high enough to absorb the overall inflow of educated workers. This results in rising over-qualification and possibly rising high-skilled unemployment. The improvement of skill levels on the supply side should be coupled with stimulation on the demand side to avoid these mismatches. Indeed, some policies enhancing innovation and research would help to increase the outlet for high-skilled labour supply in addition to improving the competitiveness of European industries. Beyond the structural policies for resource efficiency and climate change (carbon tax, rising of environmental standards, etc.), education and training systems must be more oriented towards these environmental concerns in order to benefit from the new markets that will automatically emerge under the pressure of depleted fossil energy.

Finally, with the single exception of Luxembourg, the growth rate of working-age populations is projected to be lower than the growth rate of total populations. The higher proportion of older people in the total population poses a challenge for public finances, but the fiscal burden associated with the growing pension bill and healthcare may be eased by labour market adjustments. A reduction in the working-age population does not automatically translate into a smaller labour supply – a shrinking labour supply creates pressure for wage increases, which in turn induces labour participation. In addition to migration policies, it is therefore possible to increase the number of hours worked through policies that ease the transition from part-time to full-time employment, of which improvements in childcare facilities are an example.

Bibliography

Autor, D., K. Lawrence and K. Melissa (2006), "The Polarization of the U.S. Labour Market", *American Economic Review*, Vol. 96, No. 2, pp. 189-194.

Boitier, B., N. Lancesseur and P. Zagamé (2013), "Global Scenarios for the European Socio-ecological Transition", NEUJOBS Working Paper No. D9.2 (www.neujobs.eu).

CEDEFOP (European Centre for the Development of Vocational Training) (2012), "Future skills supply and demand in Europe – Forecast 2012", Research Paper No. 26, Publications Office, Luxembourg.

Dolls, M., K. Doorley, H. Schneider and E. Sommer (2013), "Structural and behaviour al dimensions of Labour Supply in Europe in 2030", NEUJOBS Working Paper No. D10.9 (www.neujobs.eu).

_____ (2014), "Demographic Change in Europe: The Labour Market and Fiscal Effects in 2030", NEUJOBS Working Paper No. D10.8 (www.neujobs.eu).

European Commission (2013), "Growth potential of EU human resources and policy implications for future economic growth", Working Paper 3/2013.

Hemerijck, A. (2013), *Changing Welfare States*, Oxford: Oxford University Press.

Hemerijck, A., V. Dräbing, B. Vis, M. Nelson and M. Soentken (2013), "European Welfare States in Motion", NEUJOBS Working Paper No. 5.2/2013 (www.neujobs.eu).

Huisman, C., J. de Beer, R. van der Erf, N. van der Gaag and D. Kupiszewska (2012), "Demographic scenarios 2010-2030", NEUJOBS Working Paper No. D10.1 (www.neujobs.eu).

_____ (2013), "Demographic Scenarios 2010-2030", NEUJOBS Working Paper No. D10.1 (www.neujobs.eu).

Maselli, I. (2012), "The Evolving Supply and Demand of Skills in the Labour Market", *Intereconomics*, Vol. 47, No. 1, pp. 22-30.

OECD (2011), *Employment Outlook 2011*, Paris: OECD Publishing.

_____ (2013), *Skills Outlook 2013*, Paris: OECD Publishing.

Redding, S. (1996), "The Low-Skill, Low-Quality Trap: Strategic Complementarities between Human Capital and R&D", *Economic Journal*, Vol. 106, No. 435, pp. 458-470.

Timmer, M.P. (ed.) (2012), "The World Input-Output Database (WIOD): Contents, Sources and Methods", WIOD Working Paper No. 10, WIOD FP7 Project (www.wiod.org/new_site/home.htm).

Zagamé, P., B. Boitier, A. Fougeyrollas, P. Le Mouël, P. Capros, N. Kouvaritakis, F. Bossier, F Thierry and A. Melon (2010), "The NEMESIS Reference Manual" (www.erasme-team.eu).

Notes

[1] Huisman et al. (2013). As Croatia was not yet part of the European Union at the time the NEUJOBS scenarios were compiled, Croatia is not included in the scenarios.

[2] See Dolls et al. (2013, 2014).

[3] Dolls et al. (2013).

[4] See Dolls et al. (2013, 2014) and Huisman et al. (2012).

[5] For a discussion, see Dolls et al. (2014).

[6] NEMESIS (New Econometric Model for Environmental and Sustainable development and Implementation Strategies) is a macro-sectoral econometric model built to aid decision-making in the fields of energy, the environment and economic policy. It was built for two main purposes: the production of short-term and medium-term projections and the analysis of economic policy issues, especially in the fields of the environment and R&D. Co-financed by the European Commission, NEMESIS was developed by a European consortium composed of the Federal Planning Bureau of Belgium, SEURECO (Société Européenne d'Economie, Paris, France) and the Institute of Computer and Communication Systems (NTUA - University of Athens). It currently covers the whole of Europe and Norway. The rest of the world is divided into ten different geographical areas and is assumed to be exogenous.

[7] Zagamé et al. (2010).

[8] Timmer (2012).

[9] Hemerijck (2013) and Hemerjick et al. (2013).

[10] Based on 2005 data.

[11] Autor et al. (2006) and Maselli (2012).

[12] See OECD (2011).

[13] See the literature on the complementarities between R&D and human capital (e.g. Redding, 1996).

[14] European Commission (2013).

4. EXPLORING THE TRANSFORMATION OF HUMAN LABOUR IN RELATION TO SOCIO-ECOLOGICAL TRANSITIONS[*]

Human society – willingly or not, slowly or quickly – is in a transition away from the use of fossil fuels. This transition is expected to have as many and equally far-reaching implications for human labour as the previous transition to a fossil-fuel based industrial society had. To understand this phenomenon better, we develop a simple scheme that can be applied throughout history to characterise human labour according to its quantitative, qualitative and institutional features. Using this scheme, we attempt to explore historical linkages between energy regimes and the changing nature of human labour. We focus on the

Human labour and energy regimes are closely interwoven. Consequently, the new energy transition away from fossil fuels will play an important role in shaping the future of labour.

interrelationship between socio-metabolic regimes and the amount of human lifetime spent on labour, the respective critical qualitative capacities of human labour power and the institutional forms in which labour is employed. Our hope is to be able to draw some useful conclusions derived from socio-ecological analyses.

Against this backdrop we speculate about the future: What could labour look like after the ongoing socio-ecological transition is completed, or has reached a next stage? Most analyses of 'green jobs' deal with a fairly close future, and mainly with the future of gainful employment.[1] We open

---

[*] Chapter 4 was written by Marina Fischer-Kowalski and Willi Haas, Director and Researcher, respectively, at the Institute of Social Ecology at the University of Klagenfurt.

up the time horizon (which also means keeping it somewhat unspecified) and ask ourselves: As the fossil-fuel-based socio-ecological transition apparently induced such major changes to work and life, what changes can we expect from a major societal transition away from fossil fuels?

4.1 The socio-ecological character of human labour

4.1.1 Quantitative characterisation

Our starting point is the question of how to distinguish 'labour' from other human activities throughout human history. A socio-ecological perspective on this helps to circumvent some of the longstanding debates around this issue and suggests looking upon human labour as an element of human time use in a social (distributional) context. As humans live out their lives in social groups, they cooperate in various forms of 'division of labour'. It therefore makes sense to regard as 'labour' all those activities that are subject to such a division and thus constitute social interdependencies, and to only exclude as 'non-labour' those elements of time use that cannot be socially transferred to anyone else.

While traditional time-use research deals with time use on a descriptive and individual level only, a socio-ecological analysis places time use and activity categories in a functional context of system reproduction.[2] Based on functional linkages, time spent on labour can be distinguished from time spent on non-labour, as follows:[3]

1. **The reproduction of the self.** Activities such as sleeping, eating, resting, learning, having fun, etc. These classes of activities cannot be subject to a social division of labour, and thus cannot be considered 'labour'.

2. **The reproduction of household and family.** These activities also deal with personal reproduction, but in an inter-subjective mode (child-bearing and rearing, food preparation, daily chores, etc.). This clearly should be considered 'labour'.

3. **The reproduction of the community.** Participation in 'public affairs' on various scales beyond the family, such as collective decision-making, voting, participation in religious and public ceremonies, military service or shared infrastructure work. This clearly has labour-like features.

4. **The reproduction of the economy at large.** On a systemic level, this is time used for the production of goods and services for anonymous consumers. Individually, it is the time used for income generation in

a market (and therefore is close to conventional economic definitions of labour).

The share of a population's time that is devoted to each function varies widely across socio-ecological regimes. It is also related to demographic structures, since they determine the share of people who are fit for work as well as the dependency ratio. How activities are distributed among subgroups of the population by gender, age and status is highly variable. The higher the status of a group, the more time for self-reproduction (Type 1) it will typically be entitled to.

For the individual, the question is how much labour time they need to survive and to reproduce – this defines a minimum of Type 2 and 4 activities. Under favourable environmental and social conditions, this may be very little.[4] Under unfavourable environmental or social conditions, this may be more than the individual can afford over a longer stretch of time, so they will not reproduce and will not be able to survive. For the social community, demand for labour can best be seen as an economic relationship: the relationship between the benefit to the community (i.e. the marginal return to additional labour) and the cost of this additional labour. In family and community relations, an additional potential labourer (an additional child, for example, or a second wife) may be sustained, although the benefit of the labour they can deliver is lower than the costs. In strictly economic relations, additional labour will not be employed if benefits do not exceed costs. What determines both variables – the benefits to be gained by additional labour and the cost of it, beyond social relations – strongly depends of course on a society's energy regime (see Figure 4.1).

As long as labour only serves for the collection and hunting of food and its preparation for consumption, it does not require much time. Moreover, an increase in labour time under such conditions may well be self-defeating: an increase in hunting and gathering in the same area will tend to deplete the sources of food

> *Across history, the greatest time spent on labour per inhabitant and per day was under agrarian conditions. The industrialisation of agriculture relieved labour time through the use of fossil-fuel technologies.*

and force the community to migrate. As is also documented in research from cultural anthropology, the hunting-gathering regime requires the least amount of human labour from its members.[5] With the transition to the agrarian regime, the amount of labour increases, and it increases even more with the intensification of traditional agriculture (Figure 4.1).[6] The transition to the industrial regime may at first boost labour time even further.[7] Later, however, it provides relief. This storyline is reflected in the data compiled in Figure 4.1, using working hours per day per inhabitant as an indicator. Work in the economy is lowest under hunting-gathering (0.8 hours/day), rises with traditional agricultural intensification (to a value of about 3.3 hours in Germany in 1870) and then drops to a little above two hours under contemporary industrial conditions (about 2.1 hours for France, the Netherlands and Germany, and 2.4 hours for the UK).

The economic labour time being greatest under agrarian conditions is due to the increasing amount of colonising activities required to feed ever-more people on the same land.[8] With the industrialisation of agriculture, this is greatly relieved by fossil-fuel-based technologies.

Figure 4.1 Approximate daily working hours by socio-metabolic regime for an average inhabitant

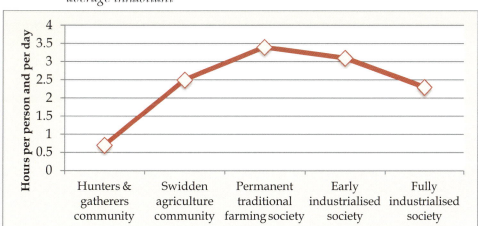

Note: Based on the following cases: Trinket (hunter-gatherers), Campo Bello (swidden/slash & burn agriculture) and Nalang (permanent farming, traditional).

Sources: Fischer-Kowalski et al. (2011); France 1998-99, Netherlands 2000, UK 2000-01: European Commission (2003), Eurostat database 2013; Germany 2001-02: Statistisches Bundesamt (2006), Eurostat database (2013).

Notwithstanding doubts about data quality and comparability, the amount of daily time spent on household and family chores seems, in contrast, to be less variable across socio-metabolic regimes (about two hours for non-industrialised communities and between two and three hours for industrialised societies).

4.1.2 Qualitative characterisation

For a qualitative characterisation of human labour, we are looking at abstract dimensions that bear a certain relationship to energy and vary across socio-metabolic regimes. One should be able to argue that these capacities are rooted in human nature, in the sense that they are part of the natural equipment of every human being and they should render themselves for social enhancement (or suppression) and training (or lack thereof). From the wide range of possible distinctions, we have selected the following three basic capacities for our analysis: physical power (as a capacity of the body), rationality/knowledge (as intellectual capacity) and empathy (as emotional intelligence or social capacity).

Physical power. Physical power is the capacity to alter physical objects through the use of force. This capacity relates to the notion of 'exergy', which is the ability to perform work in a physical sense,[9] and the concept of energy efficiency: one can look at the human body as a machine that requires a certain amount of energy input (i.e. food) to perform a certain amount of work (exergy output). Physically speaking, the human body is not a very efficient machine as it needs a high amount of energy input just for living, i.e. for its basic metabolism, and can transform only a small amount of energy input into useful work and only for a limited fraction of its lifetime. While the basic metabolic rate (BMR) depends on age and body mass (e.g. 6.2 MJ/day for a 50 kg woman and 9.6 MJ/day for an 80 kg man, corresponding to outputs of about 70-110 watts), heavy farm work or sports such as all-day cross-country skiing may double the daily energy demand. With typical kinetic efficiencies of around 20%, even eight hours of heavy physical work represents an output of only 2 MJ – equivalent to burning 1 kg of coal in an engine with 10% efficiency.[10] Another limitation is the relatively small 'installed power' of the human body – even elite athletes cannot sustain a power output beyond 500 watts for longer than an hour; their peak power delivery is 1,000 watts for several seconds.[11] Human effort, even at its best, is therefore a most unimpressive source of mechanical energy.[12]

Rationality/knowledge. This represents the intellectual capacity to correctly anticipate the effect that one's own actions have and to plan them deliberately. This capacity relates to information processing and to learning from experience as well as from communication with others. While the adult human brain accounts for about one-sixth of the basic metabolic rate, brain work is, energetically speaking, light work – even intensive intellectual activity only marginally raises the brain's metabolic demand.[13]

But more so than with physical power, the individual perspective is too narrow: rationality and knowledge should be looked upon as social properties, as being built up and maintained collectively, with individuals only having a certain share in this collective propensity. And of course, building-up and maintaining a stock of knowledge and information processing generates a certain energy (and labour) demand at the social system level.

Empathy: Empathy is the capacity to emotionally anticipate and mirror the feelings of other living beings. Modern brain research has demonstrated that it is an innate capacity of primates to sense the feelings of others and 'understand' (mirror) the intentions that guide the activities of others.[14] However, this natural capacity should be expected to be strongly influenced by cultural features at the social system level. It should be looked upon not as an *intellectual* but as an *emotional* capacity, crucial for human labour that involves and functionally relies upon communications and caring for the needs of people or other living beings. Empathy as an emotional capacity rooted in certain neuronal equipment must not be equated with a value orientation of altruism; the ability to mirror the feelings of others may just as well be used to manipulate or harm them.

These qualitative features of human labour power have three types of interlinkages with socio-metabolic regimes: they can be functionally (economically, technologically) more or less relevant for the performance of work; they may be socially (culturally) more or less valued and enhanced or suppressed (investment in education); and, finally, they may be technologically more or less supported and enhanced, or they may be substituted to a greater or lesser extent by technology. These different pathways will play a prominent role in the subsequent historical analysis.

4.1.3   Characterisation by institutional form

In some highly stratified societies, it may be considered altogether unworthy for the 'free man' to be working for his subsistence. This is well represented, for example, by Aristotle, Hesiod or Xenophon for ancient Greece and by Cicero for ancient Rome, who highly valued a life in leisure and service to the *polis* as a free and self-determined citizen, and for whom working under somebody else's command was incompatible with personal dignity. However, the conceptualisation of work is highly dependent on societal formations and varies over human history.

The following broad classifications for the various institutional forms that labour may take can be found in the historical and anthropological literature:

- **Family work** within personally interdependent household systems and mutuality of obligations – examples are subsistence agriculture, hunter-gatherers and household work in most socio-metabolic regimes.

- **Slavery,** where a master owns the labourer and has to take care of his/her reproduction or, if cheaper, buy a new one.

- **Other kinds of collective, often compulsory services** like the military, prison camps or religious orders, and sometimes voluntary work where individuals invest surplus time for the sake of a community, such as hospice services.

- **Serfs within manorial systems** – the family receives land from the lord of the manor and owes a share of its produce as taxes and/or compulsory labour in return.

- **Self-employment** in own firm/enterprise, often household-based but selling produce/services on markets.

- **Wage labour** – the individual is free to sell a certain quantity of time on a labour market. This form of labour has undergone an enormous differentiation process with regards to professional and hierarchical specialisations.

While the social science discourses about the institutional forms of labour tend to focus on self-determination, hierarchy and exploitation from the point of view of their moral and political legitimacy, a socio-ecological reflection should focus on economic and ecological functionality. Functionality as understood here refers to the effectiveness with which the natural resource base can be utilised for people's benefit at the lowest environmental cost. The institutional form of labour is at least as relevant for this functionality as the technologies used.

4.2   Human labour in different socio-metabolic regimes

While hunter-gatherers do work by the standards of the time-use distinctions, this work is still very close to what other social animals need to do to sustain themselves. With the transition to agriculture, labour becomes a much more pronounced feature of human existence specifically – both qualitatively and quantitatively. During industrialisation, the labour time required to be spent on food production is reduced significantly, allowing for the development of a highly differentiated labour market with further increased divisions of labour within and between countries.

4.2.1 Work in the agrarian regime

Quantitative features

A critical quantitative question is how many people can be sustained by a certain piece of land, and how many additional people not working the land (landlords, urban citizens, soldiers, etc.) can it subsidise. There is a tendency to develop techniques that allow more people to live off a piece of land, intensifying land use at the expense of investing in additional labour.[15] The increased labour burden creates an incentive to have more children to share the workload. This triggers population growth, lowering labour productivity even more. If population pressure on the land is reduced, for example by labour opportunities in urban centres, agricultural labour productivity may rise again and allow for increasing surplus production that then allows feeding a larger urban population.[16]

Nevertheless, working hours in mature agrarian systems tend to be very high.[17] In the agrarian regime, the overwhelming majority of the population (including children and the elderly) are occupied with food production for most of their available lifetime. This reflects the relatively low energy return on energy investment (EROI) of agriculture and the focus on humans and animals as the main source of mechanical power. Depending on land productivity, the EROI of agriculture lies somewhere between 2 and 10 units of energy return to each unit of energy invested (in a draft animal agricultural system, for example, maize has an EROI of 4.1:1).[18] The proportion of the population that can be sustained from the surplus of agricultural labour, even in advanced agrarian systems, is in the range of 5-15%. This (low) proportion is confirmed by typical rates of taxation and shares of urban populations across the pre-industrial history of countries (see Figure 4.2).

Figure 4.2 presents regional estimates for the time around the year 1500, as this is a period in which we can expect urban settlements to sustain themselves exclusively on contributions from traditional agriculture. The figure shows that the share of the population in settlements of 2,500 or more inhabitants varied between 2% and 10% across world regions. This means that it took, on average across the world, 25 peasants to feed one urban citizen; even in Renaissance Western Europe, 11 farmers had to contribute.

Figure 4.2 Share of urban population in settlements with 2,500 or more inhabitants by world region in 1500

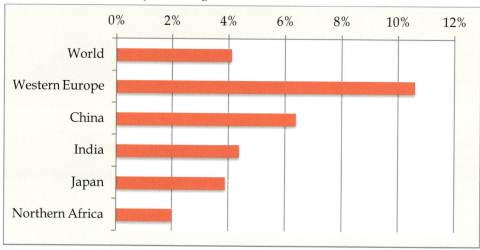

Source: Klein et al. (2010).

Qualitative features

Qualitatively, the agrarian regime relies mainly on the physical power (and physical endurance) of human labour. This applies to the rural population (constituting the very large majority) and also, for example, to slave labour in mines and infrastructure building (if we think of the Roman Empire). There is little societal effort to improve the skills and knowledge base of those 90-95% of the population engaged in agricultural labour. As long as they feed themselves and deliver their tithes and taxes, they are left to themselves to organise their work. With the fellachs (farmers) in ancient Egypt, the lower castes in India or feudal serfs in Europe, as well as with African slaves in the southern states of America, no effort is made to spread literacy or practical knowledge concerning work in agriculture.

Education, in the sense of societal investment in the skills and the knowledge capacity of physical labour, is largely absent. This investment is restricted to a small minority of privileged, usually male urban elites liberated from the need to work for their subsistence, and is largely disconnected from what may be considered 'productive work'.[19] Religious castes and organisations contribute to the education of ideological elites (universities founded in Europe from the late 11th century) and to the religious indoctrination of children (Sunday schools, Qu'ran schools, etc.), but do not convey functionally useful knowledge to those whose labour sustains society. Whatever great civilisational gains are achieved, they are rarely connected to the mass of human labour. The social tensions created by this highly unequal distribution of knowledge (albeit without any relationship to practical application) are reflected in the widespread religious conflict in 14th to 16th century Europe over the Bible and the right of everyone to read it by themselves, and in the efforts from the elites to maintain knowledge monopolies as reflected in the burning of Giordano Bruno in 1600.

Technological enhancement and substitution of human physical power were mainly sought via animal power: buffaloes, oxen and (later) horses, and in other regions elephants and camels, are used for traction of ploughs, water pumps and carriages, or for carrying heavy loads in the case of donkeys. This technological solution draws on the human labour capacity for empathy, since educating and guiding working animals requires a certain understanding and concern for their needs and feelings. Animals may be useful or even indispensable due to having a higher power density than humans, but they do not substitute quantitatively for human physical labour (as this is still required in order to work with and feed those animals).[20] In general, agrarian systems are marked by a substantial degree of public cruelty, a cultural emphasis on heroism and the use of force. Thus it should not be expected that the evolution of empathy receives much social enhancement.

Institutional forms of labour

Labour in agriculture (>90%). In peripheral or unproductive regions (such as mountainous areas, marshes or sparsely populated arid regions), agricultural or pastoral labour usually takes the form of household-based family labour, largely subsistence-oriented, according to family power structures. In more productive regions, labour is organised into some form of manorial system with bonded serfs or slaves who owe a defined proportion of the fruits of their labour in the form of produce, labour or money to the landlord.

Labour outside agriculture (< 10%). This can take the form of slave or compulsory labour, e.g. in mining or construction, or as household-based self-employment, for example in crafts and trades or transportation. The "atomisation of production was the rule...".[21] Another common and important form of 'labour' is military service, which may be considered labour in the sense of providing food, animals, slaves and treasure by looting, and by protecting one's own population from looting. However, military service cannot be considered labour in the sense of producing resources; it does so only by redistribution between enemies and friends.

4.2.2 Work in the coal-based industrial regime

Quantitative features

Quantitatively, the unfolding of the coal-based industrial regime multiplies the demand for labour. Although industrial labour is mainly the exertion of physical power, and much additional physical power is brought into the economy from coal-driven steam engines, the demand for human labour soars so much that even the rapid population growth ('first demographic transition') can be absorbed. For the industrial workforce, it is only humanitarian legal efforts that gradually achieve a reduction of daily working hours and a ban on child labour. Industrial labour is cheap, and the profits to be gained from it far surpass the surplus to be gained from land ownership.

In this phase, there is clearly a positive relationship between energy input into the economy and the number of labour hours: more energy does not substitute for, but facilitates, the use of additional human labour. In Germany and Italy, as in most industrialising European countries, the total number of labour hours in the economy rises with energy use up to the First World War. Then

> *Physical power is the key feature of human labour during the agrarian regime. The ruling classes are not interested in the majority of the population engaged in agricultural production or in improving their skills and knowledge as long as they feed themselves and deliver their tithes and taxes.*

there is a reduction of working hours while energy use stagnates; this pattern holds throughout the period of coal dominating the energy regime. In contrast, after World War II, when the use of oil became dominant, energy use in both countries increases significantly while labour hours decrease; this speaks to a substitution of labour by technical energy. After the 1970s, there is no clearly discernible relationship between energy use and labour hours (see Figure 4.3).

Historians studying time use have even documented that in the early phase of industrialisation in the UK (i.e. during the 18th century), the weekly working hours of urban labourers rose above those of the previous agrarian conditions.[22]

Figure 4.3 Primary energy consumption (PEC) and working time (hours) for Italy (left) and Germany (right), 1870 to 1998

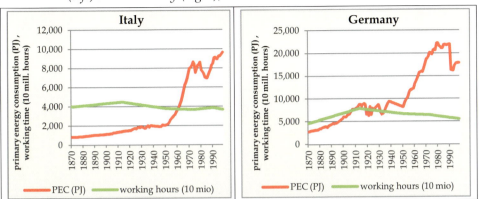

Source: Maddison (2001, 2008); Cleveland (2011); SEC database (2011).

Qualitative features

At its onset, the coal-based industrial regime mainly adds physical power through steam engines driving water pumps (in mines) and weaving looms in manufacturing. This additional physical power does not so much replace human labour as increase its demand, because production processes can take place more cheaply and on a larger scale. For agriculture, there is only an indirect impact: allowing (and in part, forcing) rural populations to migrate to urban centres and earn their living on wage labour in manufacturing.[23] Later, railways facilitate transporting coal and food over large distances into these urban centres, thus allowing them to grow and at the same time stimulating surplus rural production. In manufacturing (so-called 'proto-industry') and, later, industrial labour, the impact of steam engines is not to improve the skill component in human labour, but rather to minimise it.[24] The key capacity of human labour in agriculture, as well as in urban wage labour, remains physical power and endurance. However, small skill segments evolve further – in urban craftsmanship and engineering, in trade and finance, in the military and among civil servants.

During this regime most countries start to introduce publicly financed compulsory schooling for children (including, or even in particular, for the lower classes in urban centres). Often still under the supervision of the clergy, children are expected to learn reading, writing and simple forms of algebra, in addition to receiving religious instruction. This is largely to do with the functionalities of the modern nation state and the requirements of its military, and very little to do with "qualifying labour".[25] It does create a need for teachers, however, as maybe the first labourers to be mainly qualified by formal education.

With empathy, one can observe an increasing cultural differentiation by gender. While men, in their work and beyond, are supposed to be tough and to contain their emotions, females are supposed to be sympathetic and emotional. Empathy, one might say, becomes a female virtue, but a virtue nonetheless.[26]

Institutional forms of labour

The most spectacular change during this regime is the rise of free wage labour. Free wage labour, a minority form at first, increases to become the most dominant institutional form. Gradually, often through revolutions, serfdom and slavery are abolished. In contrast to the landed aristocracy of the agrarian regime, industrialists see themselves as hard-working, responsible for the labour process, and drivers of technical innovation. Capitalists do not see themselves as a leisure class, but feel obliged to demonstrate frugality and a strong work ethic.[27] During this phase, the separation of a sphere of production and gainful employment from the sphere of reproduction as a cosy and secluded home wisely governed by a housewife (who is not seen to be 'working', but to be exercising love and care) becomes an urban middle-class model that gradually spreads to other social strata.[28]

4.2.3 Work during the rise of the oil-based industrial regime

Quantitative features

Primary energy consumption in the economy rises, but overall labour hours decline; energy input per labour hour is no longer stagnant, but rises rapidly. This novel 'substitution' effect of mechanical energy for human labour can be clearly seen in Figure 4.3 for Italy and Germany after the World War II. With the implementation of the 'oil regime' after the World War II, human labour hours in the economy become completely dissociated from energy input. While labour hours show a slight decline, energy use soars and so does the energy intensity per labour hour. This same pattern can be seen for all European countries. An important part in the decline of labour hours is played by the decline of employment in agriculture; there, the working hours per employee had been particularly high relative to all other economic sectors.

Somewhat similar changes occur in households: electrical equipment (washing machines, vacuum cleaners, food mixers, etc.) substitutes for physical effort on the part of housekeepers and raises the intellectual requirements to handle these machines. As has been demonstrated in a number of studies, however, the overall impact is not to reduce household work, as purchasing and servicing this equipment in larger homes with higher standards of order and cleanliness are time-consuming activities. In combination with the gradual disappearance of servants, the household burden on middle-class women tends to increase.

Since the 1970s, information and communication technology has substituted for the knowledge work component of human labour. At the same time, the physical work component has been further reduced in Europe by the externalisation of industrial production to the world's periphery.

This is the 'golden age' of building up the welfare state and boosting private consumption, of steady increases in wage levels and of reductions of working time. It is also a 'golden age' when the consequences of expanding the education system become statistically visible in the rapid increase of 'white collar' over 'blue collar' labour and the near disappearance of agricultural labour.

Qualitative aspects of human labour

Liquid fossil fuels and electricity allow for the substitution of the physical power dimension of human labour by decentralised energy services. Key technologies are the internal combustion engine, used for cars, and multi-purpose electro-motors linked to electricity grids. Liquid fossil fuels used for tractors and in chemical conversion for mineral fertilisers and pesticides also substitute for a large part of physical human and animal labour in agriculture. In effect, physical strength and prowess lose much of their economic, and thus cultural, value.

Instead, the knowledge dimension of human labour becomes much more important. There is an unprecedented growth in public education and knowledge production. This is the 'golden age' for expanding the public education system, propagating equal opportunities, and building up a skilled workforce with capacities in information and knowledge management rather than physical power and endurance. Knowledge production, information processing and communications become major economic activities. For the first time in history, knowledge production and learning become no longer class privileges and ideological bastions, but evolve to become secular and rational, and functionally related to roles in the labour market.

As far as empathy is concerned, a gender-based picture predominates: toughness and rationality for men, empathy and emotionality for women. Women as loving housewives, taking care of their husbands and children, become the majority model of middle class life.

Institutional forms of labour

In this phase, wage labour becomes by far the most dominant form of labour. Self-employment, both in agriculture and in other sectors, declines while employed labour rises. The overall rates of participation in gainful employment remain largely constant, but within wage labour there is a shift from 'blue collar' to 'white collar' labour. From the end of World War II to the early 1970s, unemployment rates remain very low.

4.2.4 Work in the transition phase from the early 1970s onwards

Qualitative features of labour

One might draw the following analogy: just as technological development and increasing fossil fuel use meant internal combustion and electric motors substituting for much of human physical work, now information and communications technology (ICT) is substituting for knowledge work. Substituting for knowledge work is inherently less energy intensive than substituting for physical work, even if it is not optimised in this direction. Nevertheless, knowledge production and knowledge handling remain key features of human work.

Coinciding with the first world oil crisis in 1973, a structural change in the relationship between energy and labour becomes apparent: the trend of steeply increasing primary energy input in high-income countries is over and gives way, after some sharp fluctuations, to a more stationary energy consumption, both overall and per working hour (see Figure 4.3). There is no longer any discernible correlation between energy use and working time. This period is also characterised by a loosening of the tight ties between exergy and economic output, most likely as a result of the shift in technology towards information and communications technologies.[29]

The reduction of physical work in Europe was of course also greatly enhanced by the externalisation of industrial production to the world's periphery, where emerging economies with very low labour costs were prepared to produce the steadily increasing amount of industrial products that Europe and other rich regions of the world wished to consume. Studies of carbon emissions embodied in trade have shown, for example, that the apparent reduction in the domestic growth of fossil-fuel-based energy was – at least to a certain degree – compensated for by rising fossil-fuel combustion elsewhere.[30]

Intellectual educational standards in the labour force keep rising, as does school and university enrolment, and qualified white collar work increases while industrial blue collar work continues to decline. There are indications that – connected to the rising importance of marketing, services and communications processes – the capacity for empathy is gradually losing its exclusive female label and becoming a more important qualification for work in general.

Quantitative features and institutional form

In Europe, average annual working hours per inhabitant decline only very slightly in the early 1970s, much less than previously (Figure 4.4, left panel), but working time per employee continues to decline (Figure 4.4, right panel). This is a symptom of increasing part-time work (particularly by females), unemployment and rising flexibility in the use of labour power. While Japan shows a similar trend of declining working time to that of Europe, the US is increasing its working time per inhabitant, with stagnating numbers per employee.

More generally, one might say that there are signs of erosion of the traditional, well-established patterns of employment and signs of rising insecurity, while no new clear pattern has established itself. The family pattern that had been introduced in the course of the industrial transformation and had seen its climax in the late 1960s – namely, early marriage for the large majority and long phases of female economic dependency upon male incomes – gradually fades away. Women seek (and need) employment for their sustenance irrespective of family ties, they bear fewer children and the household division of labour slowly becomes less gender-based. Unemployment remains at a higher level than in the period before, and the main measures considered to

With the availability of decentralised energy services enabled by liquid fossil fuels and electricity, physical human and also animal labour is substituted in agriculture, and also in other economic sectors.

counter this are boosting economic growth and keeping immigration at bay.

Figure 4.4 Annual working hours per employee (left) and per inhabitant (right) in the US, Japan and EU-15 (1960-2005)

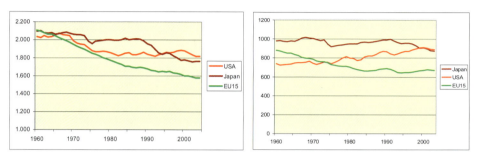

Sources: left: OECD (2001); Maddison (2001); Maddison (2008) (online data base); right: OECD Stat Extracts
(http://stats.oecd.org/Index.aspx?DatasetCode=ANHRS; Maddison (2008); own calculations).

4.3 Speculation on the future of labour

Human labour in Europe as we know it today is highly interwoven with the fossil-fuel based energy regime. In different energy regimes of the past, human labour took different shapes in terms of the features we have identified for our socio-ecological analysis. Now we venture into the future of labour with the simple but fundamental claim that the next socio-ecological transition away from fossil fuels will, in the long run, have as huge an impact on the organisation of human labour as the socio-ecological transition towards fossil fuels has had. To this end, we first briefly sketch the key features of the structural change we anticipate from a new socio-metabolic transition. We do this by speculating on possible changes in certain economic activities, from which we can deduce consequences for labour. Second, on the basis of the sectoral understanding and on the insights gathered from past transitions, we develop our – admittedly highly speculative – storyline for the future of labour.

4.3.1 *Anticipated changes in economic activities*

The starting point for our speculation is the assumption that both rising expenses for energy generation and declining energy return on investment (EROI) will make energy more costly and less abundant. This is already being observed for fossil fuels, where 'conventional' resources are becoming depleted and new, 'unconventional' resources require much higher energy investments (for example, tar sands).[31] While this phenomenon has not yet fully impacted upon energy prices, sooner or later we assume energy consumption will become quite expensive, and even more so in rural areas.

Along with these changes in the energy regime, there are further changes in framework conditions that may have long-lasting structural impacts upon work. After many decades of decline, we are now (since about the year 2000) seeing a sharp rise of prices of all raw materials (commodities). While some believe this to be a transitional phenomenon due to lagging investments, we see many indications of approaching scarcity and of rising efforts for the extraction of material and energy.[32] If this were to dominate the future of resource use, it could have two substantial impacts. First, the share of jobs in supplying society with material and energy would rise due to both lower EROI and declining ore grades. Second, if commodity prices (including energy) remain high or rise even further, this could substantially alter business strategies. One could expect a shift in the dominant mode of cost reduction from labour to resources. In this case, the increase of labour productivity would not be the key measure, but rather the saving of resources, possibly at the expense of more labour.[33] From a macroeconomic perspective, this would mean a shift in the relative prices of material goods and human labour, and consequently a decline in demand for material goods and increasing demand for human labour.

A decline in low-price commodities, including energy, could trigger significant changes in economic activities with subsequent consequences for labour. In effect, if the purchasing power of workers were to be reduced, distributional conflicts over wages and prices for basic goods could become more frequent if no countermeasures are taken.[34] Such social unrest could speed up transition processes. However, here we choose a pragmatic approach and assume incremental changes with little turbulence in sketching the future of

A scarcity of commodities is likely to shift the focus of cost reduction from labour to resources.

certain economic activities where, against our analysis of the past, changes seem to be most obvious (Table 4.1).

Table 4.1 Anticipated changes in economic activities and their consequences for human labour

Assumed changes in Europe arising from the socio-metabolic transition	Consequences for labour	Changes in			
		Quantity	Physical	Intellectual	Empathy
Energy sector		□	□	□	□
• Share of electricity in final energy use significantly increases • Power generation largely from wind, solar and hydro power • Reduced imports of fossil fuels • Demand-side management increases	• More labour force required to supply society • On average, higher skills needed • Increased maintenance work for power generation • Increased demand upon consumers to manage their energy consumption in terms of quantity and timing				
Agriculture, forestry and fishing		□	□	□	□
• Increasing quality of food due to increasing demand for 'healthy' food • More organic farming, more vegetable farming • Less production of red meat • Higher attention to animal protection and standards of husbandry • Price increases in wood and forestry products • Crisis of wild fish production requires new investments and controls, aquaculture increases	• Increasing labour demand in organic and vegetable farming with high quality standards • Stable labour demand for livestock rearing (fewer numbers, but higher standards) • Spread of 'precision farming' in response to price increases and environmental standards • More labour investment in securing ecosystem services (forestry, fishing)				
Construction		□	□	□	□
• Stabilisation of infrastructure at present levels of per capita stocks (transport, energy, building, etc.) • Gradual conversion and rebuilding of existing structures into an energy efficient, low maintenance, and slim infrastructure (insulation of buildings, compact structures	• Less overall construction activities reduce labour demand • This might be compensated by a change from extending infrastructure to converting, rebuilding and renovating, since this is more labour intensive				

concentrated in urban areas, reduction of road network and improved rail network, etc.)

- This shift leads to higher demand for manual skills (handicraft) and less machine-intensive labour

Transport

Passenger

- Further agglomeration in urban areas and reduction of rural population due to the number of productive people required for agriculture, forestry, mining and tourism
- Transport between urban areas is organised with public transport, mainly by rail
- In urban transport, cars are reduced to a minimum and replaced by walking, cycling and public transport
- Reduction of and shift to low maintenance transport infrastructure (e.g. railways, cycling, walking)

Freight

- Reduced volume of cargo because of radically reduced fossil fuel demand
- Less transport of construction materials for non-growing slim infrastructure
- With agglomeration process, material demand shifts further to bigger settlements

- Employment shifts from transport manufacturing to transport services; the net employment effect is positive, given the same mileage
- In urban areas pro-cycling policies and promotion of public transit stimulates labour demand – overall this increases physical exercise by citizens
- A reduction in mileage for both passengers and freight might reduce labour demand in the transport sector
- Improvement of logistics requires sophisticated ICT solutions and skilled labour

Body-related services
(food services, healthcare, wellness, fitness)

- 'Eating out' remains common; increased demand for 'healthy' food, differentiation of food styles
- Increased health literacy increases demand for 'soft' services (e.g. wellness and fitness programmes)
- Ageing increases demand for health services, including caretaking

- Observed trends continue
- There is a wide range of body-related services that require special skills
- The overall demand for care both within families and professionally increases and requires empathy

Supply of raw materials	☐ ☐ ☐ ☐
• Increased material management to improve material circularity • Consequent design for longer service life and easier recycling at end-of-life • Recycling where this saves energy	• More logistics skills and work • More handling of goods and waste • More challenging design tasks

4.3.2 Implications for the future of labour

The existing 'green jobs' reports, such as UNEP (2008) or the European Strategy Agenda 2020, do not elaborate on the quality of 'green' labour in terms of physical work, intellectual capacity or empathy required. Consequently, we have to venture a guess ourselves. Figure 4.5 summarises how the envisaged changes in economic activities might affect labour (it should be noted that the numerical values in this figure are only illustrative). The reference frame of 100% refers to the total number of human working hours. No statistics are available that would allow the quantitative historical comparison of the quality and institutional form of labour that we attempt in Figure 4.5.

Figure 4.5 Variation of quality of work and its institutional form in Europe, by past socio-metabolic regimes and speculation about changes during the new transition

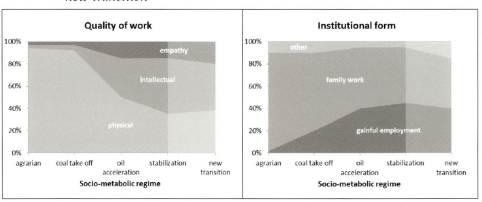

Notes: Work includes market-oriented employment and non-market subsistence work, including household and non-market community work.

According to our assumptions (see Table 4.1), the energy sector, agriculture, the construction sector, as well as body-related services and supply of raw materials will experience a quantitative increase in labour demand.[35] Since these are clearly sectors with a demand for physical labour, we assume that after a long period of decline, the proportion of physical work might rise again (Figure 4.5, left panel).

A decline in continuously available, cheap energy could lead to reduced substitution of human labour by mechanical energy, and thus an increase in the proportion of physical work in our everyday life.

The increasing share of work in caretaking, as assumed above, would play a particularly significant role in increasing physical work. Similarly, when jobs that can save resources – such as in renovation, repair, remaking and reusing – gain momentum, this also might contribute to increasing physical work.

Another line of reasoning sees the increasing frequency of extreme climate events as a source of additional physical labour, whether in the form of gainful employment, as non-market civil services ('other'), or as family labour in coping with such events. This is reflected in the left panel of Figure 4.5 as a possible increase in non-market forms of labour (family and 'other') at the expense of gainful employment.

Finally, Figure 4.5 is based on the assumption that the substitution of (particularly medium qualified) intellectual or knowledge work by ICT and – facilitated by the use of this ICT – its eventual global outsourcing to lower-income countries will continue. The only services that are very difficult to substitute by ICT and almost impossible to outsource to other countries are those involving face-to-face contact with the target population, e.g. various forms of caretaking. In the context of an aging and increasingly culturally heterogeneous and demanding population, we assume that there will be an increase in the type of work based on empathy (at the expense of medium qualified intellectual work) in the institutional forms of collective services, family work and gainful employment.

To avoid the dangers of climate change (i.e. a rise in average temperatures above 2°C), most simulations assume a global decline in primary energy use in the order of 1% annually.[36] If such an assumption were to be realised globally, the required decline in primary energy use in Europe would be much steeper.

How could Europe respond to the changing global landscape, and what would this mean for the medium- and long-term transformation of human labour? Two broad pathways can be distinguished.

One pathway would seek to carry on business as usual for as long as possible and take little action in shifting away from fossil fuels (*Energiewende*) towards a new energy regime. Economic growth and global competitiveness would be prioritised by lowering wages and social standards. This pathway may well still result in growth rates that remain too low to substantially decrease unemployment.[37] Large portions of the labour force may become marginalised, and new forms of labour (such as self-employment, deliberate part-time work or voluntary civil engagement) may be constrained due to inadequate social security arrangements. People (if they are able to) may cling to traditional jobs even if they do not find them satisfactory, and also continue to follow the traditional order: education, work and then retirement. Aggravating impacts of climate change could make the maintenance of public infrastructure substantially more expensive, and security costs could rise to cope with rising inequality and social conflict.

Another pathway would be a more pro-active and innovative response to the socio-ecological transition. There could be massive investment in renewable energy infrastructures on the one hand, and efforts to shift the tax burden from labour to resources (or carbon) on the other. There would be institutional adjustments to a future of low economic growth, but also the expectation of rising wage in emerging economies that would change the terms of trade and open up opportunities for re-industrialisation within Europe. Social policy would be directed at allowing a diversification of labour forms across the classical distinction of employment/self-employed, but also across the life cycle and the phases of education/job/parenthood/pension by providing flexible economic support for phases of little or no work.

Overall, it seems inevitable that the socio-ecological transition will impact labour, both quantitatively and qualitatively. What seems at stake is not so much the demand for labour and the availability of gainful employment, but the economic balance between the remuneration of labour, the cost of raw materials and the expectation of profits.

Bibliography

Arendt, H. (1958), *The Human Condition*, Chicago, IL: Chicago University Press.

Ayres, R.U. and B. Warr (2005), "Accounting for growth: the role of physical work", *Structural Change and Economic Dynamics,* Vol. 16, No. 2, pp. 181-209.

Badinter, E. (1980), *L'Amour en plus: histoire de L'amour maternel XViie - XXe siècle*, Paris: Flammavarion.

Bolognese-Leuchtenmüller, B. and M. Mitterauer (1993), *Frauen - Arbeitswelten. Zur historischen Genese gegenwärtiger Probleme,* Vienna: Verlag für Gesellschaftskritik.

Boserup, E. (1965), *The conditions of agricultural growth. The economics of agrarian change under population pressure*, Chicago, IL: Aldine/Earthscan.

_____ (1981), *Population and Technological Change - A study of Long-Term Trends*, Chicago, IL: University of Chicago Press.

CEDEFOP (European Centre for the Development of Vocational Training) (2009), *Future skill needs for the green economy*, Luxembourg: Publications Office of the European Union

Christ, K. (1984), *Die Römer. Eine Einführung in ihre Geschichte und Zivilisation*, Munich: C.H. Beck.

Clark, C. and M. Haswell (1967), *The Economics of Subsistence Agriculture*, London: Macmillan.

Cleveland, C.J. (2011), Podobnik energy datasets 2013 (www.digitaluniverse.net/energytransitions/view/exercise/51cbf0fa7896bb431f6a3cc8/).

Dobbs, R., J. Oppenheim and F. Thompson (2012), "Mobilizing for a resource revolution" *McKinseyQuarterly*, January.

Drucker, P.F. (1953), "The Employee Society", *American Journal of Sociology,* Vol. 58, No. 4, pp. 358-363.

_____ (1969), *The Age of Discontinuity: Guidelines to Our Changing Society*, New York, NY: Harper & Row.

Elias, N. (1939), *Über den Prozeß der Zivilisation. Soziogenetische und psychogenetische Untersuchungen*, Basel: Haus zum Falken.

Eurofound (2012), *Greening of industries in the EU: Anticipating and managing the effects on quantity and quality of jobs*, Public Policy Management Institute, Vilnius.

European Commission (2010), "Europe 2020 - A European strategy for smart, sustainable and inclusive growth", Communication from the Commission, Brussels.

_____ (2003), "Time use at different stages of life – Results from 13 European countries", Working Papers and Studies, Luxembourg.

Eurostat database (2013), Population on 1 January, extracted via source dataset August 2013 (http://appsso.eurostat.ec.europa.eu/nui/submitViewTableAction.do and http://appsso.eurostat.ec.europa.eu/nui/submitViewTableAction.do).

Fischer-Kowalski, M. (2011), "Analyzing sustainability transitions as a shift between socio-metabolic regimes", *Environmental Innovation and Societal Transitions*, Vol. 1, No. 1, pp. 152-159.

Fischer-Kowalski, M., S.J. Singh, L. Ringhofer C. Grünbühel C. Lauk and A. Remesch (2011), "Socio-metabolic transitions in subsistence communities", *Human Ecology Review*, Vol. 18, No. 2, pp. 147-158.

GEA (2012), *Global Energy Assessment – Toward a Sustainable Future*, Cambridge: Cambridge University Press and Laxenburg, Austria: International Institute for Applied Systems Analysis.

Gellner, E. (1988), *Plough, Sword and Book*, London: Collins Harvill.

Gershuny, J. (2000), *Changing Times: Work and Leisure in Post-industrial Societies*, Oxford: Oxford University Press.

Giampietro, M., K. Mayumi and H. Sorman Alevgül (2012), *The Metabolic Pattern of Societies. Where economies fall short*, New York, NY: Routledge.

Gowdy, J. (1998), *Limited Wants, Unlimited Means: A Reader on Hunter-Gatherer Economics and the Environment*. Washington, DC: Island Press.

Hertwich, E.G. and G.P. Peters (2009), "Carbon Footprint of Nations: A Global, Trade-Linked Analysis", *Environmental Science & Technology*, Vol. 43, No. 16, pp. 6414-6420.

Klein Goldewijk, K., A. Beusen and P. Jansen (2010), "Long-term dynamic modeling of global population and built-up area in a spatially explicit way: HYDE 3", *The Holocene*, Vol. 20, No. 4, pp. 565-573.

Krausmann, F. and H. Schandl (2006), "Der soziale Metabolismus der Industrialisierung. Die Überwindung der energetischen Schranken des agrarischen Wirtschaftens", *GAIA*, Vol. 15, No. 4, pp. 285-293.

Leitner, A., B. Littig and A. Wroblewski (2012), *Die Qualität von Green Jobs. Informationen zur Umweltpolitik Nr. 186*, hg. v. d. Arbeiterkammer Österreich, Vienna: Eigenverlag der AK.

Lewis, W.A. (1955), *The theory of economic growth*, London: Allen & Unwin.

Maddison, A. (2001), *The World Economy. A millenial perspective*, Paris: OECD.

_____ (2008), *Historical Statistics for the World Economy: 1-2006 AD*, online database (www.ggdc.net/maddison/).

Marx, K. and F. and Engels (1848), *Manifest der kommunistischen Partei*, Berlin: Dietz Verlag.

Mattera, P., A. Dubro, T. Gradel, R. Tompson, K. Gordon and E. Foshay (2009), *High road or low road? Job quality in the new green economy*, Good jobs first, Washington, DC.

Mudd, G.M. (2010), "The Environmental sustainability of mining in Australia: key mega-trends and looming constraints", *Resources Policy*, Vol. 35, No. 2, pp. 98-115.

Murphy, D. and C. Hall (2010), "Year in review-EROI or energy return on (energy) invested", *Annals of the New York Academy of Sciences*, Vol. 1185, pp. 102-118.

OECD/Martinez-Fernandez, C., C. Hinojosa and G. Miranda (2010),"Green jobs and skills: the local labour market implications of addressing climate change", Working Document, CFE/LEED, OECD (www.oecd.org/dataoecd/54/43/44683169.pdf?conte ntId=44683170).

Pimentel, D., M. Pimentel, M. Karpenstein-Machan, G.S. Srzednicky and R.H. Driscoll (1999), "Energy use in agriculture: an overview", *CIGR E-Journal*, Vol. 1, International Commission of Agricultural Engineering.

Randers, J. (2012), *2052: A Global Forecast for the Next Fourty Years*, White River Junction, White River Junction, VT: Chelsea Green Publishing.

Ringhofer, L. (2010), *Fishing, Foraging and Farming in the Bolivian Amazon. On a Local Society in Transition*, New York,NY: Springer.

Rizzolatti, G., L. Fogassi and V. Gallese (2006), "Mirrors in the Mind", *Scientific American*, Vol. 295, pp. 54-61.

Sahlins, M. (1972), *Stone Age Economics*, New York, NY: Aldine de Gruyter.

SEC database (2011), Data download from www.uni-klu.ac.at/socec/inhalt/1088.htm.

Sieferle, R.P., F. Krausmann, H. Schandl and V. Winiwarter (2006), *Das Ende der Fläche. Zum gesellschaftlichen Stoffwechsel der Industrialisierung*, Cologne: Böhlau.

Smil, V. (2008), *Energy in Nature and Society. General Energetics of Complex Systems*, Cambridge, MA: MIT Press.

Sohn-Rethel, A. (1970), *Geistige und körperliche Arbeil*, Frankfurt am Main: Suhrkamp.

Statistisches Bundesamt (2006), Zeitbudgets – Tabellenband I – Zeitbudgeterhebung 2001/2002, Statistisches Bundesamt, Wiesbaden.

UNEP (2008), "International Panel for Sustainable Resource Management (Resource Panel)", (www.unep.fr/pc/sustain/initiatives/resourcepanel/index.htm).

Voth, H.-J. (2000), *Time and Work in England 1750-1830*, Oxford: Clarendon Press.

WBGU (2011), *World in Transition - A Social Contract for Sustainability*, Flagship Report, WBGU (German Advisory Council on Global Change), Berlin.

Weber, M. (1920), "Die protestantische Ethik und der Geist des Kapitalismus", in M. Weber (ed.), *Gesammelte Aufsätze zur Religionssoziologie*, Tübingen: J.C.B. Mohr, pp. 17-206.

Wrigley, E.A. (1988), *Continuity, Chance and Change. The Character of the Industrial Revolution in England*, Cambridge: Cambridge University Press.

_____ (2010), *Energy and the English Industrial Revolution*, Cambridge: Cambridge University Press.

Notes

[1] For example, see Eurofound (2012), Cedefop (2009) and OECD (2010). There are some exceptions to this, such as the 2000 project by the Hans Böckler Stiftung, "Arbeit und Ökologie", which looked at a broad range of conceptions of 'labour', including household work and paid civil work.

[2] For a discussion of the traditional time use research, see Gershuny (2000). Giampietro and Mayumi have a long research tradition of placing human time use within a framework of system reproduction, and see it as a key link between demography, energy use and economic output (e.g. Giampietro et al., 2012). This chapter follows a similar perspective.

[3] See Ringhofer (2010).

[4] See Sahlins (1972); Ringhofer (2010).

[5] See Sahlins (1972); Gowdy (1998).

[6] See also Boserup (1981); Ringhofer (2010).

[7] Voth (2000).

[8] Boserup (1965).

[9] See Ayres and Warr (2005).

[10] Smil (2008, p. 138).

[11] Ibid., p. 137.

[12] Ibid., p. 138.

[13] Ibid., p. 128.

[14] Rizzolatti et al. (2006, pp. 54-61).

[15] Boserup (1981, pp. 1-255).

[16] This is at the core of the Nobel Laureate William Arthur Lewis's influential 'dual-sector model' (Lewis, 1955).

[17] Clark and Haswell (1967); Fischer-Kowalski (2011); Fischer-Kowalski et al. (2011).

[18] See Pimentel et al. (1999).

[19] Sohn-Rethel (1970).

[20] Smil (2008, p. 174).

[21] Christ (1984, p. 2).

[22] Ibid., p. 2.

[23] See Wrigley (1988); Wrigley (2010) for the UK.

---

[24] See Marx and Engels (1848, pp. 25-57).

[25] Gellner (1988).

[26] Elias (1939); Badinter (1980).

[27] Weber (1920).

[28] Bolognese-Leuchtenmüller and Mitterauer (1993).

[29] Ayres and Warr (2005, pp. 181-209).

[30] Hertwich and Peters (2009).

[31] Murphy and Hall (2010).

[32] Mudd (2010).

[33] See, for example, Dobbs et al. (2012).

[34] See also Randers (2012).

[35] This is in line with recent studies – (Mattera et al. (2009) for the US; Leitner et al. (2012) for Austria – that identify forestry and agriculture, the construction industry, waste management, and trade and transport as the main sectors of new 'green jobs'.

[36] See, for example, WBGU (2011); GEA (2013).

[37] Randers (2013).

5. JOB QUALITY IN THE EUROPEAN UNION: TRAVELLING BACK IN TIME?*

> *The academic discourse is out of touch from what is going on.... We spend our lives having theories about whether the contract of employment is green, yellow or pink, instead of asking if everybody has employment.*
>
> (A labour law expert from the UK)

T he European Union's Lisbon Strategy, launched in 2000, aimed to create "more and better jobs". The global crisis has clearly undermined the achievement of quantitative employment targets, but this chapter seeks to answer whether jobs have become "better" over the past 10 to 15 years. The Job Quality Index constructed by the European Trade Union Institute shows that there was a marked deterioration in subjective job security between 2005 and 2010. At the same time, it shows an improvement with regard to working time and work-life balance. It may be that while rising unemployment and the declining bargaining power of labour reduced the quality of existing jobs, overall job quality rose in certain respects because low-quality jobs were more likely to disappear than high-quality ones.[1]

A further challenge to understanding the relationship between quantity and quality of employment arises from the ways in which Europe

---

* János Kovács is the author of chapter 5, which builds on the work of Christoph Hilbert, Marcela Veselková and Tünde Virág as well as their co-authors, Ada Garriga, Mireia Las Heras, Esther Jimenez and Zsuzsa Vidra. The research conducted in the work package 2 (Good jobs in a good economy) is summarised in two studies (Kovács et al. 2012, 2014), in which the reader will find detailed notes and references. János is a permanent fellow at the Institute for Human Sciences in Vienna.

copes with climate change. However, the precise impact of the greening of European industry is difficult to predict. So far, greening seems to have redistributed jobs between sectors without altering the general level of employment. The effect of greening on job quality is moderate. The greatest improvement is observed in skills development, while the impact of greening on career and employment security, health and well-being, and reconciliation of working and non-working life is less clear.[2]

Assessing the development of job quality depends on the indicators used.[3] Quite frequently, the concept of 'good jobs' is examined along the dimension of intrinsic versus extrinsic features.[4] Intrinsic features include how interesting or meaningful the work is or whether the worker experiences social isolation. Extrinsic features pertain to objective, easily measurable components of quality such as the work compensation package, the regulation of working time or the contractual status of the employee. Another important distinction may be whether 'materialist' or 'post-materialist' attributes prevail in a certain job (and/or in the perception of that job by the employee). Accordingly, one is advised to contrast acquisitive and security/survival-oriented, instrumental-rational, etc. (materialist) values with autonomy/self-expression-oriented, gender- and environment-conscious, etc. (post-materialist) values.[5] The two distinctions are not necessarily mutually exclusive.

Since the middle of the past century, researchers have tended to presume optimistically that in the long run good jobs would gradually crowd out the bad ones. Simultaneously, the proportion of its materialist and post-materialist elements would change in favour of the latter.[6] 'Detraditionalisation' was one of the labels characterising this process.[7] Today, however, one may expect to witness a declining importance of attributes such as creativity, self-fulfilment, recognition, autonomy, participation and equal opportunity, but a rising significance of stable full-time employment, decent pay, and good physical working conditions in the eyes of the employees when assessing the quality of jobs. This chapter will therefore focus on 'retraditionalisation', asking whether or not time travel back to the 20th century began some time ago. Does the demand for quantity override job quality considerations ("A good job is an existing job.")? Is there a broad preference for the stability of employment ("A good job is a job that will continue to exist tomorrow.")? Do post-materialist values really not matter much in defining the concept of a good job ("A good job is a stable, well-paid job that offers agreeable physical working conditions.")?

This chapter grew out of a considerable dissatisfaction[8] with the typical research agenda in this field, which i) is preoccupied with the *quid pro quo* between job security and the flexibility of work contracts and/or physical working conditions (especially the regulation of working time); ii) regards the post-materialist elements of job quality as cushions that moderate the shocks of decreasing security or increasing flexibility of employment rather than as self-explanatory aims of 'humanising' the workplace; and iii) does not make any distinction between the 'egoistic' and 'altruistic' constituents of post-materialist aspirations.

5.1 Putting some flesh on the bones of survey-based studies

Current studies of job quality are dominated by large surveys. They begin by identifying a set of composite quality features (mixing materialist and post-materialist ones), and continue by formulating a questionnaire in which these features are presented to the respondents for evaluation/selection/ranking in the framework of impersonal (or personal, but rather shallow) surveys. In many cases, the interviewees have to choose from among answers like "safety at the workplace is unimportant/important/very important for me".[9] Frequently, these surveys are carried out by leading international organisations with a primary interest in large-scale comparisons and generalisable results.[10] They tend to observe objective and subjective variables of job quality simultaneously, as well as measure (and aggregate) even the subjective variables to construct in an extreme case, a single job quality indicator for a whole country.

As regards the subjective variables, the respondents are normally asked about their satisfaction levels rather than about their aspirations or preferences. The researcher then tries to derive the latter from the former.[11] In this way, one may produce snapshots of how 'decent' the respondents feel their existing work to be, but one cannot really learn what kind of ideals they cherish with regard to good jobs. Moreover, in most surveys the interviewees are not requested to explain the components of these snapshots. Typically, the researcher wears the hat of the 'normal employee', seeing the existing (viable) selection of the quality features from his/her perspective and pretending to know the breadth of the choices and the potential reasons for certain preferences. The researcher will generally not make great efforts to reveal the motives governing the

In-depth case studies should serve as a complement to large surveys of job quality.

decisions taken by the respondents and to confront these with their real practices. Even if the preferences are somehow revealed, their discursive environment and the underlying cultural motives remain in the dark. The respondents are inundated with a whole lot of questions (requiring short answers) even when data collection is not impersonal. Finally, the researcher has almost no opportunity to test the strength or consistency of the preferences because the respondents are not observed in the context of a given case of employment.

To address the shortcomings of such surveys, a more personal approach to the study of good jobs is suggested. It requires asking employees to explain their quality preferences and comparing these explanations with their actual practices. Also, researchers should exercise self-restraint in terms of both measurement and making normative statements. First, they have to tell whether job quality is higher or lower… and then they have to suggest a proper mix of quality features. Such an approach should not be seen as a rival to but an ally of the survey methods described above – an ally whose results are perhaps less representative and exact, but with whose help one can put some flesh on the bones of survey-based studies.

In order to explore the background of the employees' narratives with some accuracy, a case study approach was chosen. Case studies in four countries (Hungary, Slovakia, Spain and the United Kingdom) were conducted at comparable sites. One of the two case studies conducted in each country focused on a large international company in the telecom industry. For the others, we studied two huge engineering firms, a large pharmaceutical enterprise and a medium-sized company in the food industry. (The original aim to reach full comparability was hampered by the resistance of Hungarian and Slovak engineering firms.)

During 2012 and 2013, the researchers conducted a minimum of between 10 and 15 semi-structured in-depth interviews in each company to accomplish the case studies. The overwhelming majority of the respondents came from the shop floor, including low-level management. What they offered us were certainly views 'from below' of good jobs, even if many of them worked in top industries. In the first half of the company interviews the respondents were asked about their own concept of an ideal job, and in the second they were requested to choose between materialist and post-materialist features of job quality (for the questionnaire, see Kovács et al., 2014). Relevant local documents were checked and as much participant observation was undertaken as was permitted by the companies. Of course, even more than 100 interviews do not allow for the construction of any reasonable typology of quality preferences according to age, gender, profession, occupation, status, etc. – not to mention nationality.

5.2 'Retraditionalisation' and rising flexibility

In the first decade of the new millennium, one could not help but discover a large gap between the dominant rhetoric and the real world, that is, between the mounting popularity of the term 'good jobs' (which has become a catchphrase like flexicurity, employability, matching skills and jobs, etc.) in politics and academia and the vast number of people who would be satisfied with bad jobs, even with almost any kind of job. Unfortunately, the popularity of the good job rhetoric does not originate in a coherent set of arguments. If one just compares the leading definitions of job quality – ranging from the so-called 'Laeken indicators', through the ILO or the ETUC concepts of decent work, all the way down to Eurofound's 'quality features' – astonishing results occur. Fair wages and enough jobs, not to mention health and safety, are missing in many of them. One researcher or politician emphasises gender equality, the other work-life balance, and yet another career development. One praises security while the other stresses both flexibility and security, and so on. I would almost go so far as to say that the selections of quality attributes are coherent only in one single respect: one rarely finds the ideal of 'green jobs' in any of the taxonomies. However, other post-materialist features (such as participation, social responsibility, inclusion, self-fulfilment, recognition, creativity, autonomy and engagement) appear in the elite discourse on good jobs on the EU level rather frequently.

The following selection includes a few results of the most recent quantitative inquiries on job quality in the countries under scrutiny:

- Hungary, Slovakia and the UK belong to those countries in which flexibility clearly overrides security in terms of a 'composite indicator of flexicurity' based on four pillars: contractual arrangements, lifelong learning, active labour market policies and social security systems. In Spain, however, security prevails. The UK is characterised by a higher level of both flexibility and security than in the other three countries.[12]

- In considering six types of jobs (active, saturated, team-based, passive, insecure and high-strain jobs, arranged in descending order of quality), the UK has the highest share of good jobs among the four countries, followed by Slovakia, Spain and Hungary.[13]

- The 'overall job quality index' (based on the average of rankings made in the field of wages, non-standard forms of employment, working time and work-life balance, working conditions and job security, skills and career development and collective interest representation) demonstrates that the score of Spain, Slovakia and Hungary relates to that of the UK like 4 to 7.[14]

- Focusing on four sets of indicators – 1) earnings, 2) working time quality, 3) intrinsic job quality and 4) prospects of employment – the number representing 'average job quality' in terms of 1) is 1,591 in the UK, 1,414 in Spain, 844 in Slovakia and 626 in Hungary. For 2) the numbers are 61.3, 57.8, 52.4 and 56.8; for 3) they are 69.4, 68.9, 67.5, 67.1; and for (4) they are 70.9, 60.0, 64.0, 61.8, respectively.[15]

- In a taxonomy including "high-quality standard employment relationship (SER)—like", "instrumental SER-like", "precarious extensive", "portfolio" and "precarious unsustainable" jobs (in descending order of quality), the UK has the smallest share of 'best jobs' among the four countries (the Slovak share is almost twice as large). The UK also has between two and three times as many 'worst jobs' as Spain and Hungary, and about five times as many as Slovakia.[16]

The results of such (inherently incomparable) surveys warn us to be cautious when someone tells us without any reservation that job quality in country A is three times higher than in country B, flexibility killed security or that the era of post-materialism is over for good. Yet, in preparing the literature reviews, our research group encountered such generalisations in great numbers. The doubts concerning the clarity of the concept of job quality did not ebb, as demonstrated by the following working hypotheses with which the armchair research was left.[17]

Two discursive camps. When considering good jobs, the main actors of the labour market organise their employment discourses by and large along the flexibility/security axis, suggesting different mixes of the two concepts but falling roughly into two camps (discursive alliances). These camps are rather stable and include similar sets of actors in the four countries examined. Irrespective of the fact that both camps' blends of concepts frequently carry the label of 'flexicurity', they follow the old logic: typically, the employment narratives put forward by employers, the liberal and conservative parties and labour economists oppose those suggested by trade unions, the social-democratic parties, labour sociologists and most NGOs.

Shaky concepts. With the exception of the UK, concepts such as stability and security, flexibility and precariousness, internal and external flexibility, employment and job security, income security and job security, job preferences and job satisfaction, and job quality and work quality are frequently used as synonyms without further qualification. In many cases, secure jobs are regarded as good jobs while flexible jobs are seen as bad jobs, and vice versa; both discursive alliances often suffer from tunnel vision. As a consequence, important dilemmas are sometimes disregarded (such as whether the job security for the insiders of the labour market does not hurt that of the outsiders, or whether bad jobs also deserve to be maintained).

Flexibility on the rise. The flexibility and security discourses are intertwined, but on average lean towards the former. Flexibility can be interpreted as inclusion and, as such, as a contribution to a new version of security that replaces the outmoded narrative of stability with that of employability. Thus the adherents to the flexibility narrative open a door towards a novel version of security that can be attained through new, variable skills, including by those whose employment is currently insecure. In the optimal case, flexible work schedules may improve work-life balance and reduce ethnic-, gender- or age-related discrimination.

The security camp could, in principle, show a greater interest in attributes of good jobs which go beyond those related to wages, contractual rights

Is flexibility on the rise, are post-materialist values in decline?

and physical working conditions, but the leap in this direction does not seem to be made in three of the four countries. They could use attributes such as self-fulfilment, autonomy or participation as Trojan horses of the security narrative. But even in the fourth country, the UK, where a coherent narrative has crystallised around the concept of 'good work' (stressing skills, health and even green values), concern about the quantity of (secure) jobs offsets quality considerations for the major stakeholders of the security camp.

Retraditionalisation. As regards the various components of job quality, those of a post-materialist nature are the clear losers. Hence, a retraditionalisation seems to be a valid assumption, especially in Spain and to a lesser degree in the UK, while in the two Eastern European countries the same phenomenon could be described as being stuck in a traditional interpretation of job quality focusing on full-time work with permanent contracts and appropriate wages. When employees in any of the four countries choose from among the materialist elements of good jobs, one sees a strong preference for stability of employment, that is, for compromising on wages and physical working conditions, not to mention fair treatment, career development or work-life balance.

'North-south' divide. Instead of the widely-assumed 'east-west' divide in reflecting upon job quality (in which, say, the west is flexibility-prone and post-materialist, while the east is security-prone and materialist), a 'north-south' cleavage emerges, in which Hungary and Slovakia as new entrants join Spain on the southern side of the EU. This division is demonstrated in the three countries through less sophisticated employment discourses, a stronger antagonism between the two discursive camps, a quantitative rather than qualitative approach taken by the main actors of the labour market to jobs, and the relatively low value attributed by them to the post-materialist components of job quality.

5.3   Case studies: Industries, companies and job qualities

As mentioned above, the eight case studies of employee preferences for the various components of good jobs represent telecommunications (E, H, SK, UK), engineering (E, UK), food (SK) and pharmaceutical (H) industries. Evidently, the industry matters. Just like the concrete company cases do, which are strongly affected by the actual changes in the labour markets of the four countries. What do the macro data tell us?[18]

All things considered, by the end of our research period, the plight of employment was most favourable in the UK, and employment trends showed the greatest improvement in Slovakia. Of the two 'bad performers', employment trends were more critical in Spain than in Hungary in most respects.

Besides the overall employment situation in the four countries, it is the most recent developments in workplace innovation that may have influenced the quality preferences of employees to a large extent during the past 10 to 15 years. The spread of relatively new techniques of work organisation, such as teleworking, flexi-time, task rotation and multi-skilling, prompt the researcher to ask whether these counter-balanced some of the adverse trends in the labour markets during the past decade or so; trends that were probably further aggravated by the global crisis. They seem to be instrumental *sui generis* in reinforcing the post-materialist attitudes of the employees, although the 'virtualisation' and 'fragmentation' of work may promote the egoistic rather than collectivistic elements of these attitudes.[19]

How do all these changes (or lack of changes) manifest themselves in actual employee discourses on 'decent work'?

Box 5.1 What do the macro data tell us?

- During the past decade and a half, economic growth as a whole was very fast in Slovakia, fast in Hungary and moderate in Spain, while the UK underwent a slight economic decline. Hungary, Spain and the UK suffered from the global financial crisis to an almost equal measure, resulting in near stagnation over more recent years.

- The rate of employment did not change significantly in the four countries. It was higher in the middle of the past decade but decreased afterwards (in Spain until today). The rate was highest in the UK throughout the period studied. The decline in male employment was essentially counter-balanced by a rise in female employment, especially in Spain. The rate of employment fell sharply among the youth (by the least in the UK), stagnated among the middle-aged, and grew considerably among the older-age cohorts (particularly in Slovakia).

- The share of part-time employment rose, especially in the case of men (who are still two to three times less likely than women to be employed in part-time jobs. The rise was the slowest in the UK, but there the share of part-time work was already high.

- Temporary employment grew a little in Hungary and Slovakia, and fell in Spain and the UK.

- The rate of unemployment rose everywhere, except Slovakia, and particularly sharply in Spain (especially among men and the young). Long-term unemployment changed in a similar fashion.

- The unemployment trap did not grow in the UK; it decreased considerably in Slovakia, and increased in Hungary more than in Spain.

- Finally, net incomes between 2005 and 2012 more than doubled in Slovakia, rose significantly in Hungary and moderately in Spain, and stagnated in the UK. The crisis hit Hungary and the UK the hardest. By and large, as far as incomes are concerned, neither female nor young employees fared worse than their male and older colleagues.

5.4 Job quality choices in the same industry

In the telecoms companies under scrutiny – that is, in large transnational firms in a flourishing industry employing many young, well-trained professionals (with a majority of males in the sample) – the main security attributes of job quality, such as a decent salary that is paid regularly, a formal contract

> *Post-materialist values, such as team spirit, communication, pride, recognition, prestige and upward mobility, are more important in large transnational firms.*

promising longer-term employment, good physical working conditions and the like, were usually taken for granted. Perhaps more importantly, the interviewees were without exception employed at the time we met them, mostly enjoying the 'luxury' of legal certitude and an acceptable living standard. As regards flexibility, in these companies imminent dismissal is not normally a credible threat, and flexibility of working time can be associated with values such as autonomy, creativity and work-life balance rather than with the stress of precarious work. The post-materialist quality features come to the fore, and team spirit, communication, pride, recognition, prestige, upward mobility and so on may overshadow some of the classical material rewards. Employees appreciate the fact that their work is creative and challenging (according to one Hungarian respondent, *"it is unpredictable, I like that there are no two identical days"*[20]), represents a cutting-edge technology, and constantly develops their skills.

In the Hungarian telecoms firm, recognition was considered by the employees interviewed as the third most important trait of good jobs, following job security and decent pay. Besides career development resulting from (and also generating) recognition, they also valued team work, being treated as an equal, and receiving information on higher-level decisions even if they cannot actively take part in them. As a Hungarian manager remarked, *"one usually thinks it is pay but we found that the real touch point is communication"*. However, maybe he was not quite right. Irrespective of whether or not the management informed employees correctly about a crucial change in the company's work organisation introduced at the time of the case study, the employees were resisting the new scheme by saying that it disrupted team spirit by excessively individualising work activities and curbed their feeling of autonomy through a system of permanent supervision (*"they are watching us from above"*). At the same time, the employees were not complaining much about the reduction of the wage-performance ratio resulting from the organisational shift. In the opinion of the authors of the case study:

> The growing tendency of flexibilisation is perceived as a major threat to all the good qualities that they currently appreciate in the job. (...) At the end of the day, (...), the super-flexible working conditions achieved by the necessary company reorganisations may lead to the retraditionalisation of employees' values: they will regard security as the most important work value.

In other words, if flexibilisation of work organisation hurts the former post-materialist combination of autonomy and collective performance, then the employees may again attribute more significance to the materialist features of security, such as an agreeable wage and stable employment.

In the Slovak telecoms firm, career development, professional education ('progress', in their parlance) and work-life balance were given high scores by the employees. Moreover, they emphasised their own responsibility in exploiting these opportunities. At the same time, they tended to relativise the importance of material rewards against other features of work:

> Wage is important in the beginning (...) but if there is no recognition, no education, no career growth, (...) if the job is boring and you don't see the challenge, you lose motivation, you lose productivity.(...) High salary can convince you to sign that contract but you will probably try to quit after three months if you wake up in the morning and don't want to go to work although the salary is high (...).[21]

While amongst the post-materialist components of good jobs the primarily egoistic (consumerist, individualist, hedonistic, etc.) components like flexibility of working hours or work-life balance were often emphasised, the altruistic (collectivist) ones such as non-discrimination, participation or environmentalism were hardly mentioned in the interviews (again, maybe because of their self-explanatory character in a Western-based enterprise of a prestigious industry, just as in the Hungarian company). In this respect, I found the following interview excerpt extremely telling:

> I do, I do [care about the working environment] because I want to feel important. Freud says that mankind craves two things, right? The first thing is sexual satisfaction and the second is the feeling of

importance. And I agree with Freud, by the way. So as every person on earth, I want to feel important. This might not be my building, I might not own it but it is good-looking and it makes me feel important that I work at a cool place.

Studying a telecoms company in Spain revealed similar results in terms of the ranking of more and less traditional elements of job quality. Here, permanent and tailor-made contracts were appreciated more than a good salary, while the latter was also preceded by work-life balance and flexible regulation of working time. In this case, flexibility meant personal autonomy in changing traditional cultural patterns such as spending 12 hours at work (with long lunch and coffee breaks) and paying the employees *'by presence'*, which prompts them to stay at work until the managers leave. As the authors of the Spanish case study noted, their respondents would like to avoid having *'much overtime'* or *'Marathon days'* and consider the right to take part in organising their own working time as *'non-negotiable'*.[22]

Professional development shared second place with autonomous time management in the employees' preference lists. One of the respondents put it this way: *"Money is important but if you have on the table flexibility [of working time] and career development then money is not important."* Mobility within the firm as well as between regions and countries was also considered a key feature of good jobs, as was having meaningful work. Happiness is a principal requirement, as demonstrated by our interview partners: *"I do not understand why I have to be tied to a chair." "The job should be ambitious, entrepreneurial allowing you to contribute with new ideas." "I would like to enjoy doing my job and go home in peace with myself."* Hence, certain post-materialist features of decent work managed to occupy many of the upper positions in the Spanish employees' ranking. Amongst the other typical post-materialist values, equal opportunity came out as a top priority whereas other ethical, political, ecological, etc. components of job quality did not really matter.

Did experiences in the British telecoms firm differ significantly? By and large the answer is "no", but according to the case study, decent pay was not primarily compared to in-job post-materialist features (such as recognition, creativity and participation) but rather to work-life balance in general, and the time one can spend with one's family in particular. *"(...) You work to live but you don't live to work." "I think you should enjoy your free time as much as you should enjoy work." "Work is important to pay the bills but the most important thing is what's happening in your family." "It's more important to have more time for oneself than for work."*[23] Also, health and safety were valued by employees almost as much as pay, and environmental awareness was stressed in the interviews more often in the UK than in Hungary, Slovakia and Spain.

The respondents in the British telecoms firm also felt privileged as far as material rewards were concerned (or did not expect any improvement under the current economic conditions). Thus, they were also inclined to speak about their claims with regard to a good working atmosphere, recognition, independence and creativity: *"I mean we'd all want more money but I don't think (...) I would go back in the factory just for money, no." "When you're sort of governed by the clock, you feel like you're a robot." "A bad job is gonna be one way not valued, possibly grossly underpaid or mistreated. (...) A good job is exactly the opposite, so valued, you're paid well and you enjoy."*

It also transpires from the UK study, as well as from the other three, that if any of the three main pillars of security (pay, contract and physical working conditions) was to be shattered in this industry, then post-materialist aspirations would probably not assume such a prominent position in the preference lists of the respondents.

All in all, the fact that our telecom case studies do not reveal much difference in the quality preferences across the four countries, and that these preferences are slightly biased towards post-materialist values, does not mean that the 'retraditionalisation' hypothesis should be dismissed for good. In the companies we examined, the material needs of employees, including job and income security, are apparently relatively satisfied, or the employees cannot hope to achieve a substantial increase in the level of satisfaction. They are therefore ready to accept second-best solutions in the field of security. But to which amongst the non-traditional values do they subscribe? The respondents tend to embrace those post-materialist components of job quality which are of an egoistic character, such as a pleasant working environment, autonomy, work-life balance, skills and education. Altruistic values, such as participation, social responsibility, equal opportunity or greenness, remain at the bottom of their preference lists. Is a kind of 'selfish post-materialism' on the rise?

5.5   Job quality choices between industries

Employees in other – less prosperous – industries normally do not develop such a high intensity of post-materialist attitudes in defining the concept of good jobs as that experienced in the telecom firms. Of course, prosperity is only one among the possible explanations. Some of the companies discussed below are not less prosperous, but represent much older technologies and industrial culture, not to mention the fact that they have left behind the most vigorous/constructive phase of their development trajectory, in which labour shedding is less likely.

> *Materialist values are dominant in more traditional or less prosperous industries.*

Similarly, they do not attract as many young professionals who bring post-materialist values to the workplace. Undoubtedly, some of these companies can give their employees a sense of security, but frequently the technology they apply does not promise them much flexibility, creativity or autonomy.

Consider the two engineering companies. The one in the UK is equal, if not superior, to the telecom firms discussed above in terms of cutting-edge technology, size and reputation. Decent pay, long-term employment and favourable working conditions were expected by the employees as almost axiomatic features of job quality in this large multinational company that, in their view, "*would always exist*". By security they meant reliability and predictability of the firm's behaviour as well as safety stemming from the excellent brand name, and did not regard material rewards as an absolute criterion of quality. According to one respondent, "*[w]age is important. But it's again a balance between working environment and wage. I wouldn't for instance work a crazy amount of hours*".[24] His colleague put this thought in a similar way: "*I want to get paid. But it's not my number one driver. I am more driven by having a really good experience, a great challenge, and being employable.*"

Instead of talking about security, interviewees stressed how challenging, creative and socially responsible their ideal job would be, and to what extent it was expected to contribute to their own professional development. Continuous learning as a means of future employability was an important element here. Although the respondents did not face any aggressive attempts at flexibilisation of working time, they believed that, for example, longer working hours would be a fair price for attaining these values. Health and safety were important aspects of a good job, but given ample state regulation as well as a reliable company record in this field, the employees did not emphasise them in the interviews. The same applies to equal opportunity. However, while in all the above fields the company's official narrative largely matched the discourse of the individual employees, the employees ranked environmental awareness much lower than their company did. What seems symptomatic again is that, with the remarkable exception of social responsibility, altruism is not a strong driver in the domain of post-materialist considerations. However, in the other three countries our case studies have hardly identified employees who would have had ideological motives as strong as those demonstrated by the following three interviewees in a British engineering company:

> For any money in the world I wouldn't work for, I have ten companies in my head, I wouldn't work for those with a very strong 'first-world' attitude and bad working conditions or impact in the third world.
>
> Somewhere between alcohol and tobacco, there is a line that I would prefer not to cross. I worked for a bank, enjoyed working for a bank (…) but I wouldn't go back (…) I think it's just the world view that I don't subscribe to (…).
>
> I wouldn't work for a company that does animal testing or spills oil everywhere, anything like that (…).

The Spanish engineering firm shows a more traditional pattern; here materialist values are more popular among the employees. Although decent pay is not considered the top priority (coming third in the list), but some kind of pay originating in stable employment definitely is. The latter was presented, together with professional development, as the most important element of job quality in the interviews. As one interviewee said, *"I prefer to earn less and be comfortable but this does not mean that salary is not important in a job".*[25] In contrast to responses at the Spanish telecom company, here the recent employment crisis in the country has clearly exerted a major influence upon the employees' attitudes. In the opinion of one interview partner of ours:

> (…) earlier having a permanent contract meant something, now I know many cases that [the employees' position] seemed stable, and they got fired. My wife works in a bank and this kind of job seemed much more secure and stable but now not anymore, and the same happened to many good jobs in big and stable companies.

The majority of respondents thought that the stability of a job is contingent on their employability which may result from continuous education. They presumed that *"autonomy is also linked to professional development"*, *"(…) when you get promoted it goes with (…) dignity and prestige"*. In second place on the list of quality features one finds the adequate organisation of working time, leading to a better work-life balance and a shortening of the traditionally long Spanish workdays. *"Flexibility should be linked to your personal use of time"*, one of the employees noted. Another respondent contended, *"I could renounce [part of my] salary for a good team (…) I could give up my salary but not my time"*.

As for other post-materialist features of good jobs, variability of the work and mobility were frequently mentioned. Moreover, time (the authors of the case study ask whether this is not the new currency of the 21st century) was appreciated not only for self-fulfilment, but also for voluntary work outside the company. Green attitudes, however, were not popular among the respondents. One of them said with resignation, *"it is very difficult to value sustainability if you have no job"*.

The employees of the pharmaceutical company we studied in Hungary also preferred a stable contract (but also the possibly inflexible working time of eight hours and five days) to decent pay among the standard elements of employment security. In other words, they also tended to accept a 'job for pay' trade-off, as demonstrated by the following interview excerpt:

> It kills your daily life when you constantly have to worry whether there's going to be work tomorrow, whether or not the company will close in six months. This place has a stable reputation. I'm not saying they're paying the employees sky-high but the positions are secure.[26]

Primarily due to technological reasons (three-shift operation, severe work discipline) and company traditions (lifelong employment, family networks in the workforce, special welfare services), neither external nor internal flexibility were regarded by the employees as a major threat. In accepting that they are 'locked in' to a high-discipline work process, the respondents valued not only creativity and variability of work, but also trust, solidarity, intergenerational cooperation, social sensitivity, industrial peace, and so on (that is, a pleasant working atmosphere) in addition to the pride they felt working in a competitive, well-organised, clean industry of high esteem. Surprisingly for a chemical firm, health and safety did not feature highly on the priority list of job quality attributes. Furthermore, compared to the British and Spanish companies, the employees in the Hungarian pharmaceutical firm did not rank professional education and work-life balance among the top priorities when thinking about decent work. As the case study author notes, *"being penned up and having a time schedule partly or wholly in contrast to normal family schedules lend human relationships at work a far higher importance"*.

Are the above-mentioned constituents of working atmosphere - i.e. non-physical working conditions – post-materialist and if they are, do they belong to the egoistic or the altruistic segment of job quality traits? They are mostly of only an indirectly materialist nature, even if some of them remind the observer of the cultural world of a traditional (paternalist) company. ("*It's like we had two homes*", said one interviewee.) Also, altruism unmistakably occurs amongst these traits but it is also slightly old-fashioned, relating to 'love and peace' within the firm rather than participation, equal opportunity, environmentalism or obtaining time for voluntary activity outside of work.

Finally, let us have a look at a much smaller company operating in the food industry in Slovakia. As it is located in a region of severe unemployment and most of the employees are not highly qualified, it was not surprising to hear our respondents wish for more security for themselves. Although they were not satisfied with their wages, they put the ideal of having a permanent contract at the very top of their preference list, while attributing almost as much importance to acceptable pay. The author of the case study asserts the following: "*Links were drawn between low wage and underrated or under-appreciated work. Wage was thus constructed as both a source of income and a source of dignity.*"[27] Yet, resignation seems stronger: things are "*not that bad and you cannot be too picky nowadays*". This sentiment, repeated by many respondents, reflects the fact that today many employees are content to have second-best jobs rather than striving for ideal ones.

In any event, good physical working conditions were mentioned among the vital components of decent work much more often than in the seven other case studies – an understandable phenomenon if one takes into account the high intensity of work and ratio of overtime in this firm, not to mention heat and noise. "*The relationships here are disturbed. Maybe it's because of too much work, people are nervous*", said one of the respondents. Another noted: "*You have to hurry up, you have to work fast. You hurry to the work, you hurry from the work, you hurry in the work. The break is short, you just have something to eat and then you get back to work and work fast until you're finished.*"

Just as in the Hungarian pharmaceutical firm, professional education and career development were not brought up by the employees in the Slovak food company. They longed for meaningful work, team spirit and recognition – "*civility in the workplace*", as one noted – and would appreciate a family-like working atmosphere. However, they cited none of the altruistic features of post-materialism, such as participation, fair treatment and social responsibility. Despite the fact that theirs is a bio-sensitive company producing healthy food, and that the owner is proud of his commitment to green values, the highest level of adherence to environmentalism by the employees was reflected in this opinion: *"Before I started working here I wasn't concerned about [greenness]. But when you work in this company, you gain a different perspective."*

5.6 Hypotheses vs. conclusions: Which post-materialism?

How do our preliminary assumptions relate to the results of fieldwork? Is the evidence collected in the case studies convincing enough to accept the working hypotheses of our research group, above all the assumption of 'retraditionalisation'? Are the respondents' attitudes reverting to those of the 1960s, when post-materialist values were less important in defining a good job. Have the interviewees really travelled back half a century in time?

A note of caution must be made here. To understand the degree of '*de*traditionalisation' during the last century, and to establish how seriously employees began to '*re*traditionalise' their quality preferences during the past decade or so, one would have had to study their attitudes 10, 20 or 50 years ago. In want of a better solution, we took the conclusions of the 'detraditionalisation' literature for granted, which suggested that the present importance of materialist elements should have been preceded by a process of 'retraditionalisation' eroding the results of decades of 'detraditionalisation'. This section therefore captures only the outcome of that process, without making specific claims about when the process started and whether it will continue.

Similarly, our research design does not offer an answer to the question of *why* post-materialist values have lost some of their importance (although the recent economic crisis and a growing risk aversion in its wake seem to be principal reasons for this).[28] Also, as mentioned above, the small sample size of the investigation does not allow for estimates regarding the participation rates of various social groups in 'retraditionalisation' by age, gender, profession and the like. The interviewees, however, seem to confirm the truism that younger, higher-skilled employees in transnational companies of progressive industries are perhaps the most reluctant to return to traditional attitudes towards job quality.

The empirical findings nuanced much of what our research group believed they knew about materialist versus post-materialist values (or, more broadly put, cultures) in the context of the flexibility and security discourses. First, it became clear that insisting on a sharp distinction between the two kinds of culture in the context of job quality is rather difficult because of a grey zone in which they overlap. Materialist values (such as a stable contract or appropriate pay) may be regarded by employees not only as a source of material safety, but also as part of recognition, prestige and engagement, thus embodying post-materialist values. Or indeed post-materialist values such as a pleasant working atmosphere or self-fulfilment may largely depend on the quality of physical working conditions, without doubt a materialist value.

Second, both cultures consist of competing elements and are, as a consequence, not well defined. The trade-off between job (contract) and pay is probably the best-known example in the field of materialism, while in the field of post-materialism it is the rivalry between egoistic and altruistic aspirations (for example, humanising the workplace in a polluting industry) that may prevent the observer from making unambiguous statements on cultural undercurrents of employment discourses. The same applies to the concepts of security and flexibility, which are also loosely defined and may overlap. As mentioned before, flexibility may result in security (such as when flexible working time leads to more jobs or longer-term employment contracts) and vice versa (when stable employment increases employability through professional development in a classic flexicurity regime).

Materialism is defined by the trade-off between job contract and pay, post-materialism by the trade-off between egoistic and altruistic aspirations.

Third, one wonders how two or more partially defined dichotomies can be combined in a reasonable manner. The binary model of materialism versus post-materialism cannot be identified with that of security versus flexibility (or that of east versus west or south versus north). Wishing more security for oneself, for instance, is not necessarily a materialist claim and characteristic of employees in the eastern or southern countries. To put it in simple geometrical terms, let us imagine two perpendicular axes dividing the space into four quarters. One axis embodies the security versus flexibility dimension, the other stretches between the extremes of materialism and post-materialism. (For the sake of simplicity, let us forget about the fact that the extremes may overlap.) Now, if one looks for job quality features, they will be found not only in the security/materialism and flexibility/post-materialism quarters, but also in the other two.

For example, aspiring to security may go beyond materialist values (for example, if health and safety includes mental/spiritual well-being), whereas flexibility is not tantamount to post-materialism (cf. flexible employment contracts increasing job security through inclusion). Does the formalisation of informal employment contracts enhance security? Most likely it does. But maybe the employee has to pay its price by means of accepting a more flexible pattern of work organisation. At the same time, his or her job's prestige may grow as well, and the employee will cease to feel a lack of affiliation. He or she may also gain in terms of fair treatment and participation through the process of formalisation. Consequently, both materialist and post-materialist traits of the job improve.

Similarly, flexibilisation may result in 'retraditionalisation' in terms of narrowing the contractual rights of employees, or curtailing their freedom to decide on their own work-life balance, thereby also reducing their autonomy. Symbolic geography is also a slippery slope: as demonstrated above, 'eastern' employees can subscribe to post-materialist values (such as demanding more recognition and dignity), while 'westerners' may prove to be heavily materialist (regarding professional education as a means of raising wages and remaining employable rather than of increasing self-fulfilment), and so on and so forth.

These distinctions usually remain hidden in the thick of the security/flexibility discourse, in particular, if examined through impersonal surveys in which the researcher does not want to go beyond a simplistic Maslowian approach. However, the most important finding of this study is that retraditionalisation manifests itself not so much in giving preference to materialist values as opposed to post-materialist ones, but rather in an inclination towards egoistic values, whether materialist or post-materialist in nature. The low position of any altruistic approach to job quality in the preference lists of the overwhelming majority of the respondents in almost all companies (and *Hexenküchen* of labour legislation) in the four countries was nearly as representative a result as if it were presented by a large-sample survey. The ignorance and neglect of green values was probably the most obvious phenomenon, followed by a general lack of interest in social responsibility, participation and equal opportunity.

It seemed an even more striking fact that in the case of those components of good jobs which could have been interpreted as either altruistic or egoistic, the latter option prevailed. The best example is participation (social dialogue), which was not regarded by the interviewees as a (collectivist) end in itself but as a means of attaining predominantly egoistic goals like the prevention of layoffs or wage cuts. Quite frequently, employees took a passive approach to participation: the wish to be informed replaced that of having a share in decision-making. Flexible working time presents a more complicated issue. When it was popular at all, the employees defended it as an opportunity to achieve an adequate work-life balance. Nevertheless, altruism rarely exceeded the boundaries of the family; in those cases when it did, the free time gained through flexibilisation was meant to increase personal autonomy, in particular the freedom to engage in leisure activities.

5.7 Quantity and egoism win

The complexity of the underlying concepts notwithstanding, it seems possible to derive the following conclusions from the case studies:

1. *Quantity wins.* On the level of elite discussions, the flexibility narrative clearly dominates its rival in the countries under scrutiny. However, as far as employee preferences 'on the ground' are concerned, job security (in the sense of stable employment) overrides not only most of the post-materialist values, but also such traditional materialist quality features as decent pay, appropriate physical working conditions (including health and safety at the workplace) and fixed working time. This phenomenon is characteristic even of those cutting-edge firms in which the employees are also keen on many of the post-materialist values related to job quality. Sheer quantity defeats quality, whether the latter is materialist or post-materialist in nature. Therefore, paradoxically, retraditionalisation may endanger even some of the traditional components of decent work.

2. *Second-best wins.* In any event, when employees talk about the concept of an ideal job, they normally describe a "second-best" occupation that they can realistically obtain. Having lowered their aspiration levels, they mean "acceptable/agreeable" when saying "good". This overall attitude applies to the materialist and the post-materialist components of decent work almost equally. However, when it came to actual choices, our respondents pointed out a variety of trade-offs between the two but tended to sacrifice the post-materialist values more readily.

> *Policy-makers focus on job quantity, employees on egoistic aspirations.*

3. *Egoism wins.* Retraditionalisation seems to be a helpful assumption, but the post-materialist features of good jobs do not disappear entirely. They tend to assume a rather low position in the preference lists of the employees; one could perhaps say they are in a dormant state but may be reawakened, in particular in the progressive industries, at any time provided that meanwhile the overall quantity of (good) jobs grows to a sufficient extent. At this point, it is not easy to judge which among the post-materialist features may have a better chance of reaching a higher position in the future, the more egoistic or the more altruistic ones. Currently, egoism seems to be the obvious winner.

4. *The 'south' wins.* The concept of the presumed 'north-south' cultural divide in employment discourses also needs to be attenuated. This is not because, in contrast to the expectations, there are striking similarities between the formerly eastern countries or between the formerly western ones. The case studies demonstrate the strength of global/transnational impacts, including those of the EU. These cut across national borders, homogenise the concept of job quality to a considerable extent, and turn the large, cutting-edge firms into islands on which the employees order their preferences for good jobs rather independently from the dominant narratives of the countries' elites. A Slovak telecom company may be regarded as at least as 'northern' as a Spanish one. The UK is an obvious exception in all fields examined, being the most 'northern' amongst the four countries as far as the obstacles to retraditionalisation are concerned. (Evidently, this would not have been the case if our sample had included 'northern' countries, e.g. Germany and France or Sweden).

5. *Country-specific cultures lose.* Cultural dissimilarities with national/ethnic roots did not surface in the course of fieldwork in great numbers. A likely reason for this is that the recent global crisis standardised many of the former cultural specifics, and one would have had to use more sophisticated research instruments to detect their remnants. Yet, it is possible to observe some essential cultural motives (for example, regarding health in the UK, dignity in Hungary and Slovakia or time in Spain as high-priority constituents of decent work; the importance attributed to physical working conditions in Hungary and Slovakia; or professional education as a top priority in Spain and the UK) though they did not provide a solid basis for generalisation.

These 'four wins, one loss' conclusions will perhaps become a suitable point of departure for survey-makers in job quality studies in the future. Otherwise, researchers may continue to i) endlessly mix and remix the (often rather ambiguous) quality features in order to identify the best- and worst-performing countries; ii) overlook a decline in expectations concerning decent work, and a growing share of materialist and/or 'selfish' post-materialist aspirations; and iii) separate the 'east' and the 'south' too sharply. Even worse, they will ignore those fundamental value choices which transpire even from such quasi-anthropological studies such as this one.

Bibliography

Beaston, M. (2000), "Job Quality and Forms of Employment: Concepts and the UK Statistical Evidence", Invited Paper at the Joint ECE-Eurostat-ILO Seminar on Measurement of the Quality of Employment, 3-5 May, Geneva.

Clark, A. (2005), "What Makes a Good Job? Evidence from OECD countries", in S. Bazen, C. Lucifora and W. Salverda (eds), *Job Quality and Employer Behaviour*, Palgrave Macmillan

Council of the European Union (2007), Council Resolution on "Good Work" (www.consilium.europa.eu/press/press-releases/employment,-social-policy,-health-and-consumer-affairs?target=2007&bid=79&lang=en&id=).

Davoine, L. and C. Erhel (2006), "Monitoring Employment Quality in Europe: European Employment Strategy Indicators and Beyond", Centre D'Etudes de l'Emploi, Noisy-le-Grand, France.

De Bustillo, R. and E. Macias (2005), "Job Satisfaction as an Indicator of the Quality of Work", *Journal of Socio-Economics*, Vol. 34, pp. 656-673.

De Bustillo, R., E. Fernández-Macías and J.I. Antón (2009), "Indicators of Job Quality in the European Union", European Parliament (http://www.europarl.europa.eu/document/activities/cont/201107/20110718ATT24284/20110718ATT24284EN.pdf).

De Bustillo, R., E. Fernández-Macías, F. Esteve and J.I. Antón (2011a), "E pluribus unum? A critical survey of job quality indicators", *Socio-Economic Review*, Vol. 9, No. 3, pp. 447-475.

_____ (2011b), *Measuring More than Money: The Social Economics of Job Quality*, Edward Elgar.

ETUC (2007), "Decent work", European Trade Union Congress, Brussels (www.etuc.org/decent-work).

Eurofound (2002), *Quality of work and employment in Europe. Issues and challenges*, Dublin.

_____ (2012), *Trends in job quality in Europe. Fifth European Working Conditions Survey*, Dublin.

_____ (2013a), *Quality of employment conditions and employment relations in Europe*, Dublin.

Gaušas, Simonas (2013) "Greening of industries in the EU: Anticipating and managing the effects on quantity and quality of jobs", European Foundation for the Improvement of Living and Working Conditions, Dublin.

Gallie, D. (ed.) (2007), *Employment Regimes and the Quality of Work*, Oxford: Oxford University Press.

Green, F. (2005), *Demanding Work: The Paradox of Job Quality in the Affluent Economy*, Princeton, NJ: Princeton University Press.

Heelas, P. and P. Morris (eds) (1992), *The Values of the Enterprise Culture,* Routledge.

Heelas, P., S. Lash and P. Morris (eds) (1996), *Detraditionalization*, Blackwell.

Holman, D. (2012), "Job Types and Job Quality in Europe", *Human Relations*, Vol. 66, No. 4, pp. 475-502.

ILO (undated), "Decent work agenda" (www.ilo.org/global/about-the-ilo/decent-work-agenda/lang--en/index.htm).

Inglehart, R. (1977) *The Silent Revolution*, Princeton, NJ: Princeton University Press.

_____(1990) *Culture Shift in Advanced Industrial Society,* Princeton, NJ: Princeton University Press.

Inglehart, R. and P. Abramson (1995) *Value Change in Global Perspective*, Ann Arbor, MI: University of Michigan Press.

Inglehart, R. and C. Welzel (2005), *Modernization, Cultural Change and Democracy: The Human Development Sequence*, Cambridge: Cambridge University Press.

Kovács, J.M., C. Hilbert, M. Veselková and T. Virág (2012), "Jobs First? In Search of Quality", State of the Art Report, CEPS, Brussels.

_____ (2014), "Travelling Back in Time? Job Quality in Europe As Seen from Below", CEPS, Brussels.

Leschke, J. and A. Watt (2008a), *Job Quality in Europe*, European Trade Union Institute, Brussels.

_____ (2008b), *Putting a Number on Job Quality? Constructing a European Job Quality Index*, European Trade Union Institute, Brussels.

Leschke, J., R. Peña-Casas and A. Watt (2011), "Possibilities and Challenges for Building a European Indicator on Job Quality", in K. Busch et al. (eds), *Socially Unbalanced Europe: Socio-Political Proposals in Times of Crisis*, Merlin Press.

Leschke, J., A. Watt and M. Finn, Mairead (2012), "Job quality in the crisis – an update of the Job Quality Index (JQI)", Working Paper No. 2012.07, ETUI, Brussels.

Maselli, I. (2010), "Beyond Flexibility and Security. A Composite Indicator of Flexicurity", CEPS Working Document, CEPS, Brussels, May.

Sirgy, J., J. Efraty, P. Siegel and D.-J. Lee (2001), "A New Measure of Quality of Work Life", *Social Indicators Research*, Vol. 55, No. 3, pp. 241-302.

UNECE (2010), *Measuring Quality of Employment*, Geneva: United Nations.

Notes

[1] Leschke et al. (2012).

[2] Gaušas (2013)

[3] For an overview of indicators of job quality in the European Union, see e.g. Green (2005); Davoine and Erhel (2006); Gallie (2007); Leschke and Watt (2008a, 2008b); De Bustillo et al. (2009); Bustillo et al. (2011a, 2011b); Leschke et al. (2011).

[4] Beaston (2000).

[5] Inglehart (1977).

[6] Inglehart (1977, 1990); Inglehart and Abramson (1995); Inglehart and Welzel (2005).

[7] Heelas and Morris (1992), Heelas et al. (1996).

[8] Fortunately, our research design is not the only one suggesting a critical approach to the analysis of job quality. Cf. the results of the *Recwowe* and *Walqing* projects (see the *Recwowe* Working Papers and *Walqing* Working Papers).

[9] Clark (2005) or Eurofound (2012).

[10] ETUC (2007); UNECE (2010); Eurofound (2002, 2012).

[11] On the risks of using satisfaction indicators, see Sirgy et al. (2001) or De Bustillo and Macias (2005).

[12] Maselli (2010).

[13] Holman (2012).

[14] Leschke and Watt (2008).

[15] Eurofound (2012).

[16] Eurofound (2013a).

[17] Kovács et al. (2012).

[18] Kovács et al. (2012).

[19] The authors of background studies leave the question partly unanswered. Average participation in the new schemes is still very low (Spain and Hungary are at the very bottom of the country list in Europe), and has not increased over the past ten years. The only exception is performance-related pay, which is becoming increasingly common in "old" Europe. Workplace innovation tends to be stronger in countries that are developed and show a good record of employee empowerment anyway (though the UK does not perform well in innovation). For example, in 2010 the share of office workers who also work from home was a mere 4.5% in Hungary, 5.7% in Spain, 9.0% in Slovakia and only 11.0% in the UK (as compared to the leading three countries, Denmark, Sweden and the Netherlands, with their 30% to 36% records).

[20] Z. Vidra and T. Virag, Hungarian telecom company, 2013

[21] M. Veselkova, Slovak telecom company, 2013.

[22] M. Las Heras, A. Garriga, E. Jimenez and C. Hilbert, Spanish telecom company, 2013.

[23] C. Hilbert, UK telecom company, 2013.

[24] C. Hilbert, UK engineering company, 2013.

[25] M. Las Heras, A. Garriga, E. Jimenez and C. Hilbert, Spanish engineering company, 2013.

[26] T. Virag, Hungarian pharmaceutical company, 2013.

[27] M. Veselkova, Slovak food company, 2013.

[28] For more on how the crisis affected employment discourses, see Kovács et al. (2012).

6. WORKPLACE INNOVATION IN EUROPE[*]

Is the nature of work really changing, as is frequently asserted in both popular and academic literature? Before trying to sketch an answer to this question, it is important to clarify what constitutes innovation in the workplace. We believe that the best way to do this is to frame the concept around the overall phenomenon of innovation, which is normally thought of in terms of product innovation (in other words, the creation of new products). Innovation, however, can also concern processes and among these, the organisation of work.

More specifically, workplace innovation (WPI) can be understood as being a possible outcome of the intersection between human resource (HR) management, technology and skills. The three elements co-exist and are interdependent: where technology adoption is driven by HR strategic policies, managers are likely to create enough momentum to change the work process and consequently to invest in training and upgrading of skills to support the innovation. Conversely, a lack of skills coupled with static HR management will most likely present a barrier to technology adoption, and hence to workplace innovation.

What does this mean in practice? In everyday working life, workplace innovation is translated into a number of specific actions, such as flexi-time, teleworking, alternative payment schemes, employee empowerment and autonomy, task rotation and multi-skilling, teamwork and team autonomy.

Workplace innovation in practice: flexi-time, teleworking, alternative payment schemes, employee empowerment and autonomy, task rotation and multi-skilling, teamwork and team autonomy.

New modalities of working have started to appear in recent years and

[*] Miroslav Beblavý and Ilaria Maselli are the authors of chapter 6, which is based on the research report on workplace innovation conducted by CEPS and supported by Microsoft. The original report features among co-authors also Elisa Martellucci.

neologisms like 'crowd-sourcing' and 'co-working spaces' have entered our vocabulary. These new forms of work organisation involve tasks that are chopped up and outsourced to independent workers in different parts of the globe and the aggregation of workers themselves across new types of working spaces. An important driver of such change is technology: working across different states without the possibility of sharing documents or communicating instantaneously would not only be unproductive, but also a hassle.

As so often happens with change, these new modes of working generate doubts and fear. Is it really more productive to organise work in a less hierarchical and more flexible way? What are the consequences for workers? Is it happening too fast? Should policy-makers regulate it, and if so, in what way?

6.1   No single metric measures workplace innovation

How widespread are workplace innovation practices in reality? Data from the European Working Condition Survey collected by Eurofound offer plenty of insights, but it is important to bear in mind that it is impossible to summarise workplace innovation with one single number for Europe. In fact, two elements of differentiation exist. On the one hand, penetration varies enormously according to the practice – telework compared with task rotation, for instance. On the other hand, we show that each of these practices is present in the various European countries, but in a very uneven fashion. Nonetheless, for nearly all the forms of workplace innovation considered, Sweden, Denmark, the Netherlands and Finland score higher than the other countries. This is consistent not only with the traditional literature on welfare-state classifications, but also with studies that argue for the existence of a Scandinavian model of work organisation.[1]

For purposes of comparison, it is useful to look at the US experience as a benchmark, where the debate on workplace innovation has re-ignited following the decision by Yahoo's CEO Marissa Mayer to ban teleworking early in 2013. According to data from the US Bureau of Labor Statistics, one-third of all American workers have access to flexible working hours, a proportion that does not change visibly between men and women but increases rapidly with the level of education.[2] Telecommuting, however, is less widespread: a recent study shows that such practice applies to less than 20% of US workers, a percentage that remained quite constant during the 2000s after a period of growth during the 1990s.[3]

6.2   An uneven spread, both geographically and by country

The key elements of workplace innovation for which we have statistical information are: flexi-time, teleworking, alternative payment schemes, flat hierarchies, employee empowerment and autonomy, task rotation and multi-skilling, teamwork and team autonomy. Table 6.1 shows the percentage of workers involved in each of these practices in the European Union. It is clear that different practices have different average levels of penetration: almost 70% of workers, for instance, enjoy autonomy but only 12% have access to teleworking. The least diffused are the so-called 'quantitative aspects': flexi-time (37.8%), teleworking (11.7%) and alternative payment schemes (12.5%). More common are the qualitative aspects, which apply to at least four workers out of every ten.

Table 6.1 Percentage of workers involved in innovative practices in their workplace in Europe, 2010

Flexi-time	Tele working	Alternative payment schemes	Flat hierarchies	Employee empowerment
37.8	11.7	12.5	56.8	43.9
Employee autonomy	Team work	Team autonomy	Task rotation	
67.4	56.4	52.0	43.6	

Source: Authors' own elaboration based on data from the 5th European Working Conditions Survey (Eurofound, 2010).

But are these averages representative of the continent as a whole? Looking at detailed data by country, we discover that the answer is clearly "no". The Nordic countries are in the lead: Denmark, Sweden, Finland and the Netherlands rank highest in the diffusion of new ways of working, which are much more widespread in these countries than in the Mediterranean countries like Spain, Portugal, Greece and Italy. In between are the Baltics: Latvia, Estonia and Lithuania in particular occupy the middle rank, creating a model of 'post-communist almost-Nordics'. The most interesting case is Slovenia; it ranks fifth, right after the Nordics, and has the same level of diffusion across all elements.

Figure 6.1 Diffusion of innovative practices in the workplace, by country, average across nine items

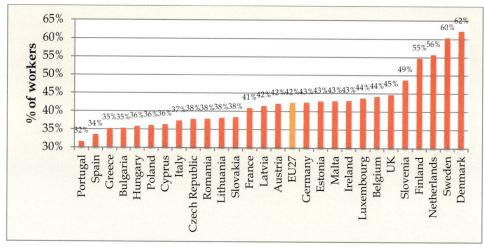

Source: Authors' own elaboration based on data from the 5th European Working Conditions Survey (Eurofound, 2010).

6.3 Flexi-time, teleworking and alternative payment schemes in Europe

Interviews conducted with workers across Europe as part of the European Working Conditions Survey 2010 indicated that in the majority (60%) of cases, working time is set by the company with no possibility of change. The exceptions to this finding were Sweden, Denmark and the Netherlands where this percentage falls significantly to the point that in only one-third of the cases does the employer set the working

> *Flexi-time, teleworking and alternative payment schemes still concern a minority of workers.*

time in a rigid fashion. The laggards in terms of working-time flexibility are the east Europeans, the Spaniards and the Portuguese.

If on average 60% of workers cannot choose their working time, this means that the remaining 40% enjoy at least some flexibility. Such flexibility can take different forms: a small minority (7%) can choose between several fixed working schedules; 16% have a margin for adaptation, which, for example, can take the shape of flexi-time whereby the worker has flexibility in terms of starting and ending hours, but with core hours when the worker's presence is compulsory. Only 16% of workers can fully determine their working hours, and a majority of these are self-employed.

Figure 6.2 Working time set by the company with no possibility for changes

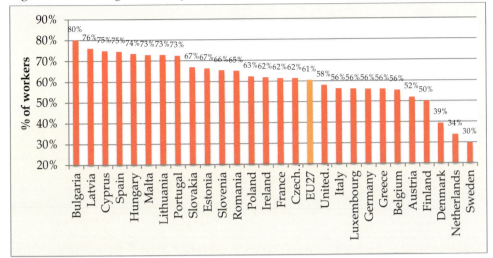

Source: Authors' own elaboration based on data from the 5th European Working Conditions Survey (Eurofound, 2010).

What type of working-time flexibility are we referring to here? The responses to two questions in the survey (Do you work the same number of hours every day/every week?) reveal that flexibility "by the day" is more widespread than flexibility "by the week". In other words, European workers often have a predetermined number of working hours per week that are adjustable by the day, with highly skilled clerical workers and self-employed people having more flexible working hours than others.

The second element of the definition of workplace innovation we selected is teleworking. Figure 6.3 shows the share of workers whose main place of work is their employers' or their own business premises, and home as a second option. On average, 12 Europeans out of every 100 engage in telecommuting. The difference between countries is again very stark: only in the Netherlands, Sweden and Denmark does this share exceed 30%. It is not by chance that these are also the countries where workers have more freedom to choose their work schedules; overall, Dutch, Swedish and Danish workers have the greatest liberty to set their own working time and their place of work. At the opposite extreme are Italy, Bulgaria, Hungary and Cyprus, where fewer than five in ten workers can work from home as an alternative to their business premises. Aggregate data for Europe (as a whole) by sector illustrate that greater numbers of workers in four particular sectors are allowed to work from home: real estate, professional and scientific activities, education, and information and communications.

Figure 6.3 Percentage of office workers that "also" work from home

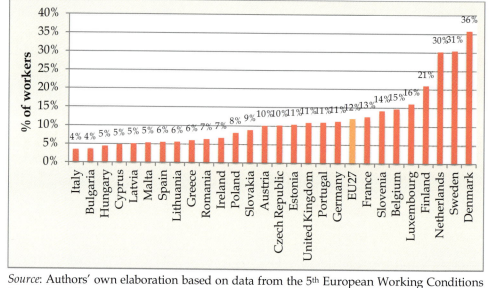

Source: Authors' own elaboration based on data from the 5th European Working Conditions Survey (Eurofound, 2010).

The third element of quantitative flexibility considered is performance-linked remuneration. Figure 6.4 plots the share of workers who mentioned, as part of their remuneration, company shares and/or payments based on overall company performance (i.e. a profit-sharing scheme). While both sub-elements increase in importance over time, payments related to performance remain by far the most important.

Figure 6.4 Diffusion of performance-linked remuneration

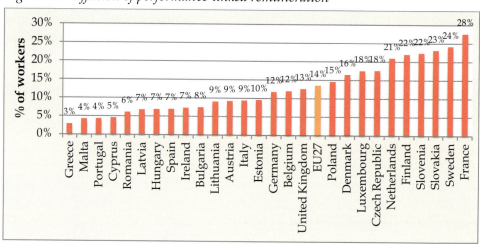

Source: Authors' own elaboration based on data from the 5th European Working Conditions Survey (Eurofound, 2010).

Both measures create a stronger link between the fate of the organisation and the worker. However, they differ in intent: profit-sharing schemes create an incentive for the worker to put in more effort, whereas employee-share ownership reflects trust and inclusiveness. Performance-linked remuneration is more widespread in France, where almost one-third of workers receive part of their salary linked to the performance of the company. The other countries above the European average of 14% are a mix of Nordic and east European countries.

6.4   Increased worker autonomy and responsibility

The seven dimensions that characterise an innovative workplace – flexi-time, teleworking, alternative payment schemes, employee empowerment and autonomy, task rotation and multi-skilling, teamwork and team autonomy – can be grouped into quantitative and qualitative dimensions. The latter aspects of high-performance workplace systems are based on allowing employees to exercise higher independence and giving more responsibility to single workers and teams. As a consequence, high-performance workplaces abandon the rigid pyramidal structure typical of Taylorist organisations and adopt a flatter structure with the intention of encouraging innovation from the bottom-up, thereby achieving greater productivity because workers feel more invested in their jobs.

European Working Conditions Survey data indicate that more than 60% of workers enjoy some degree of autonomy because they are able to choose or change their method of work. The capacity to influence company

> *More than 60% of workers enjoy some degree of autonomy, defined as being able to choose or change their method of work.*

decisions is rather more limited: even though one-half of European companies have put in place a mechanism designed to give a 'voice' to workers, only 40% of workers report having some involvement in the organisation of the work process.

The three variables in the Survey that refer to workers' autonomy are positively correlated, which means that it would be very difficult to empower workers by allowing one element and not the others. For example, it would be unnecessarily inefficient if a worker who is able to change his or her work method discovers a more efficient process but is not able to communicate it or share it with colleagues and superiors.

Another element of qualitative flexibility at the workplace is task rotation. It has its *raison d'être* in workers acquiring multiple skills that make them more flexible in the distribution of tasks. This practice involves at least one-third of all European workers. The EU average, by country, is 44%, with Sweden and Denmark among the countries exceeding 70%. Of the workers involved in rotating tasks, approximately 80% declared that different skills are needed to cope with all aspects of their work.

Teamwork and team autonomy are the last elements of qualitative flexibility. Teamwork concerns more than 50% of workers, only half whom also enjoy autonomy in terms of the internal division of tasks. This latter dimension of teamwork is more differentiated across countries: once again, Denmark, Sweden and Finland rank in the top positions, given that more than two-thirds of team workers in these countries also enjoy great autonomy in the division of tasks.

6.5 Workplace innovation as a package

Correlation analysis indicates that flexi-time and teleworking are positively correlated with all qualitative elements. In the case of alternative payment schemes, the signs of the coefficients are the same but the relationship is strong only with flat hierarchies and team autonomy. Not only is there no trade-off between telecommuting and employee empowerment, for instance, but in some cases there is a strong interdependence. This indicates that workplace innovation comes as a package.

The importance of a holistic approach to workplace innovation also emerges from the radar charts in Figure 6.5: not only do the Nordics exhibit wider diffusion across each item compared to the southern countries, but they also achieve a better balance between the different dimensions (with the exception of alternative payment schemes and teleworking, which in general display very limited diffusion). Altogether, they enable workers to decide when to work, to influence decisions relevant for the organisation, to work in teams and to exchange tasks. In the southern countries, however, there are efforts to let workers organise themselves in teams and take more responsibility, but elements of rigidity persist – the diffusion of flexi-time and task rotation remain limited and hierarchies are not smooth across the different criteria considered.

Figure 6.5 Innovative practices: Nordic vs. the southern countries

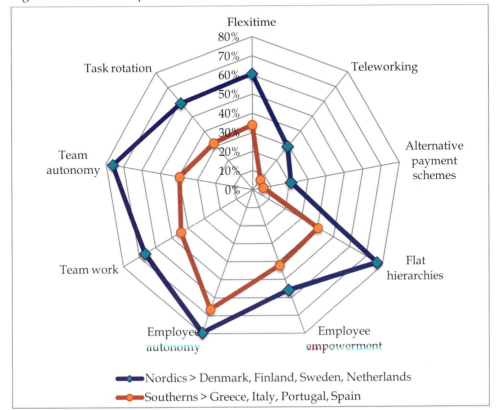

Source: Authors' own elaboration based on data from the 5th European Working Conditions Survey (Eurofound, 2010).

6.6 The slow diffusion of innovation in the workplace

We have already shown that workplace innovation still concerns only a minority of workers in most countries. Has there been any change on this front? A comparison with the same data for 2010 (only old-European countries available here) reveals that the diffusion of participatory practices made little progress much between 2000 and 2010.

It is interesting to note that the only major change across the decade was in the share of workers who receive part of their compensation linked to performance: the percentage of workers who answered positively to this question rose from 5.2% in 2000 to 13.7% ten years later. Surprisingly, diffusion of the remaining workplace innovation elements remained consistently static. On top of this, for all items except teamwork, there is divergence rather than convergence across the old-European countries (standard deviation coefficients mostly go up between 2000 and 2010).

Table 6.2 Workplace innovation in western Europe, 2000 vs. 2010 (% of total respondents)

		Tele-working	Alternative payment schemes	Employee autonomy	Team work	Task rotation
2000	Average	11.7	5.2	69.1	58.1	44.1
2010	Average	15.7	13.7	69.3	57.7	46.0

Source: Authors' own elaboration based on data from the 5th European Working Conditions Survey (Eurofound, 2010).

This finding is clearly a surprise. Between 2000 and 2010, the technology allowing workers to organise differently surely improved: it became both more widespread and cheaper. This leads to a puzzle: if technology became increasingly accessible and the gains from workplace innovation outpaced the losses in terms of productivity and job satisfaction, why do we not observe more of it? And why has it made so little headway in the past decade?

6.7 Workplace innovation and the economy

In a knowledge economy, one can expect that a major share of the output is not produced by traditional factors of production. As economies approach the technological frontier, they cannot simply rely on the accumulation of capital and labour to grow more, but rather need to innovate more and more.

Innovation is often understood as the creation of new goods and services, but that is only one element. Innovation in fact also concerns processes, including how work is organised: how hierarchical the structure of a firm is, how free workers are to decide the content and the timing of their activities, whether they need to present in the office during working hours and if their pay is linked to the fate of their company.

Measuring innovation and its contribution to productivity improvements, and therefore ultimately to growth, has been a major preoccupation of many social scientists for many years. The only point of

All inputs to production aside from capital and labour matter more and more in a knowledge economy.

agreement among them is that all those inputs excluding capital and labour compose total factor productivity, and some attempts have been made in recent years to decompose this residual and quantify how, for instance, changes in the organisation of work or the skills of workers contribute to explaining economic growth. According to this literature, summarised under the heading 'intangible capital', organisational capital constituted one-quarter of the overall intangible investment in Europe in 2005, which in itself accounts for approximately 7% of GDP.[4] These estimates obviously need to be taken with caution, but they do confirm that the ways in which work and production are organised do indeed matter, potentially in a positive way for the overall economy.

6.8   Employees' and employers' perspectives

But this is not the end of the story. Moving from macroeconomic estimates to the literature on working conditions, we discover that the view that workplace innovation can be beneficial to both the employer and the employee is rather dominant.

Some researchers have used data on Canadian establishments to test whether particular organisational structures are correlated with the likelihood of adopting process and product innovations. Their study confirms that establishments with decentralised decision-making, information-sharing programmes, or incentive pay plans are significantly more likely to innovate than other establishments.[5]

One strand of the literature argues that workplace re-organisation plays a significant role in rising productivity. A US study on manufacturers during the period 1993-96 concludes that "employers have been actively engaged in workplace

> *Workplace innovation is mostly beneficial for the economy as a whole, as well as for employees and employers.*

re-organisation and that these changes in workplace practices, along with increasing diffusion of computers, may well have played a significant role in the recent rise in manufacturing productivity".[6] More precisely, the authors find that workplace practices and re-engineering efforts accounted for approximately 30% of output growth in manufacturing over the period 1993-96. They also observe that workplace innovation is positively associated with labour productivity, especially when it has occurred in unionised establishments, possibly because workers are more willing to participate in employee involvement programmes if they feel the union will protect their employment security.[7]

Another study finds that firms with interdependent worker productivity, or more simply firms where teamwork is the rule, are more successful at keeping turnover and absent rates lower.[8] Along the same lines, it has also been documented that private sector establishments that explicitly link pay with individual performance experience significantly lower absence rates.

Overall, most research finds that an innovative workplace increases employees' influence at work and increases perceived self-realisation. Of those who have a high overall level of access to an innovative workplace, 60% regard themselves as highly satisfied and only 13% display a low level of job satisfaction. Greater control over work and the allocation of tasks within a relatively flat hierarchical system allows individuals (in an optimal case) to choose tasks according to their preferences and talents. Not only do the so-called 'organisational innovations' enhance the utility of employees in their work, but being able to voice preferences and influence work distribution highly correlate with job satisfaction. Qualitative changes in work organisation can foster creativity and let ideas emerge from the bottom. Groups with more complex tasks (i.e. task variety), autonomy, team-specific goals and feedback demonstrate higher values for the team climate for innovation than do groups with more restrictive task structures.

On the negative side, it is important to mention that higher job satisfaction practices – such as additional learning possibilities, task complexity and high levels of autonomy – lead to an increased level of stress, work pressure, increased workloads, job insecurity and poorer work-life balance. In this regard, the paradoxical aspect of these new forms of work organisation has been observed. It was trade unions that, based on the critique of 'Taylorism', requested more autonomy and control over their tasks, which was welcomed by managers. In the end, this also brought new challenges and threats for employees: risk of burn-out and the need to rethink workers' rights and job security.

If workplace innovation allows the possibility of a higher income, more interesting work, higher job discretion and better employment security for less-skilled employees, these benefits come at a price. Workplace innovations are implemented to improve performance, but this improved performance may be achieved at the expense of employees, and some experts even refer to this as "management by stress". Recent research revealed that, at least in the US, telecommuting is more instrumental in increasing working hours and blurring the boundary between work and private life than in improving work-life balance.

Among the elements of quantitative flexibility at the workplace, alternative payment schemes are perhaps the most controversial. Origo and Pagani found that the increase in job satisfaction often associated with innovative workplace systems comes more from the qualitative aspects, such as team working, than the quantitative and monetary ones:

> Workers attach great importance also to non-monetary aspects of the job, which are more likely to be improved by many forms of functional flexibility rather than numerical and working time flexibility. Given the same wage level, workers may then be more satisfied (and hence more productive) if they perceive some enhancement in the intrinsic aspects of their job (such as control over their tasks and the possibility to use their creativity).[9]

Performance payments have also been roundly criticised by those who argue that the practice is not consistent with the definition of an employee, since dependent workers are not supposed to share risks with the entrepreneur. Very recent research at the intersection of neuroscience and economics has found that if it is true that workers with variable-payment schemes are more productive, this is due not only to the incentive mechanism but also to a degree of self-selection: "When facing the alternative between variable and fixed payments, more productive workers systematically prefer the variable pay."[10] This implies that employers can use screening techniques to attract less risk-averse but more productive employees. How many workers receive alternative forms of compensation linked to their performance as part of their salary as individuals or team members?

The Karasek demand-control model provides a consolidated theory to explain employee well-being in the work context. According to the model, it is important to maintain a balance between demands in a job (i.e. workload) and the level of autonomy over that job. A job with a high workload and low autonomy (a 'high-strain' job) is considered stressful, whereas a high demanding job with a lot of autonomy (an 'active' job) results in learning opportunities. The difference between the two conditions is that whereas an active job leads to new learning challenges and a sense of mastery and self-efficacy, the former creates a high-stress job.[11]

6.9   It is not all about technology: Barriers to innovation

The accessibility and diffusion of technology that facilitates the adoption of innovative practices at the workplace indicate that other reasons than tools and software must explain the little change observed in the past decade. If email and VoIP (Voice over Internet Protocol, such as Skype and Google Talk), are widely used among workers, how can one explain that only a minority are telecommuters? We find that a set of microeconomic considerations applies in this case: risk aversion, lack of trust between social partners and costs related to the transition towards a new work environment. More specifically, we identify four key issues which together can create a formidable barrier to change.

The first is uncertainty about the success of the project. Even though the case studies in the literature as well as the broader statistical data show positive outcomes when workplace innovation is successfully implemented, they do not and cannot capture the number of failed attempts where it was not implemented in the end. Therefore the literature may be affected by a severe selection bias.

Technology is an important enabler of workplace innovation, yet it remains a necessary but insufficient condition for change.

This leads to the second factor, which we could call the 'first-mover cost'. In economic jargon, the term 'first-mover advantage' is used to denote the competitive benefit derived from being the first to enter a given field. However, with workplace innovation the effect appears to be the opposite, given all the costs and risks associated with being the first in a country or a field to implement a given aspect of workplace innovation. This is true with regard to regulatory and legal uncertainty, but also with respect to new, informal norms and technological change.

Moreover, even when the organisation in question is not a pioneer, there are significant costs of transition, ranging from investment in new equipment, through disruption of work and productivity, to training costs.

There is also an *ex-ante* uncertainty over the distribution of costs and benefits, which can be amplified by a lack of trust between managers and workers or among workers, leading to risk aversion and resistance by the parties involved. The reason why trust is so important in designing and implementing workplace innovation is two-fold. First, it touches upon the very core of the employer-employee/trade union relationship. Second, evidence shows that such a change constitutes a highly incomplete contract, i.e. it is impossible to precisely specify its terms and conditions in advance and there is a significant learning and adaptation process involved. With incomplete contracts, the presence of trust and/or of formal and informal institutions is crucial to whether parties decide to collaborate or not, even if there are mutual benefits to be obtained.

There are also some genuine risks in workplace innovation, particularly with regard to the blurred boundaries between work and private life and the potential for intensification of work instead of increased productivity. Again, this can be amplified if there is a lack of trust between employers and employees or their representatives.

With regard to the role of technology in changes related to work organisation, we conclude that technology is an important enabler of workplace innovation by lower the cost of work organisation, especially for small- and medium-sized enterprises, and creating the opportunity for workers to collaborate across different cities and countries. Yet, it remains a necessary but insufficient condition for changes in work organisation.

6.10 The public sector as leader of workplace innovation

Somewhat unexpectedly, the European Working Conditions Survey data analysed revealed that very little change took place over the past decade in terms of diffusion of innovative practices at the workplace, despite the availability and diffusion of technology that allows work to be organised in a much more flexible way. We explain this puzzle by relying on microeconomic considerations such as risk aversion, lack of trust between social partners and costs related to the transition towards a new work environment. We conclude therefore that technology is a necessary, but not sufficient, condition for the diffusion of innovative practices at the workplace.

In order to overcome barriers to innovation and in light of the fact that the balance between the advantages and disadvantages of innovative practices for employers and employees is in

Policy-makers should lead by example.

favour of the former, we contend that policy intervention is needed. In principle, this could be done in a wide variety of ways. However, in times of hard budget constraints on public finances and keeping in mind the goal of increasing competitiveness, we believe that the best way for policy to provoke change on the ground is by setting a good example.

The public sector plays an important role (although to a varying extent) as an employer in all EU member states. Public-sector institutions are generally perceived as facing more difficulty in shifting to new forms of work organisation compared to private-sector organisations.[12] Therefore, successful change in such an environment could send an important message to the wider corporate world that such change is possible. Additionally, public-sector organisations might find it easier to resolve the issues of regulatory uncertainty with other authorities than might private companies. This strategy would not only show that organising work differently is both potentially feasible and beneficial, but it would also allow the productivity of the public sector to be increased.

Box 6.1 The small revolution at the Belgian Federal Public Services

An example of a small revolution is provided by the office of the Belgian Federal Public Services (FPS), where several initiatives have been taken aimed at motivating employees, improving the working environment and inducing more cooperative and collaborative attitudes. Two main innovations were introduced: teleworking and the possibility to measure work on the basis of performance instead of working hours. These two initiatives have been accompanied by the creation of a new working space. The Belgian example also shows that since the benefits of such a change can be tangible both in financial terms, thanks to the money saved on rent, and in terms of productivity: an internal survey revealed that autonomously organised workers became more and more efficient in dealing with cases.

The Belgian case is interesting not only for its results, but also for its process. Before adopting the new office policy, the system was tested on a group of 40 employees. The results were positive, demonstrating to the FPS staff the feasibility of the dynamic office system. For all the employees based in Brussels (around 1,000), FPS now has a total of 668 desks, 154 spots for conversation and 25 meeting rooms. The initial investment was €10 million, but in the long term the dynamic office approach saved 30% in office space and €6 million is saved each year. To make the dynamic offices and teleworking a reality, in 2009 new equipment (personal laptops, USB keys, LCD screens) was given to the employees and internet connections installed in their homes, the ICT infrastructure was renovated and new communications tools introduced, such as the soft phone (a device to call from your computer) and office communicator (chat).

As a second step and with a more substantial effort, policy should address two important issues: on the one hand, overcoming the risk aversion and lack of information; and, on the other, dealing with regulatory barriers and uncertainty.

There is a role for direct government action to disseminate knowledge and assist organisations in using workplace innovation. The motivation for such action is a combination of risk aversion and information costs in the organisations involved. Risk aversion is associated with incomplete knowledge about and uncertain distribution of benefits from workplace innovation. Therefore, policy-makers can lower the risk aversion of individual companies/institutions by providing funds and knowledge and also by creating networks of companies/individuals involved in workplace innovation.

A clear example of good practice in this respect is the Finnish TEKES programme. The role designed for TEKES, a public agency, is to provide funds and knowledge to particular companies, but also to: i) push people involved in the same area towards the creation of networks, ii) mobilise resources for the creation of expertise through universities and consultants and awareness among the public and iii) include innovation in the workplace as part of the country's general innovation strategy. Even though it is not possible to simply export this model, the experience of TEKES can certainly be inspirational for similar institutions across European countries. Of course, creating an integrated, large-scale programme or a dedicated agency is not the only way to go forward, especially in times of tough budget constraints. Specific elements of this approach – for example, creating a dedicated fund for the training of managers and/or trade unionists, supporting research on the topic or financing the dissemination of information – can be undertaken on their own.

Overcoming regulatory barriers and uncertainty are essential steps that require the direct involvement of policy-makers. Many organisations contemplating workplace innovation believe that inflexible labour laws or collective agreements create significant obstacles to change, but a detailed analysis shows that these perceived obstacles are more frequently identified in general than specifically. The real problem seems often to be general uncertainty rather than negative certainty.

A key role for the authorities, therefore, is to help identify barriers in legal/regulatory uncertainty and to try to provide clear, binding answers. This concerns issues ranging from general labour legislation, through health and safety at work, to data protection and fiscal/social security issues. A proactive approach by the authorities could involve appointing liaison representatives for workplace innovation at key regulatory agencies – e.g. the labour inspectorate, the social security agency and the tax administration – empowered with a clear mandate.

Bibliography

Beblavý, M., I. Maselli and E. Martellucci (2012), "Workplace Innovation and Technological Change", CEPS Special Report, CEPS, Brussels, September (www.ceps.eu/book/workplace-innovation-and-technological-change).

Black, S.E. and L.M. Lynch (2003), "What's driving the new economy? The benefits of workplace innovation", Working Papers in Applied Economic Theory 2003-23, Federal Reserve Bank of San Francisco, San Francisco, CA.

Business Decisions Limited (BDL) (2002), "New Forms of Work Organisation: The Obstacles to Wider Diffusion", Report for the European Commission, Brussels.

Dohmen, T. and A. Falk (2011), "Performance and Multidimensional Sorting -Productivity, Preferences and Gender", *American Economic Review*, Vol. 101, No. 2, pp. 556-590.

Eurofound (2010), "5th European Working Conditions Survey", European Foundation for the Improvement of Living and Working Conditions, Dublin.

_____ (2011) "Recent developments in work organisation in the EU27 Member States and Norway", European Foundation for the Improvement of Living and Working Conditions, Dublin (http://www.eurofound.europa.eu/publications/htmlfiles/ef11461.htm).

Gustavsen, B. (2007), "Work organisation and the Scandinavian model", *Economic and industrial democracy*, Vol. 28, No. 4, pp. 650-671.

Handel, M.J and D.I. Levine (2004), "The Effects of New Work Practices on Workers", *Industrial Relations,* Vol. 43, pp. 1-43.

Heywood, J., U. Jirjahn and X. Wei (2008), "Teamwork, monitoring and absence", *Journal of Economic Behavior and Organisation,* Vol. 68, No. 3-4, pp. 676-690.

Hui-Yu, C. and N. Mamiko Takeuchi (2008), "The effect of work-life balance policies on women employees turnover", OSIPP Discussion Paper, Osaka University, Osaka.

Jona-Lasinio, C., M. Iommi and S. Manzocchi, (2011), "Intangible Capital and Productivity Growth in European Countries", LLEE Working Paper Series No. 91, LUISS Guido Carli University, Rome.

Kalmi, P. and A. Kauhanen (2008), "Workplace Innovations and Employee Outcomes: Evidence from Finland", *Industrial Relations*, Vol. 47, No. 3, pp. 430-459.

Karasek, R.A. (1979), "Job Demands, Job Decision Latitude, and Mental Strain: Implications for Job Redesign", *Administrative Science Quarterly*, Vol. 24, pp. 285-308.

Noonan, M.C. and J.L. Glass (2012), "The hard truth about telecommuting", *Monthly Labor Review*, June.

Origo, F. and L. Pagani (2008), "Workplace flexibility and job satisfaction: Some evidence from Europe", *International Journal of Manpower*, Vol. 29, No. 6, pp. 556-566.

Pouliakas, K. and N. Theodoropoulos (2011), "The Effect of Variable Pay Schemes on Workplace Absenteeism", IZA DP Number No. 5941, Institute for the Study of Labor, Bonn.

Ramsay, H., D. Scholarios and B. Harley (2000), "Employees and High-Performance Work Systems: Testing inside the Black Box", *British Journal of Industrial Relations*, Vol. 38, No. 4, pp. 501-531.

Zoghi, C., D. Mohr and P.B Meyer (2005), "Workplace Organisation and Innovation", BLS Working Paper No. 405, Bureau of Labor Statistics, US Department of Labor, Washington, DC.

Zoll, R. (2004), "The Paradoxes of Subjectivization of Work", in F. Garibaldo and T. Volker (eds), *Globalisation, company strategies and quality of working life in Europe*, Vol. 25, Frankfurt am Main: Peter Lang, pp. 107-120.

Notes

1 See Gustavsen (2007).

2 Bureau of Labor Statistics, US Department of Labor, Economic News Release, Employed persons with flexible work hours by age, sex, educational attainment, and disability status, May 2012.

3 Noonan and Glass (2012).

4 Jona-Lasinio et al. (2011).

5 Zoghi et al. (2005).

6 Black and Lynch (2003).

7 On the relationship between productivity/innovation and WPI, see, for example, Zoghi et al. (2005); Black and Lynch (2003); Heywood et al. (2008); Pouliakas and Theodoropoulos (2011); Hui-Yu and Mamiko Takeuchi (2008).

8 Heywood et al. (2008).

9 Origo and Pagani (2008).

10 Dohmen and Falk (2011).

11 On the negative spillovers of WPI see, for example, Eurofound (2011); Zoll (2004); Kalmi and Kauhanen (2008); Handel and Levine (2004); Noonan and Glass (2012); Karasek (1979); Ramsay et al. (2000).

12 Business Decisions Limited (2002).

7. FUTURE OF SKILLS IN EUROPE: CONVERGENCE OR POLARISATION?*

The importance of human capital for Europe's future and the emphasis placed by the European social model on both dynamism and inclusion have become clichés. This chapter examines whether the current trends in the areas of education and skills are pushing the European Union towards convergence or polarisation.

Polarisation or convergence can be analysed with regard to countries, but also within countries and educational systems. What can we expect as higher education is extended to the masses? Is it just lack of information that leads students to choose social sciences rather than mathematics? Is later tracking of students truly the answer to educational inequality and how likely is it to be politically successful? Is job polarisation by skills happening in Europe and why? How can low-skilled individuals improve their skills – going back to school or learning on the job? And what does it mean to be low-skilled after all?

7.1 What happens with the extension of upper secondary and higher education to the general population?

As universal primary and secondary education has been a reality for a considerable time in developed countries, efforts have been directed towards higher education. These efforts have been reinforced by the growing body of work suggesting that the impact of investment in

* Written by Miroslav Beblavý and Marcela Veselková, chapter 7 draws on research conducted within work package 4 (Education and skills) of the NEUJOBS project by a team of researchers at Centre for European Policy Studies in Brussels and the Slovak Governance Institute in Bratislava. The team also included Lucia Mýtna Kureková, Ilaria Maselli and Anna-Elisabeth Thum, as well as other individuals with minor research roles.

education and training on national economic growth is positive and significant, although difficult to quantify. In light of the recognition that higher education is crucial for economic development and job creation, the European Union agreed the target that at least 40% of those aged 30 to 34 should have a higher education qualification or the equivalent by 2020. According to the European Commission,[1] 11 EU countries have already exceeded this target. In contrast, the lowest completion rates can be found in the southern and central European countries, despite the fact that they have very high secondary education completion rates. Various projections of the extension to tertiary education suggest that higher education systems will probably continue to expand, but that the continued growth of 'massification' is beset by many uncertainties.

Instead of examining the expansion of tertiary education directly, we examined broad trends in the expansion of upper secondary education, which has to precede the expansion of tertiary education. The time span encompasses the post-World War II period, which witnessed a rapid expansion of upper secondary education in Europe. With regard to the speed of the expansion, two hypothetical benchmarks were set: i) massification of upper secondary education, characterised by a transition from 20% to 50% gross enrolment rates; and ii) universalisation of education, characterised by a transition from 50% to 80% gross enrolment rates.[2]

When looking at Sweden, United Kingdom and Slovakia, it took between 10 to 26 years for these countries to massify their upper secondary education and an additional 16 to 41 years to universalise it. Although the data should be interpreted with caution due to differences in the organisation of national school systems, it is clear that countries expanded their upper secondary sectors at various speeds. The expansion was slower in the leaders of expansion, such as the United Kingdom or Sweden. In contrast, laggards were able to catch up relatively quickly once the limiting conditions were removed. The results also suggest that universalisation of the upper secondary sector was faster than universalisation of primary or lower secondary schooling. A proxy of enrolment with literacy acquisition found that the typical country in the post-war 20th century took between 35 and 80 years to make the transition from 10% net primary enrolment to 90%.[3]

It is possible to derive several lessons about the consequences of educational expansion. As enrolment rates exceed 80%, we observe two trends. First, the demand for part-time secondary or post-secondary non-tertiary education in Slovakia and the Czech Republic declines and the demand for flexible forms of more prestigious tertiary education rises.[4] The demand for post-secondary education thus shifts almost exclusively to the tertiary level. It is possible to hypothesise that this shift occurs as a result of a combination of two factors: elimination

Generalisation of upper secondary schooling spills over to the bachelor studies.

of the quotas on the number of students in tertiary education, and a better signalling function of tertiary education as opposed to post-secondary non-tertiary education. Second, the generalisation of the upper secondary schooling seems to have spilled over to the bachelor studies. For example, in Germany, specialisation occurs only at the Masters or PhD level.[5] Both of these findings suggest that it is reasonable to assume that students will be staying on in education for longer and longer.

We observe a similar trend at the tertiary level: expansion of tertiary education in Europe occurred hand-in-hand with a redistribution of students across different fields of study. A growing number of studies have examined returns to investment in education. For example, in OECD countries, returns to an additional year of tertiary education are on average above 8% and range from 4% to 15% across different countries.[6] However, looking at average values is not satisfactory.

Our research[7] therefore asks a simple question: Is it worth studying engineering or art? To answer this question, we calculated the net present value of university studies for five European countries. The reference populations were the cohort of graduates in 2000 in France and Italy and the 2002-03 cohort in Hungary, Poland and Slovenia. It was found that with the exception of Italy, private investment in education largely repays itself after five years. However, the field of study is a

Social sciences graduates enjoy higher returns to education than STEM or humanities graduates.

source of inequality within the group of higher education graduates: both the resources needed during university and the returns five years later depend on the field of study. Surprisingly, it is not the science, technology, engineering and mathematics (STEM) faculties that ensure the highest return on investment. Rather, social sciences graduates enjoy the highest returns. Graduates of art, humanities and education enjoy the lowest net present value. These findings suggest that the expansion of enrolment in fields of study such as economics, business or law is driven by a rational choice. This is particularly true in central and eastern European countries. Gender is an additional source of heterogeneity: being a woman and enrolling in STEM is the worst option in Italy, France, Slovenia and Hungary.

Is it possible to steer students into preferred majors? The empirical evidence suggests that it is very difficult. Policy-makers in communist Czechoslovakia were able to effectively direct the expansion of secondary education into vocational tracks, thanks to the combination of a highly centralised education system and a system of administrative quotas on the number of students advanced to general upper secondary tracks.[8] In the post-communist period, the ability of policy-makers to manage expansion was undermined by the emergence of quasi-markets. Private institutions were more than happy to meet the demand not met by public providers of education. The surge in student enrolment in private education is characteristic also of the tertiary level. Regionally, it was concentrated in the part of Europe where the establishment of private higher educational institutions was prevented for several decades, namely central and eastern Europe. One of the major forces that has contributed to the expansion of private higher education in Europe has been the continuous and strong expansion of this sector globally.[9]

The rapid expansion of private education and the willingness to bear some or all of the costs of higher education suggests that tuition fees are a poor instrument to entice students to redistribute towards science majors. Using the data on all US public four-year colleges and universities from 1991 to 2006, Hemelt and Marcotte show that a $100 increase in tuition fees would lead to a decline in enrolment of about 0.25%, with larger effects at research universities.[10] The weak response of enrolment to increases in tuition fees is probably the result of a weak impact of

Higher tuition fees fail to redistribute students towards science majors.

tuition fees on the rate of return to education. A degree from the most expensive colleges translates into the highest premia in the labour market. For example, the median starting salary for graduates of 'Ivy League' schools is 32% higher than that of liberal arts college graduates – and at ten or more years into graduates' working lives, the spread is 34%.[11]

7.2 Is later tracking a necessary and a sufficient condition for equality of educational opportunities?

Our findings support the view that although elite, mass and universal access to education are sequential stages of educational expansion, they do not inevitably replace one another. The research documents examples of elite forms of education stubbornly surviving at the mass and universal stages, such as elite grammar schools in the United Kingdom, *Gymnasia* in Germany, and multi-year *gymnasia* in the Czech Republic and Slovakia. These examples suggest that expansion, if not accompanied by policies aimed at greater equality of educational opportunities, will perpetuate social stratification despite greater participation in upper secondary schooling.

Two types of educational policies are linked to equality of educational opportunities, in other words, the decoupling of educational success from family background: 1) later tracking, and 2) early childhood education. There is a

Later tracking and early childhood education might enhance the equality of educational opportunities.

growing body of literature suggesting that the earlier students are tracked, the more their family background will have an impact on their student performance. In highly stratified educational systems – characterised by early and irreversible assignment of students to a number of tracks – the future of the child may thus be decided as early as the age of ten. Consequently, there has been a strong push, associated most visibly with the OECD, for a policy change towards later tracking, especially with its legitimacy buttressed by the Programme for International Student Assessment (PISA). Our research adds to this debate by examining the association between within-school and equality of educational opportunities for differently performing students, regardless of their academic performance.

We study the issue at the country level for four OECD countries (Austria, Belgium, Hungary and Finland) that we selected on the basis of how conditional PISA performance distributions react to ability grouping.[12] Figure 7.1 reveals very different results for the countries concerned, both in average results and results for low and high performers. In Belgium, low performers are more strongly subject to inequality effects of within-school ability grouping, whereas in Austria

In reality, the effects of tracking are mitigated by other characteristics of the education system.

the high performers are more subjected to these inequality effects. In Hungary, we find that within-school ability grouping is positively correlated with equality, and more so for the high performers. In Finland, within-school ability grouping does not appear to have a significant relation with equality. In other words, the effects of tracking are so deeply mitigated by other characteristics of the education system that policy-makers should avoid global generalisations and focus on specific country situations.

Figure 7.1 Effect of socioeconomic gradient for children of different abilities in Austria, Belgium, Finland and Hungary

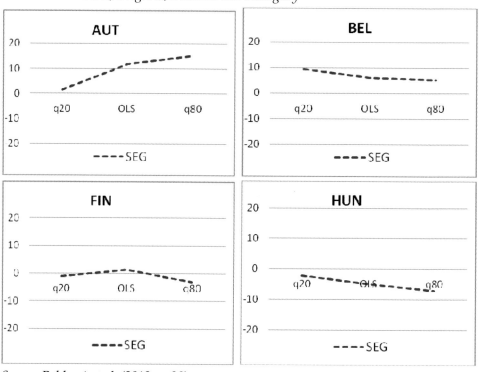

Source: Beblavý et al. (2012, p. 30).

One of the key policy puzzles is why countries adopt or do not adopt pro-equality educational policies.[13] This type of research focuses on the policy process, which introduced various elements of less selective (or comprehensive) schooling, such as later age at which children are selected to follow various tracks, elimination of dead-end educational pathways or increased mobility between tracks. Our research relies on a comparative case study of five European countries with varying degrees of success in introducing less-selective educational systems in the period following World War II: success (Sweden), failure (Germany), formal implementation of the reform and informal transfer of selection to the private schooling sector (United Kingdom), success followed by reversal (Czechoslovakia), and success associated with increased dropout rates (Spain).

There has been a gradual improvement in the equality of educational opportunities in the post-World War II period; educational systems today are less selective than they were 60 years ago. Nevertheless, there are still significant differences between countries, or rather between various educational models. A general preference towards selection is still

> *Educational systems today are less selective than they were 60 years ago, but significant differences among countries persist.*

strong within the German educational model, which favours early selection of students into academic and vocational tracks. The movement towards increased equality of educational opportunities has been accompanied by a counter-movement which is attempting to re-introduce earlier selection along the lines of increased efficiency. The importance of competition as the main driver of educational quality has been promoted under the umbrella of neo-liberalism and gained prominence in the national discourses of countries that were facing an economic downturn or financial crisis, such as Sweden in the 1990s.

What are the main drivers of the movement towards either earlier or later selection? Our study differentiates between two types of factor, which are roughly equivalent to extraordinary circumstances versus business as usual.[14] Extraordinary circumstances, or critical junctures, represent events that are beyond policy control. Typical examples include an economic crisis or a regime change. They open 'windows of opportunity',[15] which may or may not be used by policy entrepreneurs in an attempt to translate these external shocks into policy change. The above-mentioned reorganisation of education systems along neoliberal lines is an example of a shift in the 'policy paradigm'[16] in the face of widespread perception of policy failure.

External shocks are difficult or impossible to predict. From a policy perspective, it is therefore more interesting to study the policy process during ordinary times. We document three factors that enabled the introduction of less-selective schooling. First, left-leaning parties tended to be more in favour of less-selective schooling than the right-leaning political parties. The election of a strong, leftist government enabled the 'comprehensivisation' of educational systems in post-World War II Sweden and post-Franco Spain.[17] The Labour Party initiated the process of the reorganisation of the education system towards less-selective schooling in the United Kingdom. The Communist Party in Czechoslovakia introduced 'unified school ' up to the age of 15 within one year of the *coup d'état* in 1948.[18]

Second, in our study[19] we document that the dissemination of research has an impact on the prevailing beliefs about human intelligence and about the link between the age of tracking and educational performance. For that purpose, international circulation of pedagogical knowledge and models in three broad waves was examined in the research. At the beginning of the 20th century, the educational discourse was dominated by the ideas of the progressivist movement, which quickly spread to the rest of the world. Comprehensive schooling at the secondary level was introduced for the first time in the United States. A direct influence of the progressivist movement was documented in three out of five case studies (Germany, Sweden and Czechoslovakia). However, with the single exception of Sweden, these ideas did not translate into policy change despite several decades of research dissemination, the rise of reformists to decision-making positions, or experiences with experimental schools. Furthermore, whereas reform attempts inspired by the progressivist movement in Germany or Czechoslovakia culminated in the period prior to the World War II or immediately afterwards, the Swedish reform stretched from the 1950s to the 1960s.

In the post-World War II period, the prevailing beliefs about intelligence changed. Traditionally, it was believed that there are various types of intelligence suited for various types of education. Bright pupils should be educated separately from slower students, with this separation benefitting both groups. We observe these beliefs in the United Kingdom, Sweden, Czechoslovakia and Germany. The British tripartite system rested on the widely held belief, propagated by the educational psychologist Cyril Burt, that intelligence was an innate mental ability that could be evaluated through intelligence tests, and which had a strong relationship with social class.[20] These ideas were reflected in the White Paper that preceded the 1944 Education Act: "all children should receive the type of education for which they are best adapted."[21] The change in sentiment came with a paradigm shift in the field of psychology at the end of the 1950s. The prevailing theories of innate intelligence were discredited and an emphasis was placed on social factors. This perspective found resonance in subsequent official reports, including the landmark Robbins and Newsom reports which claimed that all children had an equal opportunity to 'develop intelligence '.[22] Thus, the distilling of a new orthodoxy – the psychology of intelligence – coupled with mounting evidence on the unsatisfactory operation of the tripartite system created the setting for the reforms aiming to abolish tracking.

Both the German and the German-influenced Czechoslovakian education models rested on the belief that weak students could make the strong weaker and thereby reduce quality.[23] These ideas can be traced back to the philosopher Alexander von Humboldt (1769-1859), a founding father of the *Gymnasium*. The dominating beliefs changed in the 1970s when the 'Copernican education rebound' (*Kopernikanische Bildungswende*) took place: the belief in an innate predestination for the different school types was replaced by the belief in a universal ability to be educated. This is the climate in which the idea arose of the comprehensive *Gemeinschaftsschule*.

Most recently, the PISA programme of the OECD has shown an unprecedented impact on the national educational discourses. In Germany, the PISA shock influenced educational discourse and led to a wide-ranging reform agenda; shifted the curriculum development process towards principles such as outcome control, competence orientation or external assessment; and strengthened the role of empirical research in academic discourse. Similarly, in the Czech Republic, the results of the first PISA testing debunked the myth that Czech students were above average and reinforced the belief that educational policy should address the problem of early tracking.[24] The strategic White Paper published shortly afterwards therefore called for the introduction of mechanisms such that the educational system does not further reproduce existing inequalities. These developments were mirrored in Slovakia, where the subsequent right-leaning and the left-leaning Ministers of Education endorsed the OECD's recommendations to reduce early stratification in the education system. In response, the Slovak cabinet decided to introduce quotas on the number of children allowed to enrol in elite multi-year secondary schools.

Finally, the shift in the prevailing beliefs about intelligence is a necessary but not a sufficient condition for the policy change towards less-selective schooling. The convergence towards the international model or the best practice advocated by international organisations such as the OECD or UNESCO is problematic in countries with strong national academic traditions. For example, the strong tradition of the German *Gymnasium* works as an obstacle to the reorganisation of secondary schooling.

However, the implementation of reform aimed at less-selective schooling is also complicated by other factors, notably the stable social and political balance of forces: parents with high socio-economic status and teachers from elite academic tracks vehemently oppose the comprehensivisation of education. Their typical defence strategy is to reframe the issue of later tracking as socialist or detrimental to the development of gifted children. It is therefore crucial for policy-makers to avoid the capture of the public discourse by opponents of the reform. An example of a successful strategy was the framing of comprehensive schooling as a means for the mobilisation of the country's resources and the pathway to wealth creation by the UK Labour Party in the 1960s.

Based on the above, it is possible to identify two broad trends that are likely to affect future levels of equality of educational opportunities. First, there has been a gradual shift towards greater equality of educational

Strong academic traditions and continuing privatisation are the main obstacles for the shift towards later tracking.

opportunities during the past century. Continuing advocacy of later tracking by international organisations, such as the OECD or UNESCO, will create incentives for governments to converge towards 'best practice'. However, the impetus is weaker in countries with strong academic traditions. Furthermore, the case of Czechoslovakia illustrates that policies based on later tracking are not irreversible.

Second, the continuing privatisation of educational systems will work as a counterforce to the above trend. As a result of the neoliberal revolution, the monopoly of the state as the provider of education has been eroded and we are witnessing an increasing privatisation of the public sphere. Free school choice may undermine efforts to increase equality of educational opportunities, because if "schools and children are free to seek each other out: with some caveats, this leads to perfect segregation by child quality".[25] In England, sorting by ability and by income is more prevalent, with more choices beyond attending the school determined by place of residence. In Sweden, school choice not only raised differences between schools and school areas in relation to ability, but also to social and immigrant status.

7.3 Job polarisation based on the skill content of tasks is happening in Europe

During the first decade of this century, occupational polarisation based on skills emerged across Europe, with rising demand at the upper and lower ends of the occupational skills distribution. The share of elementary occupations in total employment increased from 8.7% in 2000 to 9.6% in 2008. These findings were also supported by our research,[26] in which we analysed labour demand and supply with respect to skills and tasks and attempted to anticipate what types of skills mismatch EU countries will encounter over the next decade.

Figure 7.2 illustrates the job polarisation phenomenon in the EU-27 between 2000 and 2010. We would normally expect demand for workers to rise as the skill content of these occupations increases in a

Job polarisation occurred in 17 out of 27 EU countries between 2000 and 2010.

linear fashion. Instead the picture is U-shaped, as predicted by job polarisation, which is the result of an approximate 20% increase in the demand for low-skilled and high-profile occupations between 2000 and 2010, and a 4.5% decrease in the demand for middle-skilled occupations. This polarisation occurred in 17 out of 27 EU countries.[27]

Figure 7.2 Job polarisation in the EU-27, 2000-10

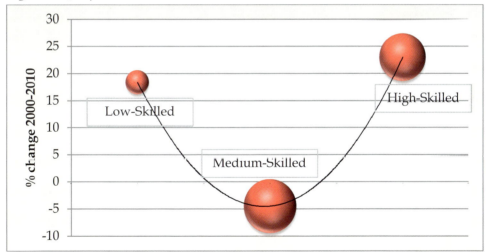

Source: Maselli (2012, p. 23).

Figure 7.3 depicts the match between labour demand and labour supply. The share of middle-skilled occupations in total employment is 50.4%, and the share of the labour supply with a secondary degree is 48.2%. However, the trends for these are to move in opposite directions: the latter has grown by 13.2%, while the former has declined by 4.5%. The share of low-skilled workers is small (22.2%) and rapidly decreasing (-15.2%), most probably due to a phasing-out of the older and less educated generation from the labour force. The percentage of low-skilled occupations increased by 18.4%, resulting in a 9.8% share of these types of jobs in the economy.

One-third of the total labour force is highly educated, and the size of this group grew by 44.9% over the period 2000-10. Meanwhile, demand for these workers grew more modestly (23%), but still accounted for 39.8% of total employment. However, one should bear in mind that there are significant differences between countries (see Table 7.1).

Figure 7.3 Demand and supply of work with respect to skills/tasks in the EU-27, 2000-10

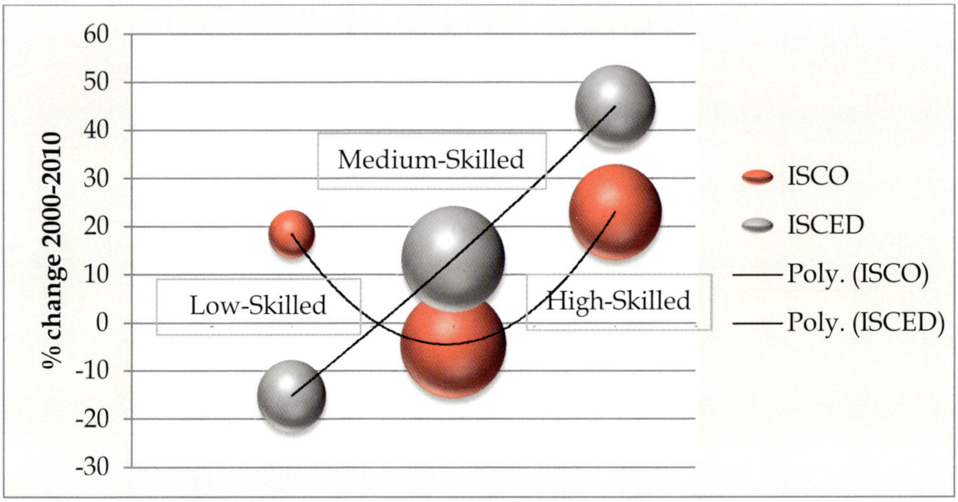

Source: Maselli (2012, p. 26).

Table 7.1 Static and dynamic match between the labour demand and labour supply by country

		Dynamic				
		Shortage of low-skilled	Low-skilled unemployment	Middle-skilled "displacement"	Over-qualification of high-skilled	Equili-brium
Static	Equili-brium	PL		DE, ET, LV, LT, HU, AT, SI, SK, UK	BG, IE	EU27, BE, FI, RO, SE, FR
	Tension		EL, IT, PT, MT, DK		CY	CZ, NL, LUX

Source: Maselli (2012).

The literature identifies several possible drivers of polarisation: skill-biased technological change, educational expansion, growth of the service sector, trade liberalisation, employer preferences and organisational change.[28] CEDEFOP attributes the occupation polarisation in Europe to three factors: macroeconomic and structural changes (between sectors), the demand-driven increase in specific service activities (e.g. private households) and the increasing labour supply of non-national workers. CEDEFOP suggests that the relative increase in elementary occupations is bound to persist in the near future because of the continuous shift towards a tertiary-based economy,[29] and forecasts that by 2020 there will be job opportunities in all occupations but their distribution will be uneven. New jobs will be concentrated in higher and lower skill-level jobs, with slower growth in middle occupations.[30]

Job polarisation is a key contributor to inequality. The concentration of wage growth among high-skilled workers, combined with disproportionate job growth at the upper and lower ends of the skill distribution, has resulted in a more unequal economic environment in the United States.[31] The literature on educational expansion suggests that with a general extension of education, the demand for less-educated workers declines. As the low-skilled become a minority, they are perceived as increasingly incapable: while educational attainment acts as a signal for the applicants' productivity and their ability to learn, the lack of it acts as a signal for failure. This phenomenon has been termed *stigmatisation by negative selection*,[32] and was confirmed empirically by showing that in countries with a low share of low-educated workers (e.g. in Norway or Switzerland), the unemployment risk of the low-skilled (defined as ISCED0/1/2) is highest. Conversely, in countries with high shares of low-skilled workers (e.g. Portugal or Spain), the unemployment risk of this group is low. In conclusion, the job market opportunities of the low-skilled depend crucially on employers' beliefs and perceptions about the relationship between applicants' education and their future productivity. It is therefore reasonable to assume that with the expanding education sector, we will see a continuing replacement of the low-skilled by the medium-skilled.

For the medium-skilled, this means that they might temporarily assume positions for which they are overqualified. Over-education and mismatches in the labour market receive a great deal of policy attention. However, Ramos et al.[33] argue that even when qualified workers are unable to find suitable jobs, they are still more productive at the aggregate level than their unqualified counterparts. This implies that there is a good case for public investment in education and its further expansion, even though a number of recent studies fail to provide favourable evidence regarding the link between human capital and growth. They warn that regions might not benefit directly from their investment in education in the context of high geographical mobility.

The final lesson to be derived is that the skills content of low-skilled jobs has increased, leading to the phenomenon of 'upskilling'.[34] The characterisation 'low-skilled' should therefore be viewed as a fluid concept, whose definition depends on the context. Job polarisation may therefore be a misleading concept, because 'low-skilled' workers are present in a wide range of jobs.

7.4 The surprisingly demanding nature of 'low-skilled' jobs

Our research identifies the competences and characteristics demanded in the labour market in selected low- and medium-skilled occupations. The research was conducted in the context of continuing high unemployment across the developed world and a debate about what role skills and upskilling can play in alleviating this problem. The focus on the lower-skilled segment was motivated by several factors: their generally lower employment rates; reports of skill polarisation towards high- and low-skilled occupations, accompanied by a process of displacement of the low-skilled by more educated workers; as well as the rising skill requirements and task complexity within all occupational categories and skill levels.

To this end, we analysed labour demand at the micro level by studying the content of job adverts to identify specific skills and characteristics that are demanded for selected low- and medium-skilled occupations in four countries: the Czech Republic, Denmark, Ireland and Slovakia.[35] Our work is innovative in exploring data from online job adverts and quantifying different skills, personal attributes and characteristics. It shows that online portals can potentially become a very useful source of information about the content of demand and for improving generally weak statistics on vacancies generated through other sources. We contribute to those works that emphasise the need to analyse labour market demand at the micro level and use job adverts as a source of information about the employer's demand. The implications of our work spill over to a number of areas and contexts. [36]

The analysis of online job adverts suggests that the specific skill-set demanded in service occupations differs from other, mainly industry-connected, jobs in the greater focus given to non-cognitive social skills and personal characteristics. There is a great variation in the content of skill demand across the analysed labour markets. For example, Danish employers focus on non-cognitive skills – such as customer approach, precision, loyalty, flexibility, empathy and the ability to communicate – whereas in the Czech Republic, employers appear to give priority to formal qualifications and diplomas. The amount of information available on the job portal Profesia.sk allowed us to dig deep into the labour demand and led us to discover that employers in the Slovak labour market are quite demanding. Language abilities are required to a large extent across a majority of occupations, including those where a low-level of education is expected, such as chambermaid and cleaner. Among non-cognitive personal skills, being responsible and flexible are the most pronounced characteristics. Among social skills, the ability to communicate is the most requested across occupations, on average.

> *The specificity of skill requirements differs considerably across countries.*

As far as formal qualifications are concerned, Slovak employers now tend to require an upper secondary education even for jobs that are marked as 'elementary' in the International Classification of Occupation (ISCO). Overall, our research indicates that the term 'low-skilled jobs' might be a misnomer, both with regard to the actual skills required as well as the formal educational credentials demanded. In a number of new occupations, such as courier, caretaker or au pair, employers requested a complete secondary education (four-year general or specialised with a leaving examination). This suggests that demand in the labour market might have adapted to the supply, which continues to be better and better educated.

The review of the literature and the analysis of the data allowed us to clearly understand that 'low-skilled' does not only mean low-educated. We have suggested that 'low-skilled' is not a static state but a dynamic process.[37] In the past, we observed the de-skilling of some occupations, such as accounting, and the upskilling of others, such as journalism. We conceptualise 'low-skilled' as a process rather than just regarding it as a status characterising workers alone.[38] Such an approach enables us to cast doubt over the existing conceptualisations of who is 'low-skilled', which typically do not move beyond the measurement of the low-skilled through the lowest attained level of qualification (ISCED 0-2). Such a conceptualisation ignores the heterogeneity of the low-skilled. To overcome these deficiencies, we propose an alternative typology. In addition to the typically included 'low-educated', the typology includes categories of workers who might be formally well-educated, experienced and trained, but have been drawn into becoming low-skilled as an outcome of structural forces or institutional barriers. Examples include people with obsolete skills, displaced workers or 'temporarily low-skilled' migrant workers. The proposed categories are then used to empirically test the quantitative differences across the EU countries. The aim is to understand how the low-skilled as a group differ internally and how structural processes and individual characteristics interact in various ways in the dynamic labour market.

We find that formal qualification levels are valued differently in different labour markets. This conclusion arises from the fact that while low (ISCED 0-2) and medium (ISCED 3-4) qualifications are substitutes in employment across the EU countries, the low- (ISCO 9) and middle-skilled (ISCO 4-8) occupations do not retain this property across the EU countries. This implies that people with the same educational level are employed in occupations with different skills requirements across the EU labour markets.

As shown in Figures 7.4 and 7.5, competition for jobs takes place within the age cohorts across different levels of formal education, and not between age cohorts. Among young workers, competition for jobs takes place between the medium-educated and low-educated, while among older workers, the medium-skilled compete with highly educated workers in the same age groups. Contrary to the literature and general policy discourse, we found that it is the young workers who tend to suffer more in the labour market. Specifically, the young are always at greater risk of unemployment than the old, regardless of their qualification level.

> *Competition for jobs takes place within the age cohorts across different levels of formal education, and not between age cohorts.*

Figure 7.4 Relative unemployment in the EU member states

Panel A: Relative unemployment of young age group Y15-24

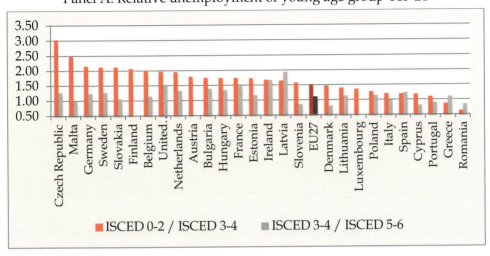

Panel B: Relative unemployment of old age group Y50-59

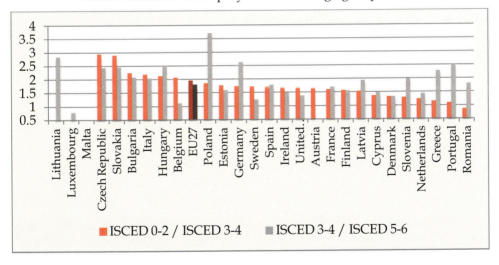

Panel C: Unemployment of young (15-24) versus old (50-59) cohort

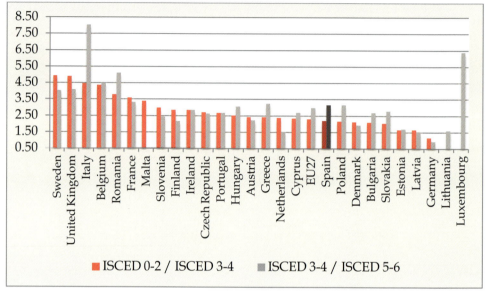

Source: Kureková, Haita and Beblavý (2013a, p. 62).

In most countries, the elementary occupations (ISCO 9) appear to shrink more than the middle-skilled occupations (ISCO 4-8), but this is linked to the overall shrinkage in the labour demand of the country. This is in contrast to the literature, which argues for the presence of skill polarisation and a decline in middle-level occupations. We interpret our finding as suggesting that a displacement of the employed in elementary occupations into unemployment by workers from the upper-skilled occupations is taking place.

With respect to skill obsolescence, we analyse unemployment and inactivity rates of the cohort of 35-39 years of age in 1995 (i.e. 50-54 years old in 2010) to provide a dynamic view. As shown in Figure 7.5, the given age cohort not only becomes less employable as it advances in age, but a large share of its members drops out of the labour market into inactivity by the end of their working life. The sharpest changes are found in Romania, Poland, Slovenia, Bulgaria and Slovakia, which experienced a rampant structural change and reformed their economic systems from socialist into market economies.

Figure 7.5 Labour market status in the EU: Old vs. prime age

Panel A: Unemployment (%)

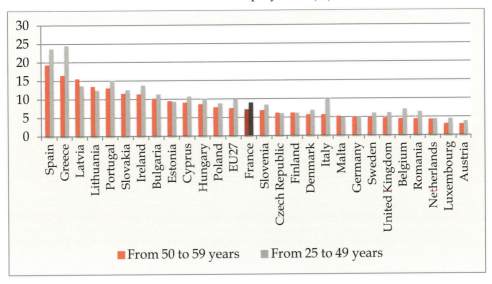

Panel B: Inactivity (%)

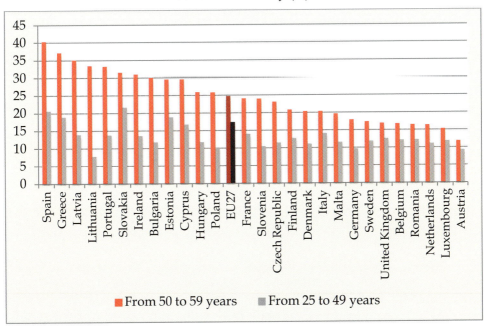

Source: Kureková, Haita and Beblavý (2013a, p. 79).

At the subjective level, however, skills obsolescence (measured as the need for further training in order to be able to perform job tasks) is reported more by young people than by older workers. Equal shares in all generations perceive themselves to have skills enabling them to perform more demanding tasks. This should not be seen as contradictory to the earlier finding, as older workers might be out of the labour market (and therefore not captured in the survey) while, with respect to the youth, it signals a lack of experience or practical skills rather than skills obsolescence as such.

Detachment from the labour market (defined as being unemployed for four years or longer) resembles the structure of the overall working population in a given country. This implies that the issue of which labour market segment is most affected by detachment is influenced by the overall educational structure of population, which justifies our proposition to go beyond the ISCED 0-2 measure in empirical investigations of 'low-skilled'.

7.5 Back to school? How people upskill during their lives differs across Europe

Our research[39] also explored different aspects of lifelong learning, i.e. adult on-the-job or informal training and formal training leading to an increase in ISCED. We wanted to examine: 1) whether lifelong learning differs across age cohorts; and 2) whether adult learning takes place through 'going back to school' (ISCED level upskilling) and/or only through training. To answer these questions, we constructed synthetic panels based on the European Labour Force Survey 2000-2010 waves for 27 European countries.

The results imply that older-age cohorts are less likely to participate in training. However, this effect is less significant for going back to school. The probability of obtaining a higher education degree after 20 years of age sharply decreases with age. However, this does not hold true for lower ISCED levels: obtaining an upper secondary degree is more common for people with greater on-the-job experience. Furthermore, lifelong learning is also determined by individual characteristics. Whereas

Men and immigrants are more likely to obtain an upper secondary degree in their adult life; natives are more likely to pursue higher education.

men and immigrants are more likely to obtain an upper secondary degree in their adult life, natives are more likely to achieve tertiary educational achievement. Contrary to the existing literature, our results imply that higher-educated individuals tend to participate less in training than those in other educational ranges.

Although individual characteristics – such as age, gender, educational level and professional activity – account for a large part of country heterogeneity, the preference of training over formal ISCED upgrading and vice versa suggests that these individual characteristics are influenced by the institutional setting. When we grouped countries by level of upskilling either through training or formal ISCED upgrade, we found that – relative to the base country, Austria – three types of country emerged: those that score highly on both dimensions, and those that score highly on one dimension but not the other (see Figure 7.6).

Figure 7.6 Training and ISCED upskilling: A comparison of European countries with Austria

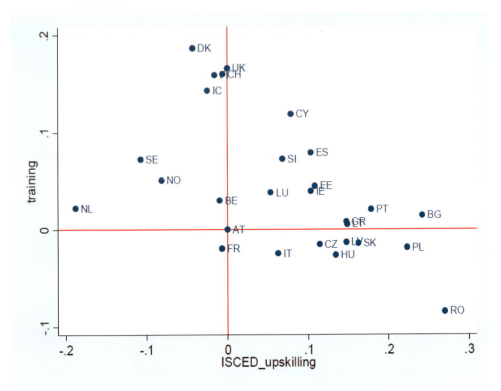

Source: Beblavý, Thum and Potjagailo (2013c, p. 26).

Scandinavian countries and the Netherlands score highly on the training dimension, but poorly on ISCED upskilling. This may be a result of educational levels that are already high or training that does not lead to a degree that upgrades the ISCED level. Relatively high levels of upskilling but low levels of training can be found in the post-communist 'Visegrad Four' countries (Czech Republic, Hungary, Poland and Slovakia), Romania and Italy. This suggests that a formal degree is highly valued in the labour market, so that people are willing to make this 'lumpy' investment.

These inter-country differences should be kept in mind by both EU and national policy-makers. In the countries of central Europe, a focus on quality and accessibility of upper secondary and higher education appears also to be the most effective lifelong learning policy, whereas in the Scandinavian countries, the focus should be on employers and the training they provide.

These patterns of upskilling also have implications for equality. Firms tend to invest in training of those workers whose training leads to the highest increase in productivity, i.e. managers and skilled workers.[40] The position of low-skilled, older or immigrant workers will therefore be more favourable in countries with a tradition of publicly funded lifelong and adult learning. Furthermore, it is reasonable to assume that with the expansion of tertiary education and the growing competition from educated younger cohorts, older cohorts and/or less-educated workers will seek further education to remain competitive in the labour market.

7.6 Moderate convergence accompanied by an impetus for polarisation

There are undoubtedly powerful forces pushing for more polarisation, particularly in the labour market. In most European countries, the destruction or lower growth of routine, middle-skill jobs can be observed. This also has important implications for the low-skilled, as the displaced middle-skilled individuals are more likely to compete with them and push them out. As employers adjust job content and requirements to this fact, and the population undergoes a gradual upskilling, nominally 'low-skilled' jobs can be surprisingly demanding. However, the demands can be manifested in very different forms, and the skill-intensity of a position and its formal educational requirements are often far apart.

This leads to reassessment of what a skill is and how people acquire it. We have demonstrated that there is increasing complexity in what constitutes a 'low-skilled' person and how well (or poorly) he or she fares in the labour market. The accelerating upskilling of populations in developed countries points to a not-too-distant future in which higher education will be somewhere between a mass and a universal phenomenon. At the same time, the importance of experience is likely to grow, with implications for the prospects of labour market entrants.

How policy-makers handle these developments and contribute to more rather than less equality of opportunity is a question to which there are no easy answers. Polarisation is likely to increase socio-economic inequalities within societies along ethnic, gender and age lines. Our research has confirmed that early childhood education plays an important role, and it also appears to be increasingly uncontested as a policy prescription. However, the other frequently emphasised remedy – less selection in secondary education, particularly later division of children into separate tracks – is more problematic. Its effectiveness depends on the country in question and the target group, while education systems are extremely difficult to shift even on a long-term basis. A different, more nuanced warning to policy-makers is delivered in our research on returns to higher education by field of study, which showed hidden rationality in how students choose their major. It is always tempting to assume people do not know what they are doing, but that assumption should always be carefully checked. European policies also need to be mindful of different ways in which national systems deal with upskilling.

Bibliography

Abel, J.R. and R. Deitz (2012), "Job Polarization and Rising Inequality in the Nation and the New York–Northern New Jersey Region", *Current Issues in Economics and Finance,* Vol. 18, No. 7, pp. 1-7.

Beblavý, M., Thum, A. and G. Potjagailo (2012), "Do the Effects of Pro-Equality Education Policies Differ across the Performance Distribution?", NEUJOBS Working Paper No. 4.5.3, July (www.neujobs.eu).

Beblavý, M. and M. Veselková (eds) (2013), "From Selectivity to Universalism: Political Economy of Pro-Equality Educational Reform", NEUJOBS Working Paper No. 4.5.2, July (www.neujobs.eu).

Beblavý, M., S. Lehouelleur and I. Maselli (2013a), "Useless Degrees or Useless Statistics? A Comparison of the Net Present Value of Higher Education by Field of Study in Five European Countries", NEUJOBS Working Paper No. 4.4.2a, NEUJOBS FP7 Research Project, July (www.neujobs.eu).

Beblavý, M., A. Thum, G. Potjagailo and M. von Werder (2013b), "A closer look at the effects of within-school ability grouping in secondary schools: How are different performers affected? An investigation into four OECD countries", unpublished manuscript.

Beblavý, M., A. Thum and G. Potjagailo (2013c), "Where and when does adult learning happen? A Cohort Analysis of Adult Education in Europe", NEUJOBS Working Paper No. 4.3.2, NEUJOBS FP7 Research Project, May (www.neujobs.eu).

Boarini, R. and H. Strauss (2010), "What is the private return to tertiary education? New evidence from 21 OECD countries", *OECD Journal: Economic Studies,* Vol. 2010, p. 1.

CEDEFOP (2011), "Labour-Market Polarisation and Elementary Occupations in Europe. Blip or Long-Term Trend?", CEDEFOP Research Paper No. 9, Publications Office of the European Union, Luxembourg.

_____ (2012), "Europe's Skill Challenge", Briefing Note, March.

Clemens, M.A. (2004), "The Long Walk to School: International Education Goals in Historical Perspective", Working Paper No. 37, Center for Global Development, March, p. 15.

European Commission (2011), Progress towards the common European objectives in education and training (2010/2011) – Indicators and benchmarks, Brussels (http://ec.europa.eu/education/lifelong-learning-policy/indicators10_en.htm).

Hall, P.A. (1993), "Policy Paradigms, Social Learning, and the State: The Case of Economic Policymaking in Britain", *Comparative Politics,* Vol. 25, No. 3, pp. 275-296.

Hemelt, S.W. and D.E. Marcotte (2011), "The Impact of Tuition Increases on Enrollment at Public Colleges and Universities", *Educational Evaluation and Policy Analysis,* Vol. 33, No. 4, pp. 435-457.

Kingdon, J. (1994), *Agendas, Ideas, and Policy Change,* 2nd edition, New York, NY: HarperCollins.

Kureková, L., C. Haita and M. Beblavý (2013a), "Being and Becoming Low-Skilled: A Comprehensive Approach to Studying Low-Skillness", NEUJOBS Working Paper No. 4.3.1, NEUJOBS FP7 Research Project, December (www.neujobs.eu).

Kureková, L., M. Beblavý, C. Haita and A. Thum (2013b), "Demand for Less-Skilled Workers across Europe: Between Formal Qualifications and Non-Cognitive Skills", NEUJOBS Working Paper No. 4.3.3, NEUJOBS FP7 Research Project, February (www.neujobs.eu).

Kureková, L., M. Beblavý and C. Haita (2013c), "Qualifications or Soft Skills? Studying Job Advertisements for Demand for Low-Skilled Staff in Slovakia", NEUJOBS Working Paper No. 4.3.3, NEUJOBS FP7 Research Project, August (www.neujobs.eu).

Maselli, I. (2012), "The Evolving Supply and Demand of Skills in the Labour Market", *Intereconomics*, Vol. 47, No. 1.

Mertlík, R. (1947), *Nebezpečí jednotné školy*, Prague: Nakladatel Václav Petr.

Pensiero, N. (2013), "Education Reform in Spain: Actors and Consequences of an Incomplete Transformation", in M. Beblavý and M. Veselková (eds), ‚From Selectivity to Universalism: The Political Economy of Pro-Equality Educational Reform", NEUJOBS Working Paper No. 4.5.2, NEUJOBS FP7 Research Project, July, pp. 183-203 (www.neujobs.eu).

Peterson, E. (2013), "Education Policy Reform in Sweden: Towards a Comprehensive School - and Back Again?", in M. Beblavý and M. Veselková (eds), "From Selectivity to Universalism: The Political Economy of Pro-Equality Educational Reform", NEUJOBS Working Paper No. 4.5.2, NEUJOBS FP7 Research Project, July, pp. 31-67 (www.neujobs.eu).

Ramos, R., J. Suriñach and M. Artís (2009), "Regional Economic Growth and Human Capital: The Role of Overeducation", IZA Discussion Paper No. 4453, Institute for the Study of Labor, Bonn.

Robertson, D. and J. Symons (2003), "Self-Selection in the State School System", *Education Economics,* Vol. 11, No. 3.

Robinsohn, S.B. and J.C. Kuhlmann (1967), "Two Decades of Non-Reform in West German Education", *Comparative Education Review,* Vol. 11, No. 3.

Solga, H. (2002), "Stigmatization by Negative Selection. Explaining Less - Educated People's Decreasing Employment", *European Sociological Review,* Vol. 18, No. 2, pp. 159-178.

Thum, A-E. (2013), "Educational tracking in Germany: six decades of hesitant and disaggregated reform?", in M. Beblavý and M. Veselková (eds), "From Selectivity to Universalism: The Political Economy of Pro-Equality Educational Reform", NEUJOBS Working Paper No. 4.5.2, NEUJOBS FP7 Research Project, July, pp. 68-115 (www.neujobs.eu).

Toubeau, S. (2013), "The Politics of Educational Reform in Great Britain (1945-2010). The process and implementation policy change and its consequence for educational inequality", in M. Beblavý and M. Veselková (eds), "From Selectivity to Universalism: The Political Economy of Pro-Equality Educational Reform", NEUJOBS Working Paper No. 4.5.2, NEUJOBS FP7 Research Project, July, pp. 116-144 (www.neujobs.eu).

Trow, M.A. (2006), "Reflections on the Transition from Elite to Mass to Universal Access: Forms and Phases of Higher Education in Modern Societies since WWII", in J.F. Forest and P.G. Altbach (eds), *International Handbook of Higher Education*, Dordrecht: Springer, p. 244.

van Wieringen, F. (1999), "Scenario Planning for Vocational and Adult Education", *European Journal of Education,* Vol. 34, No. 2.

Veselková, M. (2013), "Political Economy of Comprehensive School Reforms: Czech and Slovak Lands after World War I", in M. Beblavý and M. Veselková (eds), *From Selectivity to Universalism: The Political Economy of Pro-Equality Educational Reform*, NEUJOBS Working Paper No. 4.5.2, NEUJOBS FP7 Research Project, July (www.neujobs.eu).

Zymek, B. (2009), "Prozesse der Internationalisierung und Hierarchisierung im Bildungssystem. Von der Beharrungskraft und Auflösung nationaler Strukturen und Mentalitäten," *Zeitschrift für Pädagogik,* Vol. 55, No. 2, pp. 175-193.

Notes

1 European Commission (2011).

2 Boundaries are set at 15% for a transition from elite to mass education and 50% for a transition from mass to universal (Trow, 2006).

3 See Clemens (2004).

4 See Veselková (2013).

5 Zymek (2009).

6 Boarini and Strauss (2010).

7 Beblavý et al. (2013a).

8 See Veselková (2013).

9 Ibid., pp. 211-214.

10 Hemelt and Marcotte (2011).

11 *Wall Street Journal*, "Ivy leaguers' big edge: Starting pay", 31 July 2008 (http://online.wsj.com/article/SB121746658635199271.html).

12 Beblavý et al. (2013b).

13 Beblavý and Veselková (2013).

14 Ibid., p. 7.

15 According to Kingdon (1994); see also Beblavý and Veselková (2013, p. 215).

16 See more on the theory of policy paradigms in Hall (1993).

17 Although in that case, the regime change and the eagerness to negate the past played some role. For the Swedish case, see Peterson (2013), and for the Spanish case, see Pensiero (2013).

18 Veselková (2013).

19 Beblavý and Veselková (2013).

20 Toubeau (2013).

21 White Paper: Educational Reconstruction (1943), London: Board of Education, p. 7 (www.educationengland.org.uk/documents/wp1943/educational-reconstruction.html).

22 The Newsom Report (1963), "Half our future", report of the Central Advisory Council for Education, London: Her Majesty's Stationery Office, p. iv (www.educationengland.org.uk/documents/newsom/newsom1963.html).

23 On the German case, see Thum (2013) or Robinsohn and Kuhlmann (1967); on the Czechoslovak case, see Veselková (2013).

24 See J. Kotásek, "Bílá kniha po pěti letech", 18 November 2009 (www.ucitelske-

listy.cz/2009/11/jiri-kotasek-bila-kniha-po-peti-letech.html); P. Holub (2010), "Daň za gymnázia pro elitu. České děti ve světě propadly", 8 December 2010, (http://aktualne.centrum.cz/domaci/spolecnost/clanek.phtml?id=685014); P. Holub, "České školství se nelepší, ukázalo mezinárodní srovnání", 4 December 2007 (http://aktualne.centrum.cz/domaci/spolecnost/clanek.phtml?id=515634); R. Mertlík (1947).

[25] Robertson and Symons (2003).

[26] Maselli (2012); Kureková et al. (2013a).

[27] Diversified occupational polarisation across countries and its concentration of polarisation in service sectors was documented also by CEDEFOP (2011).

[28] For a review of literature, see Maselli (2012) or Kureková et al. (2013b).

[29] CEDEFOP (2011, p. 12).

[30] CEDEFOP (2012).

[31] Abel and Deitz (2012, p. 6).

[32] Solga (2002).

[33] Ramos et al. (2009, p. 11).

[34] See Kureková et al. (2013c); Kureková et al. (2013b).

[35] In the first three, the analysis is based on the EURERS website. For Slovakia it is based on the Profesia.sk job portal.

[36] Kureková et al. (2013b).

[37] Maselli (2012, p. 28) and Kureková et al. (2013a, p. 25).

[38] Kureková et al. (2013a).

[39] Beblavý et al. (2013c).

[40] van Wieringen (1999, p. 164).

8. THE ROLE OF THE STATE: REFORM PRESSURES AND WELFARE REFORM TOWARDS SOCIAL INVESTMENT[*]

States have evolved over time in response to a multitude of challenges and diverging socio-economic situations. The emergence of the post-industrial economy and the societal change that brought about new social risks has created the necessity for another recalibration of the welfare state.[1] Central to this new agenda is an emphasis on policies that aim at 'preparing' rather than 'repairing'.[2] The rationale behind this approach is the idea that preventive services prevent larger economic and social costs arising in the future. This so-called 'social investment' perspective therefore aims to "strengthen people's skills and capacities and support them to participate fully in employment and social life" (European Commission, undated). The key areas of interest include education, quality childcare, training, job-search assistance and rehabilitation.

The scale of social investment required is challenged by the economic crisis and the demographic shift. In the wake of the crisis, European economies are struggling with high unemployment and poverty levels, as well as fiscal pressures. At the same time, aging populations and shrinking working-age populations pose a threat to the sustainability of social security systems. It remains to be seen whether the long-run social challenges will be sacrificed for the short-term goals of deficit and debt reduction in the aftermath of the financial crisis.[3]

[*] Verena Dräbing is the author of chapter 8, which is based on work conducted in work package 5 (Work life balance and welfare transformation) of the NEUJOBS project by Anton Hemerijck, Moira Nelson, Menno Soentken, Barbara Vis, Anne Gauthier, Bent Greve, Giovanna Vallanti, Angela Cipollone and Eleonora Patacchini. Verena is a PhD candidate at the VU University Amsterdam.

The question that arises is whether or not welfare states are opting for social investment. This chapter contributes to recent research in that it offers a detailed overview of general investment trends over time. In order to answer the question of whether there is a shift to social investment, the chapter first gives a short overview of welfare state changes prior to the timeframe of investigation and then introduces the concept of social investment. As a second step, the chapter considers change more empirically – indicators on social investment expenditure are compared to other social expenditure and changes in different policy fields are traced. Then, it briefly addresses the topic of how investment in family policies matters. The conclusion sums up the findings on policy developments and offers an outlook on how social investment might matter in the future.

8.1   The evolution of European welfare states

Research often points to several phases of welfare state development.[4] With the end of World War II, a new era of increasing social expenditure emerged, providing unemployment benefits, pension benefits, survivor and disability benefits, public healthcare and an expansion of publicly provided education. The predominant focus was on the male-breadwinner model, where women stayed at home to care for children and elderly family members. The dominant economic paradigm of this phase was Keynesianism, which regards the state as a crucial actor for economic growth. According to Keynesian ideas, state investment boosts the economy in times of recession to buffer economic cycles. Thus, the state focuses on job creation via public investment while at the same time providing benefits for those in need.[5]

With the onset of the oil shocks in the 1970s, this model came under pressure. Surging unemployment rates, inflation and public debt, combined with increasing criticism of the rigid labour market and the strong role of trade unions, led to the rise of neo-liberalism as the dominant economic paradigm. Contrary to Keynesianism, neo-liberalism is in favour of a limited role for the state. The free market is supposed to provide wealth, which automatically materialises if barriers are removed. Privatisation, flexibility of the labour market and retrenchment of public spending have been the result. The market and the family are supposed to replace the welfare state in the provision of welfare. Examples of policies include private pension schemes and tuition fees for education.[6]

In the early 1990s, a new set of challenges created increasing pressure for the European welfare states. The rise of post-industrial capitalist societies has brought about major social changes, so-called new 'social risks'.[7] Among these social risks are risks related to changes in family structure and gender roles: a higher prevalence of single-parenthood and frail relatives as well as difficulties in reconciling work and care. In addition, the shift from an industrial to a service economy rendered some skills obsolete and subsequently resulted in the dismissal of employees. The need for low-skilled workers decreased, creating a new risk group of workers with low and superfluous skills. Changes in the labour market structure contributed to the risk of insufficient social coverage, where employees with temporary and flexible contracts fall through the social net.[8] Apart from the rise of new social risks, ageing societies increased the pressure on the welfare state while at the same time raising the question of how economic productivity levels can be retained while the workforce shrinks. The resulting debate on how much welfare is affordable and which productivity-increasing measures are available sparked the rise of the social investment debate.[9]

8.2 Social investment as a source of socio-economic development

The underlying assumption of social investment is that welfare spending on certain policies can contribute to economic development. Contrary to earlier policy paradigms, social investment does not regard welfare expenditure as a burden on the state finances *per se* (neo-liberalism) or as solely a measure to buffer cyclical economic development (Keynesianism), but as a necessary investment in future socio-economic development. Its core goals are to equip citizens with the capacity to help themselves across their lifetime and to reduce their risk of neediness. Secondary expected outcomes of social investment are an increase in the workforce, a positive impact on economic growth, a reduction of intergenerational transmission of poverty and a greater ability to reconcile work and care.[10] The selected tools are consequently not just benefit payments, but the provision of services and access to support. The image of the welfare state is shifted from a safety net or a burden on state finances to an investor in human capital, a facilitator of human development and a service provider.[11] In short, the main differences between a social investment welfare state and a welfare state oriented towards passive spending can be summarised up as follows:[12]

1. *A focus on societal development*. Social investment addresses the long-term problem of aging societies by focusing on the need to increase

the productivity of the workforce and to reconcile work and care to finance pension schemes. The main tools are childcare provision, re-skilling and the promotion of flexible jobs.

2. *A focus on human development and making citizens capable of caring for themselves.* Social investment recognises that unemployment might not only result from a temporary lack of work, but also from a lack of skills demanded by the labour market. Therefore, instead of focusing merely on benefit payment, it tries to actively support employability, invest in human capital development and prevent skill depletion of the unemployed.

3. *A focus on long-term reduction of neediness instead of short-term mitigation.* While passive transfer payments focus on short-term goals, social investment is a long-term strategy aiming at human capital development from an early age. The ultimate aim is to diminish the risk of poverty and increase an individual's chances throughout life.

8.3   Social investment in three types of welfare states

Path-dependency theory is often used to analyse change in the welfare state. It emphasises the role of existing institutions and investments that render departure from previous policy paths unlikely, as it is easier and less costly to implement change in line with existing structures. Therefore, change in the welfare state is assumed to be incremental rather than radical and induced by outside pressures.[13]

Among the pressures that might result in change in the welfare state are not just the new social risks; Hemerijck (2013) pinpoints four existing challenges. First, globalisation augments competition in trade and taxes, shifts the macroeconomic focus towards austerity, increases financial interdependence and consequently frames the political discourse. The second challenge is the rise of new social risks caused by the emergence of post-industrial labour markets and a shift in gender roles and family structures. Third, the legacy of social insurance commitments to a growing group of elderly represents an increasing financial strain. Fourth, European integration reduces the leeway for domestic socio-economic policy-making. Given path-dependence theory and the existence of these pressures, we would expect that a move towards social investment might be slow and stepwise, and only add up over time to a real shift.

Given the differences across Europe in terms of spending levels, the question is whether one or several types of social investment exist. The literature at least distinguishes a more 'third-way' type of investment and a more social-democratic type of investment, with the latter combining services and generous benefits while the former focuses more on activation and services and less on benefit provision.[14] This chapter keeps this distinction in mind and thus does not equate social investment with one welfare regime.

To enable a comparison, the welfare regime approach distinguishes welfare states according to their investment patterns, with the distinction generally made according to levels of de-commodification, generosity and stratification.[15] Esping-Andersen differentiates three types: the social-democratic, the conservative and the liberal regime.[16] Other authors propose an additional southern regime or discuss the difficulties of integrating the newer EU member states into this categorisation.[17] Similar to Hemerijck (2013), to compare developments across social models, this chapter categorises countries into the social-democratic, Christian-democratic, liberal and southern regimes with a residual category for the post-communist countries in order to better account for diversity.[18]

> *European welfare states differ in their degree of de-commodification, generosity and stratification.*

The time frame considered is 1997 to 2009. As the financial and the European sovereign debt crises had a severe impact on government finances, 2007 is used as an indicator for the investment levels prior to the onset of the crisis. It is clear that the crisis has dramatically influenced the financial situation of governments, but it is too early to estimate the long-term impact on social spending, especially as detailed data are only available up to 2009.

8.4   Measuring social investment

There are several approaches to the measurement of social investment.[19] This chapter focuses on overall expenditure on 'capacitating' policies as well as the per capita expenditure per policy field, because together they give an encompassing view. The overall indicator is calculated by summing up the different sub-indicators given in Table 8.1. Capacitating spending here refers to policies with a clear social investment focus. Care services for the elderly and children are included as they facilitate female employment. For family policies, it is debatable which policies to include. Services and leave policies are often seen as important for female employment,[20] while child allowances are more controversial and are therefore counted as compensating spending. Expenditure on education and active labour market policies are included due to their clear focus on human capital development, as well as public research funding. Incapacity-related benefits in kind are included as they comprise, among others, rehabilitation services.

This chapter compares spending on 'capacitation' with spending on compensation. The aim is to show how much social expenditure is directed towards benefits and how much is spent on services and work and family reconciliation. Other authors would call this distinction "old" and "new" spending,

Spending on compensation is associated with income replacement, whereas capacitating spending is directed towards services and work and family reconciliation.

referring to traditional welfare policies and policies addressing new social risks.[21] This chapter prefers the terms "compensating" and "capacitating", as this is more in line with social investment ideas where different types of social investment might exist – one that combines high levels of both compensating and capacitating spending, and one that might focus more on only capacitating expenditure.[22] Compensating spending concerns policies that clearly aim at income replacement, such as benefits to cover unemployment, old age, incapacity, survivors and family allowances, as well as other cash benefits on families.

In order to compare expenditure levels across countries, expenditure is often measured as a percentage of GDP.[23] However, percentage of GDP does not give any information about the level of expenditure per person and is affected by sudden fluctuations in GDP. Therefore, additional information on per person expenditure by policy fields is provided later on.

Table 8.1 Measurement of capacitating social spending and compensating social spending

Measurement capacitating social spending	Data source
Active labour market policies (ALMP) expenditure as % of GDP	OECD Social Expenditure database
Family policy expenditure as % of GDP, except for family allowances and other benefits	OECD Social Expenditure database
Total public expenditure on education as % of GDP	OECD Education at a glance OECD Research and

Public expenditure on research and development as % of GDP	Development Statistics
	OECD Social Expenditure database
Old-age: Expenditure on residential care as % of GDP	OECD Social Expenditure database
Incapacity: Benefits in kind as % of GDP	
Measurement compensating social spending	**Data source**
Expenditure on unemployment as % of GDP	OECD Social Expenditure database
Family allowances and other cash benefits as % of GDP	OECD Social Expenditure database
Old-age expenditure excluding residential care as % of GDP	OECD Social Expenditure database
Incapacity expenditure excluding benefits in kind as % of GDP	OECD Social Expenditure database
Expenditure on survivors as % of GDP	OECD Social Expenditure database

8.5 Overall trends in welfare expenditure

In general, several investment patterns are visible: the social-democratic regime has the highest capacitating and medium-to-high compensating expenditure levels; the Christian-democratic regime has a strong focus on compensating expenditure and medium capacitating expenditure levels; the liberal regime starts from low expenditure levels on both policy types and has increased its expenditure in general over time; the southern regime has medium levels of compensating expenditure and rather low capacitating investment levels; the former communist countries exhibit considerable variation in their investments, with Poland and Hungary lying in between the southern and Christian-democratic regimes and other countries exhibiting generally lower social expenditure levels.

As can be seen in Figure 8.1, the social-democratic regime exhibits the highest levels of capacitating spending in 1997, 2007 and 2009. In addition, the regime exhibits moderate-to-high levels of compensating spending, although compensating spending decreased between

Overall welfare expenditure trends show an increase in social investment expenditure.

1997 and 2007. Nelson shows in a couple of case studies that Sweden started early by expanding reforms focused on capacitating policies combined with generous benefits.24 Reforms in recent years have shifted the focus in Sweden more to childcare services and investment in education, while reducing the generosity of benefits. However, the country still scores high in international comparisons. Denmark, on the other hand, started its investment in the 1980s and 1990s. Here, the focus has been on increasing active labour market policies (ALMPs), for instance, in subsidising employment, education and retraining for the unemployed. Family policy reforms have included an extension of parental leave and efforts to increase the quality of daycare and possibilities to reconcile work and care. Thus, it is clear that while the Nordic countries face less pressure to reform, they have already been investing in social investment for decades, albeit in a policy mix that emphasises the combination of generous compensating spending with high capacitating spending.

Figure 8.1 Compensating spending vs. capacitating spending in 1997, 2007 and 2009: Social-democratic regime

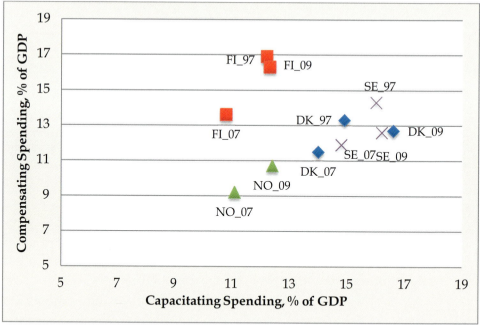

Source: Own calculations based on OECD SOCX, OECD education at a glance, OECD research spending.

Countries under the Christian-democratic regime (Figure 8.2) show in general high compensating spending and moderate capacitating spending. Within the Christian-democratic regime, the Netherlands represents an outlier with much lower levels of compensating expenditure and a strong decrease in compensating expenditure between 1997 and 2007. The effect of the financial crisis is also visible for the Christian-democratic regime through an increase in compensating and capacitating spending between 2007 and 2009. While for some countries such as Germany, higher investment in family policies plays a role, decreasing GDP might also play a role. Spending is measured as a percentage of output, therefore keeping absolute spending at previous levels might increase the share of GDP spent on certain policies in case of recession.

Figure 8.2 Compensating spending vs. capacitating spending in 1997, 2007 and 2009: Christian-democratic regime

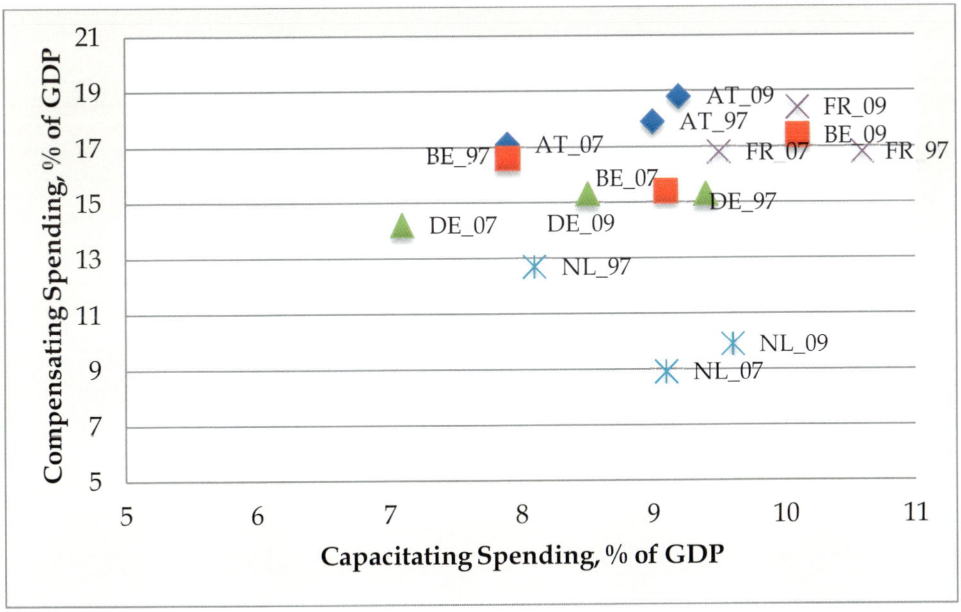

Source: Own calculations based on OECD SOCX, OECD education at a glance, OECD research spending.

Dutch reforms in activation focused more on training provision, job offers and guidance from the sixth month of unemployment onwards. In addition, job search requirements for the elderly unemployed were introduced. Disability policies were reformed, reducing replacement rates for partially disabled while providing more possibilities for training. Dutch reforms of family policy focused on the right to take leave, implementing the EU directive for parental leave, increasing access to childcare and subsidising childcare attendance. Germany's development can be explained by a major reform of labour market policies, including active labour market policies, reform of unemployment benefits, job creation and in-work benefits. In addition, family policy has been expanded with a focus on increasing access to childcare. The reform of the parental allowance scheme copied the Swedish model with a 67% replacement rate for 12 months and a limit of €1,800.[25]

The liberal welfare regime (Figure 8.3) has comparably low compensating spending levels and moderate capacitating spending. With the onset of the financial crisis, spending increased for both types of policies. Case studies show that the UK and Ireland expanded their activation policies in combination with a strong focus on implementing conditions and sanctions.[26] In both countries, the labour market policies promoted making work pay through in-work benefits while family policy expansion has taken place in early childhood care and education, as well as parental leave schemes. In the UK, a special focus was on child poverty.

Figure 8.3 Compensating spending vs. capacitating spending in 1997, 2007 and 2009: Liberal regime

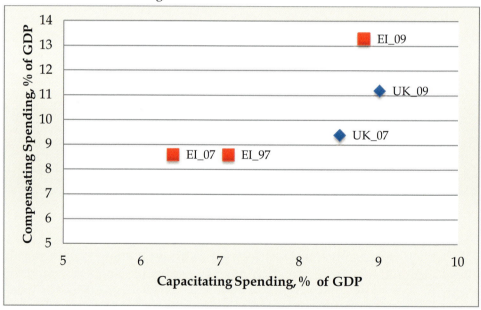

Source: Author's calculations based on OECD SOCX, OECD education at a glance, OECD research spending.

The southern welfare regime (Figure 8.4) exhibits comparably low capacitating spending and high compensating expenditure levels, with quite some fluctuation. For instance, Italy has rather high compensating spending (16-18.7% of GDP), while Portugal steadily increased its compensating expenditure from 11% of GDP in 1997 to 16.3% in 2009. Up to 2007, Spain slightly increased its capacitating spending, with the highest increase taking place after the crisis (although this might be an artefact due to decreasing GDP). Reforms in Spain between 1997 and 2007 focused on extending parental leave and making leave more flexible with the possibility for men to also participate in leave schemes.[27] On the labour market, the focus was on improving the situation for flexible and temporary workers and implementing conditioning and activation measures for the unemployed.[28] Italy focused more on increasing benefits on unemployment and family, though in 2000 the Berlusconi government switched to a stronger emphasis on family and community networks and less state funding for social services and family policy.[29]

Figure 8.4 Compensating spending vs. capacitating spending in 1997, 2007 and 2009: Southern regime

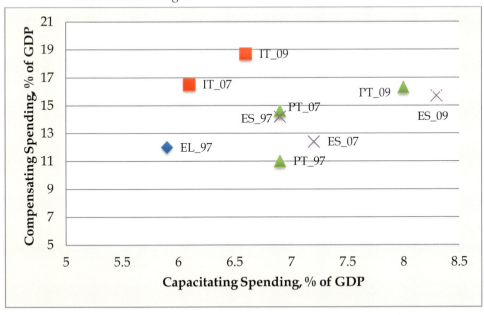

Source: Author's calculations based on OECD SOCX, OECD education at a glance, OECD research spending.

The new EU member states show low levels of capacitating expenditure, comparable to the southern regime, and low-to-medium levels of compensating spending. General expenditure as a percentage of GDP has increased for both policy types since the crisis. In terms of policy reforms, the new EU member states have to be considered in light of the transition from communism to capitalism and democracy. Many countries faced recession in the early 1990s and moved towards liberalisation, privatisation and retrenchment (especially of family policies at first), but have slowly put family policies back onto the agenda in recent years due to declining fertility rates.[30]

Figure 8.5 Compensating spending vs. capacitating spending in 1997, 2007 and 2009: New EU member states

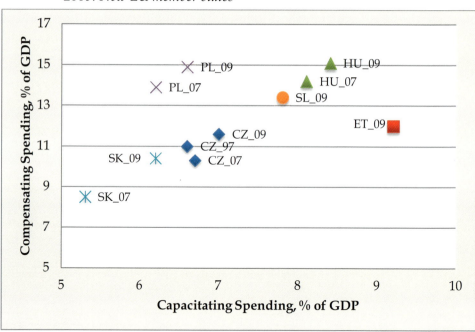

Source: Author's calculations based on OECD SOCX, OECD education at a glance, OECD research spending.

8.6   In which policy fields did most changes take place?

Table 8.2 considers spending per head of the population for incapacity-related benefits in kind, active labour market policies, benefits in kind on old age and family and cash benefits

Investment in family policy, especially childcare, has been on the rise.

on family policies. If capacitating policies (incapacity-related benefits in kind, active labour market policies, benefits in kind on old age and family) are considered, in-kind spending on families stands out as the policy field with the biggest expansion in expenditure across all welfare regimes. Only a few countries have increased their expenditure more in other policy fields, including Denmark and Sweden, which focused on incapacity related benefits in kind between 1997 and 2007, and Austria, which increased expenditure on active labour market policies in the same period.

In most European countries, increasing investments in family policy have led to an increase in expenditure on daycare and home-help services (see Table 8.3). Apart from this trend, considerable differences exist in the family policy mixes across welfare regimes. Concerning the influence of the crisis on investment, we observe that only a few countries retrenched on capacitating spending between 2007 and 2009.

8.7   Patterns in family policy by welfare regimes

The social-democratic countries have continued their capacitating investment. In social-democratic regimes, in-kind expenditure on family policies increased the most between 1997 and 2009 in Iceland, followed by Sweden, Norway and Finland. However, Iceland started from much lower spending levels than the rest of the Nordic countries. After 2007, all the Nordic countries continued to increase their expenditure on family services, especially Norway. However, for the period 1997 to 2007, family cash benefits were cut back to nearly the same extent as family services were increased in Norway. This is only the case in Norway, and only for this period. Iceland, Sweden and Denmark increased their spending in the same period and following the onset of the financial crisis, only Sweden exhibits a slight downward trend in family cash benefit expenditure. Within the social-democratic regime, there is a stronger tendency towards high investment in daycare and home-help services, and family and parental leave, compared to investments in other policies.

The Christian-democratic regime is characterised by increasing investment in care facilities. Christian-democratic welfare states – except for Austria and Germany – increased their in-kind expenditure on family policies significantly between 1997 and 2007 (see Table 8.2).

Table 8.2 Change in expenditure per head at constant (2000) PPP-adjusted US dollars

	Incapacity-related benefits in kind		Active labour market programmes		Old age benefits in kind		Family benefits in kind		Family cash benefits	
	1997-2007	2007-2009	1997-2007	2007-2009	1997-2007	2007-2009	1997-2007	2007-2009	1997-2007	2007-2009
Denmark	175.6	53	-42.8	66.4	-40.1	65.9	61.3	37.7	51.5	7.1
Finland	115.6	32.9	-48.4	-9.8	120.8	38.3	111.7	43.2	-16.6	12.6
Iceland	85.6	-8.9	3.8	-5.4	-246.9	2.4	607.7	31.4	176.3	20.6
Norway	-49.1	-72.9	-78.5	-47.8	85.9	108.3	184.6	126.3	-187.9	10.4
Sweden	372.6	13.1	-165.8	-19.5	161.9	11.7	195.9	47.2	150	-10.9
Austria	55.3	26.2	109.5	53.1	69.1	30.9	30.9	36.1	93	47.6
Belgium	-96.6	19.1	89.1	60.2	27.3	6.5	258.5	20.8	-46.6	10.5
France	-62.2	0.9	-30.2	3.2	45.2	10.1	204.9	5.4	-12.1	12.4
Germany	19.1	24.2	-61.9	71	0.4	0.5	19.2	38.3	-8.3	9.5
Netherlands	74.7	10.1	-18.8	31.7	130.3	28	376.8	-163.1	-24	58.5
Ireland	29.6	10.1	-77.2	54.1	70.5	29.7	211.6	58.8	449.7	245.1
United Kingdom	57.4	12.4	17.9	-3.1	47.4	2	290.8	27.9	251.2	82.7
Greece	10.7	-0.1	-16	14.2	4.1	-0.7	50.5	-2.2	62.5	75.9
Italy	-4.4	5.1	30.4	-13.1	7.3	5.4	185.8	-1.2	70.1	21.6
Portugal	3.9	2.9	19.8	50.9	8.4	15.2	75.1	4.2	53.9	52.8
Spain	36.2	8.1	143.8	7.1	88.3	44.3	174.5	26.1	90.5	29.4
Czech Republic	-15	-1.2	41.9	-8.5	-1.1	2.1	94.3	25.3	82.5	-58.5
Hungary		-3	-6.4	33.1		-6.5		-6.4		5.5
Poland	-23.8	1.5	28.3	26.5		0.4		10.1	33	1.3

	Family - Daycare / Home-help services			Family - Other benefits in kind			Family - Family allowances			Family - Maternity and parental leave			Family - Other cash benefits		
	1997	2007	2009	1997	2007	2009	1997	2007	2009	1997	2007	2009	1997	2007	2009
Denmark	608.6	633.6	661.9	33.7	70	79.4	299.1	330.5	332.7	173.7	193.7	198.6			
Finland	263.1	301.6	328.8	67.1	140.2	156.2	308.9	258.3	250.6	178.2	208	224.4	17.8	22.1	26
Iceland	225.6	664.3	695.4	86.7	255.7	256	288.6	271.4	278.1	112.8	265.6	274.3	32.8	73.5	78.8
Norway	327.6	453.4	565.9	184.7	243.6	257.3	463.3	299.8	288.5	258	275.3	300.1	111	69.2	66.1
Sweden	446.6	625.8	670.4	30.5	47.2	49.8	197	268.7	249.5	145.3	240.7	251.4	41.2	24.3	21.8
Austria	116.3	146.7	183.1	12	12.5	12.2	499.7	691.5	735.1	148.9	48	51.6	11.3	13.5	13.7
Belgium	22.8	269.9	279.5	38.7	50.1	61.3	523.5	509.9	516.3	48.9	59.5	63	44.7	1.1	1.7
France	188.1	377.2	376.8	109.2	125	130.8	309	309.2	321.4	103.8	91.1	90.8	0.4	0.8	1.4
Germany	104.4	114.5	140.6	95.2	104.3	116.5	226.7	239.4	236.9	60.7	65	73	46.4	21.2	25
Luxembourg	234.4	278.7	294.6		75.5	74.1	855.1	1330.2	1755.1	289.2	296.1	319.5	3	375.6	355.6
Netherlands	127.9	504.7	341.6				252.7	221.1	279.3	0	0	0	0	7.7	7.8
Ireland	41.5	249	306.9	1.3	5.4	6.3	265.1	559.7	676.5	17.8	58.6	78.5	263.2	377.5	486
United Kingdom	0.9	348.7	364.5	124.6	67.6	79.7	230.4	258.6	272.4	18.1	124.5	116.8	210.3	326.9	403.6
Greece	27.3	33.8	32.3	31.7	75.7	74.9	106.3	113.9	139.5	15	26.6	41.1	10.8	54.1	89.9
Italy	25.8	190.9	186.2	16.3	37	40.5	96	119.4	115.1	30.3	55.9	57.2	4.2	25.3	50
Portugal	3.2	77.2	81.6	16	17.2	17	75.7	94.5	135.1	16.7	55.2	66.2	17.2	13.7	15
Spain	9.9	164.5	177.5	30.2	50.1	63.2	32.4	51.3	55.2	26.5	69.4	96.5	9.8	38.5	36.9
Czech Republic	8.7	103.2	127	12.3	12.1	13.5	109.2	67.2	29.4	88.5	241.1	231.8	65.8	37.8	26.4
Hungary		134.1	131.1		102.9	99.5		302.3	293.8		154.2	162.3		19.9	25.7
Poland		45.3	55.4				54.1	67.1	51.1	28.8	42.3	56.1	10.3	17	20.4
Slovak Republic	9.2	80	90.1	1.8	0	2.4	167.5	182.8	203.6	93	98.6	111.7	0.9	13.1	12.4

Source: OECD Social Expenditure Database, extracted December 2013.

Their cash expenditure on families decreased to a much lesser degree. For Germany and Austria, it is clear that they embarked on this trend later, as the increase in their investment in family policies in kind between 2007 and 2009 is higher than the increase between 1997 and 2007. The Netherlands is the only country in the sample with a significant decrease in spending on benefits in kind on family policy between 2007 and 2009.

Does this change follow a social investment logic? It should be noted that while Christian-democratic countries are increasingly investing in childcare services, they are doing so without giving up their traditional high investment in family allowances, which still receive the majority of funds in all of these countries except for France and the Netherlands (see Table 8.3). Between 2007 and 2009, investment in cash benefits on family policies increased in all Christian-democratic countries, and in Austria and the Netherlands even more than investment in kind. Yet, expansion of daycare and home-help services had already taken place since 1997 in some countries, such as France and the Netherlands.

In the Liberal regime, it is clear that the surge in investment in services is part of a wider trend for increasing investment in family policies. In the Anglo-Saxon countries, increases in expenditure on family benefits in kind were accompanied by an increase in family expenditure in cash between 1997 and 2007. They increased their investment in daycare and home-help services from very low expenditure levels (between $0.90 and $41.50 per head) to medium levels (between $306.90 and $364.50). Ireland has also focused much more on family allowances. Expenditure on other cash benefits is highest in the liberal regime compared to other regimes (e.g. $486 per head in Ireland in 2009). Reforms in the UK have focused in particular on child poverty,[31] so this development might be in line with a stronger focus on social investment and especially child development.

> *Investments in different types of family policy still vary considerably between countries with a strong focus on childcare, and countries with a stronger focus on child allowances.*

In the southern European countries, expenditure on family policy has been rising, although it has traditionally been low due to their focus on family networks and less state involvement for providing care. The southern regime shows an upward trend in in-kind and cash expenditure on families between 1997 and 2007. Except for Greece, this trend is stronger for in-kind than for cash transfers, and is especially pronounced in Italy and Spain. Italy and Spain also increased considerably their expenditure on daycare and home-help services (Italy from $25.80 in 1997 to $186.20 in 2009). However, they departed from rather low levels and their expenditure therefore still remains rather low in the overall comparison. Between 2007 and 2009, Italy and especially Greece slightly decreased their in-kind expenditure while they kept on increasing their expenditure on cash benefits. In Portugal and Spain, expenditure on in-kind and cash benefits increased further between 2007 and 2009, with cash benefits increasing more than in-kind benefits.

The new EU member states are a rather heterogeneous group. Hungary exhibits much higher expenditure on families with a focus on family allowances and maternity and parental leave payments, while Poland spends considerably less and the Czech Republic focuses much more on maternity and parental leave as well as daycare and home-help services. The Czech Republic and Slovakia augmented both in-kind and cash benefits expenditure on families between 1997 and 2007, but with a stronger focus on in-kind expenditure. Both countries continued to increase their in-kind expenditure between 2007 and 2009, and Slovakia increased its cash transfer expenditure even more, while the Czech Republic started to retrench on cash benefits.

Although family policy investment has been on the rise, the investment patterns differ considerably across Europe. Based on survey data, Danish citizens are much more able to combine work and care than citizens in the Czech Republic, Germany or the UK. Family-friendly environments in particular play a role, as well as childcare facilities.[32] The ability to combine work and care has a significant impact on female labour market participation; the presence of children under the age of four reduces female labour market participation, while mothers' labour market participation slowly increases when the child starts school.[33] Married women with children are more often employed in flexible part-time jobs than other groups, as these jobs are more easily combined with care responsibilities.[34] In social-democratic countries, which have a long tradition in investment in childcare and leave schemes, the negative impact of having a young child on mothers' labour market participation has been decreasing significantly, while for continental and southern Europe this decreasing trend is less pronounced.[35] The OECD also stresses the poverty-reducing effect of female employment as well as the positive correlation between high fertility and high female employment.[36]

What role do social policies play? Job guarantees for mothers on leave increase women's labour market attachment.[37] Maternity and paternity leave schemes also play an important role in young women's labour market attachment, and are especially important for medium and higher educated women.[38] The OECD points out that while many developed countries have witnessed a decrease in fertility, the developed countries with high fertility rates are those with high availability of childcare for 0-3 years and other policies that contribute to the reconciliation of work and care.[39]

8.8   Persistent disparities in active labour market policies expenditure

If levels of *active labour market expenditure* per head are considered (see Table 8.4), the social-democratic regime has the highest expenditure, followed by the Christian-democratic regime. Yet within the social-democratic regime large differences persist, with Finland and Norway spending much less than Denmark and Sweden. The Netherlands and Belgium stand out with expenditure levels more comparable to Sweden than to other Christian-democratic countries. Ireland's expenditure is more than double that of the UK and within the southern regime, expenditure in Spain was more than four times higher than in Greece in 2009. In addition, trends over time show considerable increases in expenditure in Portugal, Spain and Poland. In the social-democratic regime, a trend towards less expenditure is visible, while in continental Europe spending fluctuates between 1997, 2007 and 2009.

Table 8.4 shows that the Nordic countries exhibited a downward trend before the crisis, except for Iceland. Spain, Austria and Belgium increased their expenditure in the same period, while Germany, Czech Republic and France

Most continental and Nordic welfare regimes show a trend towards convergence in ALMP expenditure levels.

decreased theirs. Sweden is the country with the most pronounced decrease in expenditure on active labour market policies. The downward trend in ALMP expenditure continues after the crisis in the Nordic countries, except for Denmark. The UK, Italy and the Czech Republic also exhibit a slight downward trend in expenditure. Ireland and the Netherlands, which retrenched their ALMP expenditure before the crisis, reverse these trends in the following period while Belgium, Portugal and Austria continue their upward trend in spending.

In terms of a move towards social investment, it is clear that for active labour market policies, the Christian-democratic regime has been catching up while the social-democratic regime has been scaling down, and Spain, Portugal, Austria and Belgium have increased their absolute spending tremendously. However, it has to be kept in mind that the measurement is spending per capita in terms of population and not unemployed. As Scandinavian countries have comparably lower unemployment rates than Ireland or Spain, their expenditure per unemployed might still be comparably high.

Table 8.4 Spending on active labour market policies per capita, at constant (2000) prices and constant (2000) PPPs($)

	1997	2007	2009
Denmark	503.1	460.3	526.7
Finland	333.2	284.8	275
Norway	342.8	264.3	216.5
Sweden	557.9	392.1	372.6
Austria	126.8	236.3	289.4
Belgium	309.7	398.8	459
France	311.5	281.3	284.5
Germany	281.5	219.6	290.6
Netherlands	433.4	414.6	446.3
Ireland	351.7	274.5	328.6
United Kingdom	91.6	109.5	106.4
Greece	58.8	42.8	57
Italy	107.9	138.3	125.2
Portugal	90.7	110.5	161.4
Spain	92.5	236.3	243.4
Czech Republic	17	58.9	50.4
Hungary	63.6	57.2	90.3
Poland	51.2	79.5	106
Slovak Republic	79.2	46.4	47

Source: OECD Social Expenditure Database, extracted December 2013.

8.9   Trends in other capacitating policies

Incapacity-related in-kind expenditure (see Table 8.2) increased the most in the social-democratic regime (except for Norway) between 1997 and 2007. After 2007, Norway and Iceland retrenched their investments, while Denmark in particular continued the expansion of its expenditure. While Belgium and France retrenched in 1997-2007 and slightly reversed their expenditure trends in 2007-2009, the Netherlands and Austria in particular increased their expenditure between 1997 and 2007. After the crisis, the Christian-democratic regime maintained its spending levels or even increased them by more than previously, as was the case in Germany. The Anglo-Saxon countries show an upward trend for both periods; within the southern regime, decreases and increases are comparably low except for Spain, which increased its expenditure between 1997 and 2007. Poland and the Czech Republic decreased their incapacity-related in-kind expenditure between 1997 and 2007, while Slovakia strengthened its upward trend in 2007-2009.

Old age in-kind expenditure (see Table 8.2) increased the most in Sweden, the Netherlands and Finland between 1997 and 2007, followed by Spain, Norway and Ireland, while Iceland and Denmark show an opposite trend. Between 2007 and 2009, Norway and Denmark expanded the most, while the positive trend also remains in other countries such as Finland, Austria, the Netherlands, Ireland and Spain. Within their regimes, Germany represents an outlier with little change in expenditure, while Spain is exceptional for the southern regime due to its very pronounced upward trend.

Public expenditure on *education* per student is highest in the social-democratic regime, followed by the Christian-democratic regime and then the liberal and southern regimes (see Table 8.5). The new member states are very heterogeneous. In most countries, expenditure per student as a percentage of GDP has continuously increased, the exceptions being Norway and Estonia. Within the regimes, one observes that Iceland has much lower expenditure levels than the rest of the social-democratic regimes, while Portugal stands out in the southern regimes with much higher levels (29.2% in 2009).

Table 8.5 Total public educational expenditure per pupil as a percentage of GDP per capita, all levels*

	1998	2007	2009	2010
Denmark	36.0	31.0	34.8	
Finland		25.0	29.6	29.7
Iceland	22.9	24.8	26.3	
Norway	30.5	25.4	28.3	26.6
Sweden	28.8	28.0	31.4	30.0
Austria	30.1	26.4	29.4	29.3
Belgium		26.7	29.3	
France	24.4	24.2	25.8	
Netherlands	22.0	23.3	26.0	26.0
United Kingdom	21.9	25.2	25.7	
Italy	24.3	22.8	25.5	24.5
Portugal		26.2	29.2	
Spain	19.1	21.7	24.7	23.8
Czech Republic	17.3	20.2	22.1	21.5
Estonia	25.1	20.0	27.2	25.8
Hungary	20.5	24.7	24.7	23.6
Latvia	28.6	22.0	27.0	25.3
Lithuania		18.9	23.8	23.3
Poland	19.6	21.4	23.3	23.9
Slovakia		16.1	19.0	20.1
Slovenia		24.9	28.2	28.4

* 1997 had too much missing data to be included.

Source: UNESCO Institute of Statistics, 2013.

8.10 Is there a shift in social investment?

To sum up, while European welfare states differ considerably in their policy mixes as well as in their welfare expenditure levels, one can observe a tendency towards an increase in social investment expenditure on families, active labour market policy and education. However, a clear divide across countries is also apparent. Eastern European and southern European welfare states continue to spend much less on social investment per capita. While Nordic countries have been the forerunners of social investment, Christian-democratic countries, and to some extent Anglo-Saxon countries, have been catching up.

It is clear that investment in family policies is on the rise, especially in childcare services, but regime patterns mostly still persist. Consequently, a slow but general shift towards a stronger reconciliation of work and care is taking place, although the overall levels of investment are still lower in southern Europe and some eastern European welfare states. In addition, investment in active labour market policy in countries with traditionally little or no activation, such as Spain and Austria, has been increasing. The move towards social investment is slow and varies by regime in the degree of the combination of capacitating policies and compensating expenditure, as well as in the speed and the initial level of investment. Southern and former communist countries in particular lag far behind.

Nordic countries are the forerunners of social investment, southern and central and eastern European countries are the laggards.

The gap in social investment levels might be problematic, as there is plenty of evidence suggesting positive effects of social investment. For example, policies supporting the reconciliation of work and care seem to be improving female employment rates.[40] Greater access to childcare services and a family-friendly atmosphere are highlighted by parents in the Czech Republic, Denmark, Germany and the UK as being important for the ability to reconcile work and care.[41] If the premise that social investment contributes to growth is correct, a lack of investment might also represent a barrier to future growth and development. Social-democratic countries are less in debt and have higher fertility levels; they fare better than many other European countries. The contribution of social expenditure and the policy mix should not be underestimated or even disregarded when reforms to tackle the crisis are considered.

Bibliography

Adema, W. and P. Whiteford (2007), *Babies and Bosses - Reconciling Work and Family Life: A Synthesis of Findings for OECD Countries*, Paris: OECD.

Aidukaite, J. (2010), "Welfare reforms in central and eastern Europe: A new type of welfare regime", *Ekonomika,* Vol. 89, No. 4, pp. 89-84.

Bonoli, G. (2005), "The politics of the new social policies: Providing coverage against new social risks in mature welfare states", *Policy Politics,* Vol. 33, No. 3, pp. 431-449.

_____ (2012), "Active labour market policy and social investment: A changing relationship", in N. Morel, B. Palier and J. Palme (eds), *Towards a Social Investment Welfare State?: Ideas, Policies and Challenges*, Bristol: The Policy Press, pp. 181-204.

Cipollone, A., E. Patacchini and G. Vallanti (2012), "Women Labor Market Performance in Europe: Trends and Shaping Factors", NEUJOBS Working Paper 5.3 (www.neujobs.eu).

Dräbing, V. (2013), "Welfare transformation and work and family reconciliation: What role for social investment in European welfare states? ", NEUJOBS Policy Brief 5.6, pp. 1-18 (www.neujobs.eu).

Esping-Andersen, G. (1990), *The Three Worlds of Welfare Capitalism*, Cambridge: Polity.

_____ (2009), *The Incomplete Revolution: Adapting to Women's New Roles*, Cambridge: Polity.

European Commission (undated), "Social investment" (http://ec.europa.eu/social/main.jsp?catId=1044&).

Ferrera, M. (1996), "The 'Southern model' of welfare in social Europe", *Journal of European Social Policy,* Vol. 6, No. 1.

Gauthier, A. (2012), "Cross-national differences in the labour force attachment of mothers in Western and Eastern Europe", NEUJOBS Working Paper 5.4 (www.neujobs.eu).

Greve, B. (2012), "Reconciliation of Work and Family Life in Four Different Welfare States", NEUJOBS Working Paper 5.5 (www.neujobs.eu).

Hemerijck, A. (2011), "The social investment imperative beyond the financial crisis", *Challenge Europe*, May, pp. 11-19.

_____ (2013), *Changing Welfare States*, Oxford: Oxford University Press.

Hemerijck, A., V. Dräbing, B. Vis, M. Nelson and M. Soentken (2013), "European Welfare States in Motion", NEUJOBS working paper 5.2.

Jenson, J. (2012), "Redesigning citizenship regimes after neoliberalism. Moving towards social investment", in N. Morel, B. Palier and J. Palme (eds), *Towards a Social Investment Welfare State? Ideas, Polices and Challenges*, Bristol: Policy Press, pp. 61-90.

Meeusen, L. and A. Nys (2012), "Are new social risk expenditures crowding out the old? ", CSP Working Paper No. 1208, University of Antwerp, Antwerp.

Morel, N., B. Palier and J. Palme (eds), (2012), *Towards a Social Investment Welfare State?: Ideas, Policies and Challenges*, Bristol: The Policy Press.

Morgan, K.J. (2009), "Child Care and the Social Investment Model: Political Conditions for Reform", in J. Palme (ed.), *What Future for Social Investment?*, Stockholm: Institute for Futures Studies, pp. 45-54.

Nikolai, R. (2011), "Towards social investment? Patterns of pulbic policy in the OECD world", in N. Morel, B. Palier and J. Palme (eds), *Towards a Social Investment Welfare State? Ideas, Policies and Challenges*, Bristol: Policy Press.

Pierson, P. (2001), *The New Politics of the Welfare State*, Oxford: Oxford University Press.

Vandenbroucke, F. and K. Vleminckx (2011), "Disappointing poverty trends: Is the social investment state to blame? ", *Journal of European Social Policy*, Vol. 21, No. 5, pp. 450-471.

Wren, A. (2013), *The Political Economy of the Service Transition*, Oxford: Oxford University Press.

Notes

[1] Bonoli (2005); Esping-Andersen (2009); Hemerijck (2013).

[2] Morel et al. (2012, p. 1).

[3] Hemerijck (2011, pp. 11-12).

[4] Pierson (2001); Hemerijck (2011).

[5] Hemerijck et al. (2013).

[6] Hemerijck (2013).

[7] Bonoli (2005).

[8] Ibid..

[9] Hemerijck (2013).

[10] Morel et al. (2012).

[11] Jenson (2012).

[12] Dräbing (2013).

[13] Pierson (2001).

[14] Morel et al. (2012).

[15] Esping-Andersen (1990).

[16] Ibid.

[17] For the former, see Ferrera (1996); for the latter, see Aidukaite (2010).

[18] *Social-democratic regime*: High levels of de-commodification, high generosity of benefits, low stratification. In this study: Sweden, Denmark, Norway and Finland. *Christian-democratic welfare state*: Stratified, high generosity, medium de-commodification. In this study: Austria, Belgium, France, Germany and the Netherlands. *Liberal welfare states:* Low generosity and de-commodification, high stratification. In this study: Ireland and the United Kingdom. *Southern welfare states:* Low de-commodification, high stratification. In this study: Greece, Italy, Portugal and Spain. *New EU member states:* Cannot be easily categorised according to existing schemes due to communist legacy but do not represent one regime either.

[19] For example, Bonoli (2012) and Morgan (2009) focus on one policy field, Nikolai (2011) focuses on total expenditure, and Meeusen and Nys (2012) and Vandenbroucke and Vleminckx (2011) focus on personal spending.

[20] See Cipollone, Patacchini and Vallanti (2012); Gauthier (2012).

[21] Meeusen and Nys (2012); Vandenbroucke and Vleminckx (2011).

[22] This term was introduced by Hemerijck (2013).

[23] Nikolai (2011); Vandenbroucke and Vleminckx (2011).

[24] See Hemerijck et al. (2013).

[25] Ibid.

26 Ibid.

27 Ibid.

28 Ibid.

29 Ibid.

30 Ibid.

31 Ibid.

32 Greve (2012).

33 Cipollone et al. (2012).

34 Ibid.

35 Ibid.

36 Adema and Whiteford (2007).

37 Gauthier (2012).

38 Cipollone et al. (2012).

39 Adema and Whiteford (2007).

40 Gauthier (2012); Cipollone et al. (2012).

41 Greve (2012).

9. LABOUR MARKET INSTITUTIONS IN EUROPE: DIFFERENCES, DEVELOPMENTS, CONSEQUENCES AND REFORMS[*]

Governments devise various labour market institutions to enhance the functioning of the labour market or to correct and overcome negative consequences that the labour market may have. One of the reasons is that, as is the case with all markets, the market for labour may not function as efficiently as predicted in neoclassical economics. As a result, many countries and economic sectors observe longer or shorter periods of high unemployment. In addition, all kinds of other mismatches can occur, for example if people work more or less hours than they would like, if they are unable to find jobs for which they are qualified, or if displacement takes place. The occurrence of these outcomes and the desire to prevent their consequences can result in government intervention in the labour market. Besides these considerations of market failure, normative and ideological forces may play a role, meaning that the public can be in favour of the government always taking a strong role in the labour market.

Researchers investigating labour market institutions can focus on different aspects of the labour market. To begin with, they can look at the outcomes or at the policies contributing to these outcomes, or both. With regard to the outcomes, full employment may be regarded as the ultimate goal of the labour market and if this is achieved, one may conclude that the labour market is functioning efficiently. Others who focus on government policies are more interested in learning how governments can contribute to

---

[*] Chapter 9 was written by Ferry Koster, Associate Professor at the Erasmus University in Rotterdam, and Olaf van Vliet, Assistant Professor at the Leiden University.

achieving full employment. This chapter examines how governments intervene in the labour market and the consequences of this intervention.

9.1 Labour market institutions: Employment, income and labour market protection

There are several approaches to defining labour market institutions. First, one can take a very broad approach in which the labour market is viewed as an institution, that is, a coordination mechanism aimed at matching labour supply and demand. By taking such a starting point, questions arise about the foundation of the labour market. This approach is too broad for understanding the actions that governments take to correct market failures. Taking instead government intervention in the labour market as our point of departure, there is a second choice to be made, again between a broader or a more specific understanding of labour market institutions as forms of government intervention. In the broadest sense, the institutions include any form of government intervention related to the labour market. According to this definition, wage-setting and the regulation of working conditions are also considered labour market institutions. To arrive at a more useful definition, however, one needs to have a somewhat less-inclusive conceptualisation and to only focus on the institutions aimed at dealing with the negative outcomes of the labour market process and those intended to enhance the efficiency of the market.

Based on these considerations, we distinguish three kinds of labour market institutions, each intended to deal with a specific form of market inefficiency. The three labour market institutions of interest are hence distinguished on the basis of their intended function or policy goal:

1. Reducing the risk of unemployment. This set of institutions includes the policies and regulations that increase the security of workers.
2. Preventing income loss. These institutions contribute to the income security of workers, in the sense that they guarantee an income in the event of unemployment.
3. Enhancing labour market transitions. A final set of institutional arrangements aims at increasing the chances that someone finds employment after unemployment (or assisting the transition from inactivity to activity more broadly).

The three aspects of labour market institutions – employment protection, income protection and enabling labour market transitions –form the core of discussions on the functioning of labour markets. And, as a result, many well-developed indicators are available that have been debated and tested at length, meaning that there is quite some consensus about their applicability. In the following, the most recent versions of these existing measures are presented and examined to provide an overview of the differences between countries and the changes that have occurred over the last 10 to 20 years.

Box 9.1 Labour market institutions

Employment protection: EPL

The level of employment protection in a country is usually measured with the Employment Protection Legislation (EPL) indicator developed by the OECD, which measures "… the procedures and costs involved in dismissing individuals or groups of workers and the procedures involved in hiring workers on fixed-term or temporary work agency contracts".[1] Hence, information is available for two groups of workers: those with regular contracts and those having temporary contracts.

Income protection: URR

The institutions securing the income of workers have been measured in several ways. A common approach focuses on the generosity of the unemployment benefits in a country - or more specifically, the ratio between an individual's income and the replacement income if that individual becomes unemployed. Since unemployment replacement rates (URRs) can differ across occupational groups and household situations, several of these indicators are developed. For the present analysis, a recently constructed database is examined.[2]

Labour market policies: LMP

Governments can take different kinds of actions to assist the unemployed to find work. Here the analysis is based on the indicators provided by EUROSTAT.[3] This measure includes spending on several labour market policies, such as 1) labour market services, 2) training, 3) job rotation and job-sharing, 4) employment incentives, 5) supported employment and rehabilitation, 6) direct job creation, 7) start-up incentives, 8) out-of-work income maintenance and support and 9) early retirement.

Actual unemployment, labour market transitions and other labour market outcomes are not the main topics addressed here, having been examined elsewhere.[4] Only the link between protection and innovation will be discussed in more detail in this chapter. The focus is not on the outcomes of the institutions, but rather on whether countries differ with regard to the use of these institutions and the extent to which their use has changed over time. Besides discussing the institutions separately, we examine their interrelationship. This means that the analysis relates to more general labour market models, such as approaches to transitional labour markets or flexicurity.[5]

Finally, it should also be noted that labour market institutions concern the policies devised by governments and aimed at employees and workers, either by protecting them or by assisting them in the job-matching process. In addition, the preferences and behaviour of these actors may be affected if labour market institutions are established, which in turn can lead to additional adoption processes. Such side effects are not considered in the present analysis, as this chapter is restricted to the purposively designed government institutions.

The remainder of this chapter is structured as follows. First, some specific questions regarding labour market institutions are explored: 1) Do western and eastern European countries differ regarding labour market institutions? 2) What are the consequences of labour market institutions for employment in innovation industries? 3) What role do active labour market policies play in processes of labour market reforms? We then present an overview of the most recent country differences and trends in EPL, URR, and LMPs, in order to shed light on how these institutions have developed and may develop in the near future.

9.2 Modest convergence between western and eastern European countries

One central question in general debates about social policies in the EU is whether the policies of individual countries are diverging from or converging into a single European Social Model.[6] Regarding labour market institutions, the question is whether the labour market institutions of central and eastern European (CEE) countries are becoming more similar to those in western European countries as a result of Europeanisation.[7] Clearly, it should

> *While the social policies of EU countries have converged somewhat, we cannot speak of a single European Social Model.*

be noted at the outset of such analyses that there is some doubt over whether the western European countries have converged into a single model; this may only partly be the case as national models remain relatively stable across time due to national differences, path-dependency and so on. Nevertheless, there is evidence that the labour market institutions have become somewhat more alike across time.

First, country descriptions show that benefit systems are insurance-based and characterised by defined benefits (implying a promised specified monthly income) in the CEE countries.[8] Furthermore, the variation in the country profiles makes it impossible to state there is anything like a single labour market model for CEE countries. Rather, these countries show similar differences to those usually found across western European countries. Hence, just like the diversity in welfare state typologies and regimes in western European countries, the CEE countries can be classified according to different welfare state models. In other words, national-level characteristics remain important in understanding national labour market institutions.

A closer look at developments over time, based on quantitative data, allows us to investigate whether there have been changes in these models with regard to the labour market institutions.[9] Tables 9.1 and 9.2 provide insights into the answer to that question. They show the coefficient of variation[10] for EPL, active labour market policies (ALMP) and URRs, for three time periods – 1990, 2000 and 2009.

Table 9.1 Convergence of employment protection legislation and active labour market policies

	EPL			ALMP as % GDP		
	1990	2000	2009	1990	2000	2009
Mean 25 countries	2.2	1.9	1.8	0.7	0.7	0.6
Coefficient of variation	0.5	0.5	0.4	0.7	0.7	0.6
Mean EU-18 countries	2.4	2.2	2.0	0.8	0.8	0.7
Coefficient of variation	0.4	0.4	0.3	0.7	0.7	0.5

Notes:

Around 1990 =average 1990-93; around 2000 = average 1998-2001; around 2009 = average 2006-09.

25 countries: Australia, Austria, Belgium, Canada, Czech Republic, Denmark, Finland, France, Germany, Greece, Hungary, Ireland, Italy, Japan, Netherlands, New Zealand, Norway, Poland, Portugal, Slovak Republic, Spain, Sweden, Switzerland, United Kingdom and the United States.

EU-18 countries = Austria, Belgium, Czech Republic, Denmark, Finland, France, Germany, Greece, Hungary, Ireland, Italy, the Netherlands, Poland, Portugal, Slovak Republic, Spain, Sweden and the United Kingdom.

Table 9.1 only enables a comparison of EU and non-EU countries. It shows that there has been a decrease in variation in both sets of countries. Hence, there may have been some sort of Europeanisation in EPL and ALMP, but this trend cannot be distinguished from a wider development of convergence of these labour market institutions.

Focusing on URRs allows us to make a broader comparison than is possible with the EPL and ALMP indicators, by separating the effects for a large set of countries and distinguishing between western European and CEE countries. Table 9.2 shows that if all countries are taken into account, there has been an overall trend towards convergence. Zooming in on the EU countries, it is clear that this trend has been somewhat stronger within the EU (the overall decrease in variation is two times higher in this subset compared to the change in all countries). This means that the URRs of EU countries became more alike in the period between 1990 and 2009. Furthermore, the variation dropped more strongly in the CEE countries than the western European countries. Within this subset of countries, the least variation is found.

Table 9.2 Convergence of unemployment replacement rates (single and couple)

	Single person			One-earner couple with two children		
	1990	2000	2009	1990	2000	2009
Mean 34 countries	0.57	0.54	0.53	0.65	0.63	0.62
Coefficient of variation	0.33	0.32	0.30	0.24	0.21	0.20
Mean 27 EU	0.58	0.54	0.53	0.64	0.62	0.61
Coefficient of variation	0.34	0.32	0.28	0.27	0.22	0.20
Mean 15 West-EU	0.59	0.57	0.56	0.66	0.66	0.66
Coefficient of variation	0.35	0.32	0.29	0.26	0.18	0.16
Mean 10 CEE-EU	0.54	0.51	0.51	0.59	0.55	0.53
Coefficient of variation	0.33	0.28	0.24	0.29	0.25	0.19

Note: Around 1990 =average 1990-93; 2000 = average 1998-2001; around 2009 = average 2006-09. See Appendix A for more data years.

Sources: Adopted from van Vliet et al. (2012). Unemployment replacement rates dataset among 34 welfare states 1971-2009 (van Vliet and Caminada, 2012)

The research presented above leads to a nuanced answer to the question of the extent to which the labour market institutions in western

European and CEE countries have converged. While the quantitative data show patterns of convergence and lead to the conclusion that the labour market institutions of these countries have become more alike, the qualitative analysis underlines that national differences between these countries still exist. Furthermore, the quantitative analysis also shows that national differences matter in understanding labour market institutions. This means that the countries may have grown closer to each other in some regards, but that national circumstances still have a strong impact on them. Hence, there is little evidence of a single European Social Model of labour market institutions of the member states.

9.3   Do labour market institutions influence innovation?

Another relevant issue – both for social policies and scientific research – concerns the question of how labour market institutions relate to the innovativeness of countries. Two positions can be taken in this debate. On the one hand, it can be argued that labour market institutions hinder the development of innovations, for example because they decrease flexibility in the labour market and take away incentives for improvement. On the other hand, it can be argued that labour market institutions provide a secure environment in which innovations can flourish, for example because the consequences of failure are less severe and employers and employees are able to invest in human capital.

Murphy, Siedschlag and McQuinn suggest that EPL and innovation intensity are negatively related to each other.[11] In countries where EPL is stricter, the overall level of innovation is lower. Furthermore, the overall effect of EPL is different if the indicator is decomposed into the EPL for regular workers (EPLR) and the EPL for temporary workers (EPLT).[12] While the first indicator is not related to innovation intensity, the second is. This means that employment protection of regular workers does not explain the innovation intensity of

There is little evidence that labour market institutions increase the innovativeness of countries.

industries, but that the employment of temporary workers does. This, in turn, seems to indicate that countries where companies have more external flexibility, meaning that they can more easily hire and fire temporary workers, are more innovative. Second, it turns out that the levels of EPL matter, but not the changes in EPL. This seems to indicate that countries that have increased or decreased their levels of employment protection have not gained or lost in terms of innovativeness. Over and above the effects of EPL on innovation intensity, the extent and duration of unemployment benefits led to lower innovation intensity in industries with a higher job reallocation propensity, while higher coordination and higher centralisation of wage-setting led to higher innovation intensity in the same group of industries.

In contrast, Beblavý, Drahokoupil, Myant, Kureková and Domonkos, in their case studies of the automotive and software industries in CEE countries, show that labour market institutions were relatively unimportant in relation to the innovations within these two industries.[13] Other factors, like past experience, the availability of financial resources and access to networks, matter more in that regard. This is, however, not to say that labour market institutions do not have an impact on innovation at all. This is evidenced, for example, by the notion that the acquisition of human capital, which may be enhanced by labour market institutions, plays a role. Nevertheless, the main conclusion of this qualitative study is that more employment protection does not necessarily lead to improvements in term of innovation.

The differences between the results of the studies by Murphy et al. and Beblavý et al. are – at least to some extent – due to different research designs and the selection of different countries. However, there is at least one conclusion that they have in common: innovativeness is not enhanced or improved by labour market institutions. And, more strongly, there may even be a negative relationship between EPL and innovation. So, while there may be all kinds of reasons for introducing such institutions, increased innovativeness does not seem to fit that list.

9.4 Are unemployment benefits and job protection substitutes?

The interrelationships between different labour market policy instruments are important for policy reforms. A single labour market policy instrument is embedded in a large number of welfare state institutions in a country. These interrelationships have been taken into account in the welfare regime literature, in which welfare states are regarded and conceptualised as configurations of various policy instruments.[14] However, in the quantitative comparative political economy literature, welfare state institutions are generally treated as isolated policy instruments. When it comes to unemployment benefits, EPL and active labour market policies (ALMPs) are particularly relevant. Unemployment benefits and employment protection are often considered as substitutes in terms of providing income protection to employees.[15] Hence, when EPL decreases, it can be expected that unemployment benefits become more generous.

The trade-off between unemployment benefits and EPL is the main axis of the flexicurity model of the EU. At the EU level, the concept of flexicurity is integrated in the European Employment Strategy, which is aimed at increasing employment and reducing unemployment. The main characteristic of flexicurity is that it is intended to overcome the tensions between labour market flexibility on the one hand and the provision of social security for workers on the other.[16] Flexibility and security are viewed as complementary. The flexicurity model builds on the combination of flexible labour markets, generous unemployment benefits and a strong emphasis on activation. Flexible labour markets can be seen as beneficial for job creation, especially during periods of recovery after a recession, but they generally imply lower levels of economic security. Welfare state programmes, such as unemployment benefit schemes, provide economic security, but they can have adverse effects, such as longer unemployment spells and thus higher public expenditure and less mobility in the labour market. Furthermore, ALMPs such as labour market training, services of employment agencies and subsidised employment are aimed at increasing labour market participation and at reducing the adverse effects of generous unemployment benefit schemes.

> *There is a trade-off between unemployment benefits and employment protection legislation.*

Flexicurity is presented as a package of policy reforms for the labour market. Lower levels of employment protection for employees are compensated by more generous unemployment benefits and with high efforts on ALMPs.[17] Such reform packages could be successful, as they can be expected to overcome the opposition from employees.[18] Hence, we test the hypotheses that the strictness of EPL is negatively related to the generosity of unemployment benefit schemes and that efforts on ALMPs are positively related to the generosity of unemployment protection.

To examine the role of ALMPs and EPL in unemployment benefit reform, we ran pooled time series regression analyses.[19] The models include conventional political economy variables, such as measures for political parties, corporatism and globalisation. The results are presented in Table 9.3.

Table 9.3 Fixed effects regressions of net unemployment benefit replacement rates,
1990-2009

	Model 1 18-EU countries	Model 2 18-EU countries	Model 3 18-EU countries
Left government (t-1) x	-0.005***	-0.006***	-0.005***
Unemployment rate (t-1)	(0.002)	(0.002)	(0.002)
Left government (t-1)	0.076***	0.083***	0.077***
	(0.022)	(0.026)	(0.023)
Right government (t-1) x	-0.005**	-0.007***	-0.004*
Unemployment rate (t-1)	(0.002)	(0.003)	(0.002)
Right government (t-1)	0.057**	0.072***	0.048**
	(0.024)	(0.028)	(0.024)
Corporatism (t-1)	-0.034	0.154	-0.158
	(1.058)	(1.191)	(1.100)
Capital mobility (t-1)	-0.035***	-0.051***	-0.045***
	(0.012)	(0.017)	(0.015)
Trade openness (t-1)	-0.054*	-0.072**	-0.043
	(0.031)	(0.030)	(0.032)
Unemployment rate (t-1)	0.210	0.267	0.208
	(0.164)	(0.190)	(0.177)
GDP per capita (x 10^{-2}) (t-1)	-0.024	-0.017	-0.008
	(0.020)	(0.023)	(0.021)
Age dependency ratio (t-1)	0.538***	0.662***	0.560***
	(0.154)	(0.132)	(0.167)
EPL (t-1)	-3.357***		-3.758***
	(1.293)		(1.337)
ALMP expenditure (t-1)		2.477**	0.190
		(1.232)	(1.036)
Constant	53.742***	38.385***	48.585***
	(12.520)	(11.720)	(13.945)
Rho	0.651	0.599	0.632
N x T	303	293	285
Adj. R-Squared	0.909	0.910	0.913

Notes: Unstandardised coefficients; panel-corrected standard errors in parentheses;
Prais-Winsten transformation [AR (1) disturbances].

Each regression includes country and year dummies (not shown here).

EU-18 countries: Austria, Belgium, Czech Republic, Denmark, Finland, France, Germany, Greece, Hungary, Ireland, Italy, Netherlands, Poland, Portugal, Slovak Republic, Spain, Sweden and the United Kingdom.

* p<0.10; ** p<0.05; *** p<0.01.

Source: Adopted from van Vliet et al. (2012).

As expected, the strictness of EPL is negatively associated with the generosity of unemployment benefit schemes, and ALMP expenditures are positively related to unemployment protection. However, the result for ALMP expenditure does not hold when EPL and ALMP expenditure are both included. The results suggest that EPL and unemployment benefits can be considered substitutes. This provides support for the idea behind the flexicurity model, i.e. that lower levels of EPL for employees can be compensated with more generous unemployment benefits.

9.5 Labour market regulation: Recent trends

As the previous sections show, labour market institutions may have a certain impact on the functioning of labour markets. Hence, zooming in on cross-national differences as well as developments across time can provide information on how these institutions and their outcomes may develop.

9.5.1 Employment protection

Country differences

We first investigate the level of employment protection using the Employment Protection Legislation Index. The indicator is based on 18 items, which are converted into an index ranging from 0 to 6 (higher scores indicate stricter regulation). As Figure 9.1 shows, the average level of employment protection for regular and temporary workers varies considerably across Europe. Furthermore, from Figure 9.1 it can be seen that countries scoring high on protection of regular workers are not necessarily the ones in which the protection of temporary workers is also high. According to the figure, the employment protection of regular workers is high in Portugal, the Czech Republic and the Netherlands, and low in Switzerland, Ireland and the UK. With regard to the employment protection of temporary workers, Portugal, the Czech Republic and the Netherlands have a far lower score compared to the other countries, while Switzerland, Ireland and the UK are also among the low-scoring countries on EPL for temporary workers. Belgium and Luxembourg stand out, as the employment protection of regular workers is below average while EPL for temporary workers is high in these two countries. Finally, it should be noted that in most countries the EPL of temporary workers is lower than the EPL of regular workers, but there are some exceptions such as Greece, where the average EPL for regular workers is 2.70 and 3.63 for temporary workers.

Figure 9.1 Employment protection legislation

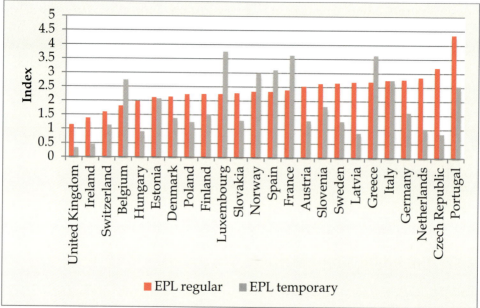

Source: OECD (2013).

Time trends

By presenting the changes in EPL for regular workers between 1995 and 2003 for a selection of countries, Figure 9.2 illustrates some of the core developments that took place in that period. In addition to showing that EPL levels tend to remain stable for longer periods of time, the figure also indicates that if there are changes, they are in a downward direction. The clearest example of this trend is found in the two countries with the highest average level of EPL for regular workers. In 1995, the EPL of Portugal was 4.58, but this dropped to 3.18 by 2013. Likewise, the EPL for regular workers decreased in the Czech Republic from 3.31 in 1995 to 2.92. In other countries, like Belgium for example, the strictness of EPL remained the same.

*Figure 9.2 Employment protection legislation for regular workers,
trend 1995-2013*

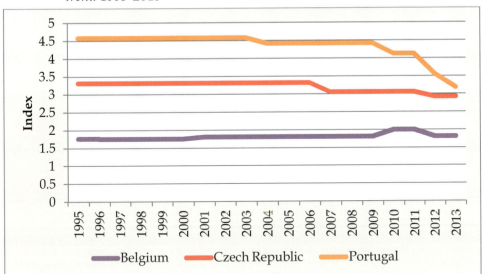

Source: OECD (2013).

In Figure 9.3, the trends are presented for temporary workers. It can be concluded from the figure that the EPL for temporary workers also decreased in the period between 1995 and 2013. For example, in the 1990s the EPL for temporary workers was comparatively high in Greece (around 4.75). By 2013, this figure had decreased to 2.25, also meaning

*While the level of employment
protection decreased particularly
for temporary workers…*

that the difference in EPL between regular workers and temporary workers disappeared in that country. Italy and Belgium followed a similar path: in Italy, EPL for temporary workers dropped from 4.75 in 1995 to 2.00 in 2013; in Belgium it fell from 4.63 to 2.38 in the same period. A clear example of a country moving in the opposite direction is Poland. In the 1990s, the EPL for temporary workers in Poland was 0.75, and by 2013 this dimension of the EPL had increased to 1.75.

Figure 9.3 Employment protection legislation of temporary workers, trend 1995-2013

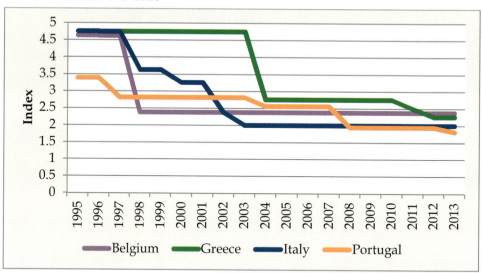

Source: OECD (2013).

The two EPL indicators show that the level of employment protection varies considerably across European countries. Furthermore, some countries tend to put more emphasis on the protection of regular workers and others more on protecting temporary workers. As the trends show, these are not communicating vessels, in the sense that if protection of regular workers goes down, temporary workers will have higher employment protection, and vice versa. On the contrary, the trends show that apart from the stable patterns and some exceptions, there has been a decline of employment protection in those countries with the highest levels of EPL in the 1990s.

9.5.2 Unemployment benefits

Country differences

Next, we turn to the level of unemployment benefits, measured by unemployment replacement rates (URR). Although there are different ways of measuring this indicator (for example, a distinction is made between net and gross replacement rates), a comparison of the URRs provided by van Vliet and Caminada shows that the rank order of these measures is quite stable.[20] Because the ordering of the countries is largely the same, only one indicator is used to get an impression of how the countries score on this dimension. Since URRs may vary across different household types, the results are presented for single workers and couples with two children. Overall, one-earner couples with two children have higher URRs than single workers. The data are shown in Figure 9.4.

Figure 9.4 Net unemployment replacement rates (average production worker), 2009

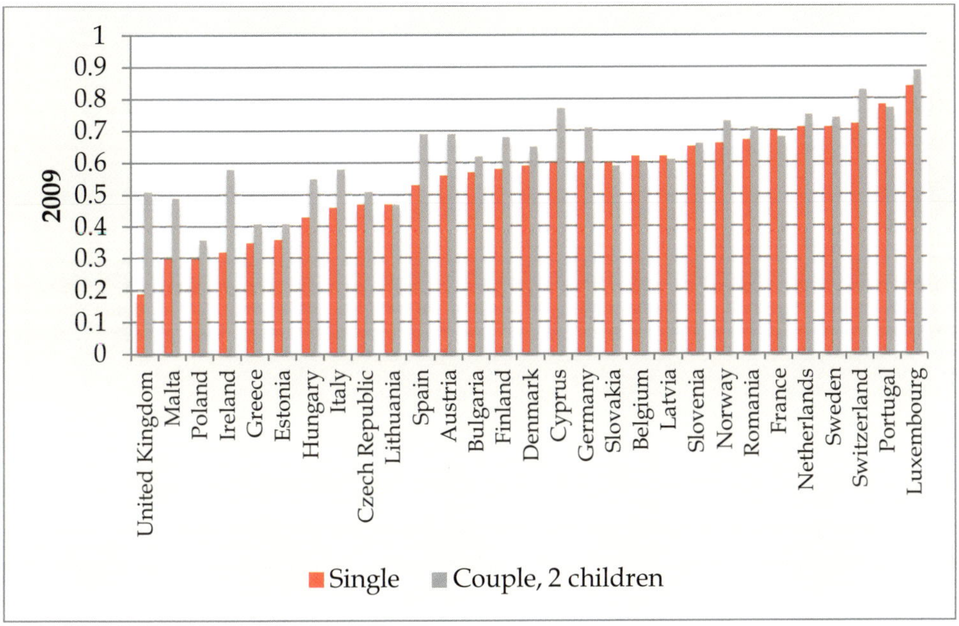

Source: van Vliet and Caminada (2012).

Time trends

Figures 9.5 and 9.6 show the developments over time for the different URR indicators for a selection of countries. The figures show that in some countries there is considerable stability of URRs across time, the main example being Luxembourg where URRs remained high for the whole period investigated. The Czech

...unemployment benefits are remarkably stable...

Republic is also among the countries with little changes in URRs. Furthermore, there are some countries in which URRs have increased sharply. For example, the URR tripled in Estonia between 1995 and 2000, and stayed at that level afterwards. A further notable pattern is found in Sweden, where URRs were amongst the highest in the 1990s, then declined before returning to the highest level again at the beginning of the 2000s, only to decline after that again.

Figure 9.5 URRs for average production worker (single), 1995-2009

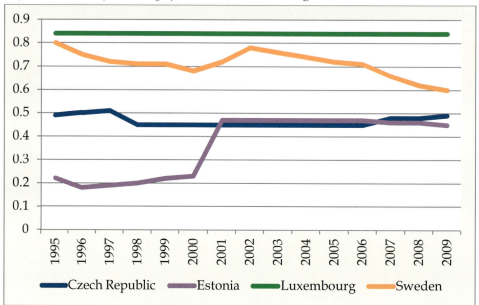

Source: van Vliet and Caminada (2012).

Figure 9.6 URRs for average production worker (couple), 1995-2009

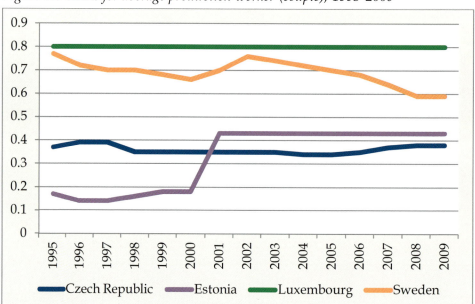

Source: van Vliet and Caminada (2012).

9.5.3 Labour market policies

Country differences

Looking at Figure 9.7, it is clear that government spending on labour market policies varies considerably across the European countries. Several countries spend around 0.5% of GDP on such policies (Romania, Lithuania, Malta, Czech Republic and Estonia), while other countries spend about six times as much (Finland, the Netherlands, Belgium and Denmark).

Figure 9.7 Spending on labour market policies as a % of GDP, average 1998-2011

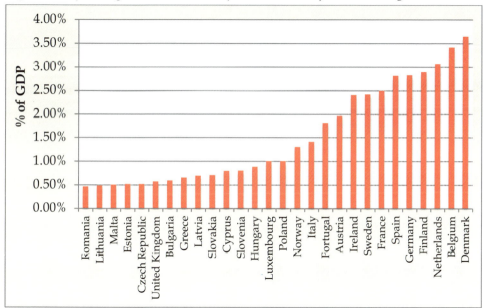

Source: Eurostat (2013).

Time trends

If we turn to the time trends of labour market policies, some noteworthy patterns emerge, as Figure 9.8 shows for a number of countries. From the beginning of the 2000s, those countries spending the most on labour market policies started to spend less. This is evidenced by the patterns that Finland, Sweden and Denmark show, for example. At the same time, the countries spending less began spending more, which is the case with Luxembourg and Norway, for example. As a result, the countries came closer to each other around 2007. As the economic crisis hit, spending

...and labour market policies have been related to the economic crisis.

on labour market policies started to increase in all countries again. Because the countries that had the highest levels of spending spent comparatively less, the countries have diverged somewhat. Nevertheless, immediately after 2008, spending on labour market policies started to decline in almost every country.

Figure 9.8 Spending on labour market policies as a % of GDP, 1998-2011

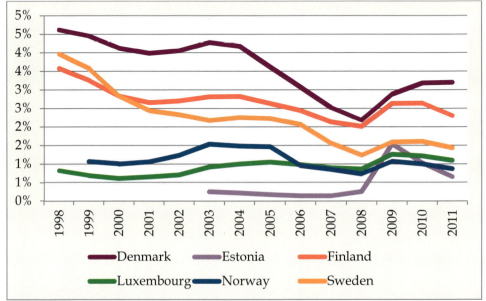

Source: Eurostat (2013).

9.6 Decline in spending on protection reversed by the crisis

The labour market institutions of EU countries have witnessed considerable changes. Most of these trends are in the direction of decreasing levels of protection and of spending on social arrangements, apart from the relative stability that is also found in some countries. However, one particular trend that stands out concerns the development of labour market policies. While spending on these arrangements also decreased for a while, they increased as the economic and financial crises hit Europe and the world. Whether this recent upsurge is permanent or temporary is hard to tell yet from the data. Addressing this issue requires a longer timeframe – that extends into the future – than can be investigated here.

With regard to policy recommendations, only a few conclusions can be drawn from the analysis. To evaluate the functioning of the labour market institutions and to formulate policy advice would require focusing more on their outcomes, while the emphasis in this chapter is on the development of labour market institutions. Extending the analysis would allow us to say more about the resilience of welfare states, for example.[21] It is likely that changes in labour market institutions can have an impact on the behaviour of individuals and companies.[22] However, as Koster and Fleischmann show in their multi-level analyses of 13 European countries, these conclusions are far from unambiguous as some policy goals are not met through the use of labour market institutions, while at the same time the application of the labour market institutions can have consequences for parts of the labour market other than those targeted.[23] Hence, the most valuable policy advice that can be formulated in that regard is that policy-makers should be aware that there is a complex relationship between labour market institutions and the labour market behaviour of individuals (and companies). Therefore, they should monitor closely what is happening in the labour market and whether labour market institutions are adapting, either in the direction of more spending and protection or in the other direction.

Given the mixed findings with regard to labour market institutions, constant monitoring of policies and outcomes is required.

There is at least one area in which labour market institutions seem to have an unequivocal outcome, namely with regard to the impact that employment protection legislation has on innovation intensity in countries. Here we see that labour market institutions do not support innovation and may even hinder it. In that regard, the observed trend towards lower levels of employment protection may be a step towards more innovative behaviour of European companies. However, whether this prediction will hold will only be seen in the future, once the impact of labour market reforms is more visible.

Overall, it can be concluded that the efficiency and impact of labour market institutions, and hence the advice for policy-makers, crucially depends on which outcomes are preferred. While extending labour market institutions may have desired consequences in one domain, they may lead to unwanted consequences in others. As a result, continuing research into these complexities will be required to monitor labour market developments. This particularly holds for the reforms that are being undertaken in a large number of countries; these may support both social and economic goals, but to what extent and why needs to be continuously investigated.

Bibliography

Beblavý, M., J. Drahokoupil, J. Draxler and M. Myant (2011), "Labour relations in Central and Eastern Europe", NEUJOBS State of the Art Report 3 D6.1 (www.neujobs.eu).

Beblavý, M., J. Drahokoupil, M. Myant, L. Kureková and S. Domonkos (2012), "Linking labour regimes and technological innovation in Central and Eastern Europe: The case of automotive and software industries", NEUJOBS Working Paper D6.2 (www.neujobs.eu).

Bigos, M., W. Qaran, M Fenger, F. Koster, P. Mascini and R. Van der Veen (2013), "Review essay on labour market resilience", INSPIRES WP 1.

Blanchard, O. and J. Tirole (2004), "Redesigning the Employment Protection System", *De Economist*, Vol. 152, No. 1, pp. 1-20.

_____ (2008), "The Joint Design of Unemployment Insurance and Employment Protection: A First Pass", *Journal of the European Economic Association*, Vol. 6, No. 1, pp. 45-77.

Boeri, T., J.I. Conde-Ruiz and V. Galasso (2006), "The Political Economy of Flexicurity", FEDEA Working Paper No. 2006-15, Fundación de Estudios de Economía Aplicada, Madrid.

Draxler, J. and O. van Vliet (2010), "European Social Model: No Convergence from the East", *Journal of European Integration*, Vol. 32, No. 1, pp. 115-135.

Eichhorst, W. and R. Konle-Seidl (2005), "The Interaction of Labor Market Regulation and Labor Market Policies in Welfare State Reform", IZA Discussion Paper No. 1718, Institute for Labor Studies, Bonn.

Esping-Andersen, G. (1990), *The Three Worlds of Welfare Capitalism*, Princeton, NJ: Princeton University Press.

European Commission (2006), *Employment in Europe 2006*, Brussels.

_____ (2007a), "Towards Common Principles of Flexicurity: More and Better Jobs through Flexibility and Security", Brussels.

_____ (2007b), "Employment in Europe 2007", Brussels.

Eurostat (2013), Brussels (http://epp.eurostat.ec.europa.eu/).

Giddens, A. (2007), *Europe in the Global Age*, Cambridge: Polity Press.

Koster, F. and M. Fleischmann (2012), "Labour market transitions in Europe: a multilevel analysis of age cohorts and institutions across 13 countries", NEUJOBS Working Paper D6.5 (www.neujobs.eu).

Koster, F. and M.E. Kaminska (2012), "Welfare state values in the European Union, 2002-2008. A multilevel investigation of formal institutions and individual attitudes", *Journal of European Public Policy*, Vol. 19, No. 6, pp. 900-920.

Koster, F., J. McQuinn, I. Siedschlag and O. van Vliet (2011), "Labour market models in the EU", NEUJOBS Special Report No. 1 (www.neujobs.eu).

Madsen, P.K. (2007), "Flexicurity – Towards a set of common principles?", *International Journal of Comparative Labour Law and Industrial Relations,* Vol. 23, No. 4, pp. 525-542.

Murphy, G., I. Siedschlag and J. McQuinn (2013), "Employment protection and innovation intensity", NEUJOBS Working Paper D6.4 (www.neujobs.eu).

OECD (1999), *OECD Employment Outlook,* Paris: OECD Publishing.

_____ (2013), http://stats.oecd.org/, Paris: OECD.

Paetzold, J. and O. van Vliet (2014), "EU Coordination and the Convergence of Domestic Unemployment Protection Schemes", *Journal of Common Market Studies*, Early View, DOI:10.1111/jcms.12139.

Schmid, G. (1998), "Transitional labour markets: a new European employment strategy", WZB Discussion Paper, WZB (Social Science Center), Berlin.

van Vliet, O. and K. Caminada (2012), "Unemployment replacement rates dataset among 34 welfare states, 1971-2009: an update, extension and modification of the Scruggs' welfare state entitlements data set", NEUJOBS Special Report No. 2 (www.neujobs.eu).

van Vliet, O., K. Caminada and K. Goudswaard (2012), "The political economy of labour market policies in Western and Eastern European Countries", NEUJOBS Working Paper D6.3 (www.neujobs.eu).

van Vliet, O., M. Beblavý, K. Caminada, S. Domonkos, J. Drahokoupil, K. Goudswaard, F. Koster, L. Kurekova, J. McQuinn, M. Münderlein, G. Murphy, M. Myant and I. Siedschlag (2013), "Labour relations and modes of employment", NEUJOBS Policy Brief D6.6 (www.neujobs.eu).

Viebrock, E. and J. Clasen (2009), "Flexicurity and welfare reform: A review", *Socio-Economic Review*, Vol. 7, No. 2, pp. 305-331.

Wilthagen T. and F. Tros (2004) "The Concept of 'Flexicurity': A New Approach to Regulating Employment and Labour Markets", *Transfer*, Vol. 10, No. 2, pp. 166-186.

Notes

[1] OECD (1999).

[2] van Vliet and Caminada (2012).

[3] Eurostat (2013).

[4] Koster and Fleischmann (2012).

[5] For the discussion of transitional labour markets, see Schmid (1998). For the discussion of flexicurity, see European Commission (2006).

[6] Giddens (2007); Koster and Kaminska (2012); Paetzold and van Vliet (2014).

[7] Draxler and van Vliet (2010).

[8] Beblavý et al. (2011).

[9] van Vliet et al. (2012).

[10] The standard deviation rises with the mean of the corresponding dataset. Therefore, we use the coefficient of variation as a measure of dispersion. The coefficient of variation is defined as the standard deviation divided by the mean of the corresponding dataset.

[11] See Murphy et al. (2013).

[12] The results from the base model are presented, but they are similar to the more extensive models, which are therefore not reproduced here.

[13] Beblavý et al. (2012).

[14] Esping-Andersen (1990).

[15] For example, Blanchard and Tirole (2004, 2008); Boeri et al. (2006).

[16] Viebrock and Clasen (2009).

[17] European Commission (2006, 2007a, 2007b); Boeri et al. (2006); Wilthagen and Tros (2004); Madsen (2007).

[18] Eichhorst and Konle-Seidl (2005).

[19] van Vliet et al. (2012).

[20] van Vliet and Caminada (2012).

[21] For example, see Bigos et al. (2013).

[22] For example, see Koster and Fleischmann (2012); Murphy et al. (2013).

[23] Koster and Fleischmann (2012).

10. THE FUTURE OF LABOUR IN EUROPE: KEY MESSAGES FOR POLICY-MAKERS*

The Hollywood mogul, Sam Goldwyn, is renowned for having claimed "I never make predictions, especially about the future". It can sometimes seem as though elected politicians, so often focused on the next election, are equally uninterested in longer-term outcomes, preferring to concentrate on what will appeal to voters today. Yet, as the NEUJOBS project takes as its starting point, European economies and societies face daunting long-run challenges that will require all levels of government to formulate and implement policies to facilitate the transformations needed to respond to these challenges.

The aim of this chapter is to draw together the findings presented in the preceding chapters and to explore their ramifications for policy-makers at the EU and national level. It starts by examining these daunting challenges and discussing the conditions that might lead to the sort of paradigm change implicit in the NEUJOBS project. The following sections explore the policy implications of the NEUJOBS research on, respectively, the evolving market for jobs, energy and climate change, labour markets, skills and the welfare state. In each of these sections, key messages for both EU and national policy-makers are summarised. Section 6 looks at EU policies and the long-run policy agenda.

10.1 The principal policy challenges

The transitions examined in this book will occur on timescales measured in decades rather than months or years, but there is also an inexorable logic to them, which means that they need to be addressed. For example, even Sam

---

* Iain Begg, Professorial Research Fellow at the London School of Economics and Political Science, is the author of chapter 10.

Goldwyn would be obliged to recognise that predictions of ageing of the population are about as robust as it is possible to be. Europeans are not only living longer, but will have to respond to the straightforward arithmetic that without change, a relatively smaller working-age population will have to provide for a larger cohort of the elderly. The impact of carbon emissions on climate change is broadly accepted and, despite the apparent ability of fossil fuels to defy gravity by continuing to find new sources of supply, a substantial shift to renewables is unavoidable, even if when it happens is hard to gauge. Societal changes tend to occur slowly and often without great fanfare, but it needs only a moment's reflection to consider how much has changed over a couple of decades in, for example, attitudes towards equality or social inclusion.

In some respects, the policy imperatives associated with the NEUJOBS transitions explained in the introductory chapter are well known. Europe needs to accelerate adaptation to a new energy model, to boost its labour supply, to equip workers with the skills demanded by the jobs of the future and to facilitate the further societal transformations required, including rethinking its approach to the welfare state. A broad understanding of what needs to be done is not, however, the same as knowing how to do it or how to build support for what, in some cases, will be politically difficult policy measures.

10.1.1 The 'crisis' and its aftermath

Although the focus of the NEUJOBS research has been on transformations with long-term consequences, a perspective that would normally be expected to abstract from cyclical trends in the economy, the duration and intensity of the crisis affecting the EU over the period 2008-13 arguably now have to be considered as sources of an additional transition to post-crisis. There have been substantial, even dramatic, changes in the circumstances of some member states, with profound effects on the labour market,[1] while others seem to have emerged largely unscathed. Just as many of the countries of central and eastern Europe had to effect a huge transition during the 1990s, the crisis has made it clear that several of the countries of southern Europe now have to undertake wide-ranging reforms.

Without concerted action, the legacy of the crisis could be a decline in growth potential, while the progress of the previous decade in boosting employment rates has been brutally reversed. Yet contrary to perceptions, the pace of governance reform has been considerable, both at the EU level[2] and in some of the countries that were worst affected by the crisis.[3] The architecture of economic governance has been reshaped, giving greater powers to the EU level to monitor and steer member state macroeconomic policies, backed up by a more credible threat of financial sanctions. There is a permanent rescue fund in the shape of the European Stability Mechanism, and following the agreement at the end of 2013 on further steps towards banking union, some progress on dealing with the toxic interaction between banking problems and public finances. But other proposals from the Commission,[4] aimed at putting in place a 'genuine economic and monetary union', are still on the drawing board, with the result that vulnerabilities remain.

At the national level, despite inauspicious macroeconomic conditions, the reforms introduced during the crisis are already altering the economic and social fabric, even if there is as yet little sign of progress in outcome indicators such as employment or GDP. The danger for these economies is that they become subject to a vicious cycle in which stagnation begets low investment and divergences in economic performance become accentuated. There is a parallel danger of reluctance to accept the urgency of reform, leading to delayed action. At the same time, 'reform fatigue' has set in with evident social and political tensions.

By the beginning of 2013, dealing with the social dimension of the crisis had manifestly moved up the policy agenda. In part, this was because of greater clarity about the longer-term consequences and legacies of the negative shocks that have afflicted the Union since 2008, as well as about some of the difficult policy choices and compromises that will have to be confronted. There was also a growing recognition that too little attention had been devoted to the social and distributive aspects of governance.

The aphorism that a crisis is too good to waste has been widely used since 2008 and it is undeniable that it has led to unprecedented policy activism. According to the Lisbon Council in its December 2013 "Euro plus monitor" assessments, Greece continues to make significant adjustment in the four areas examined – external, fiscal, labour cost and 'reform drive' – and is adjudged to be the EU economy doing most to deal with its shortcomings, followed by Ireland, Spain, Portugal and Slovakia.[5] Perhaps counter-intuitively, the Lisbon Council rankings place the most successful economies (including Sweden, Finland and Germany) at the bottom. This apparent paradox can be reconciled by looking at the Lisbon Council's Fundamental Health Indicator, which places Cyprus, Portugal and Italy at the wrong end of the table, but records a tangible improvement for Greece from its last place in 2012.

10.1.2 Is a paradigm shift on the horizon?

Underlying the policy efforts to secure recovery is a broader policy question about whether the sorts of transitions investigated by the NEUJOBS project will lead to a major paradigm shift akin to that seen when the post-war Keynesian model was eclipsed in the late 1970s. In a widely quoted analysis, Hall[6] argued that paradigm change is a "social learning" process in which three distinct types of change can occur, in ascending order of significance: in stage 1, policy settings are changed; in stage 2, the policy instruments are altered; and in stage 3, the policy goals themselves are transformed. He previously wrote of the conjunctions needed to achieve change emanating from new ideas, again identifying three: the economic ideas being attractive to policy-makers; the bureaucracy being able to translate the ideas into policies; and the scope for building a coalition of interests able to make change happen.

Commenting on the whether the crisis of recent years may induce a paradigm change, Hall observes that "today, some of the preconditions for another major shift of policy are in place and perhaps presage a new era".[7] There is a widespread sense of grievance in much of Europe and North America about rising levels of income inequality, intensified in some countries by high levels of unemployment and stagnant incomes. However, what is noticeable about much of the discussion on whether there will be a shift away from the market-orientated paradigm, dominant since the early 1980s, is that the terms of debate are about inequality and fiscal sustainability (especially around the implications of ageing), but only tangentially about the socio-ecological dimension.

10.1.3 Key messages for policy-makers

At the EU level

- The crisis will have a legacy that is likely to mean that for the EU as a whole, pre-crisis patterns of growth are unlikely to be restored.

- The EU will be characterised by greater diversity in socio-economic 'performance', implying that attempts to develop common policy solutions will have to be better attuned to such differences.

At the national level

- Extensive governance reforms introduced at the EU level have created new expectations around policy coordination that will circumscribe national room for manoeuvre.

- The policy solutions to the challenges of long-run transformations are, in many respects, very obvious, if politically highly challenging, as will be seen in subsequent sections.

- Public resources face extended pressures, which entail increasing savings today (by reducing both government and private-sector debt) while also building up funds for future costs associated with ageing and with an energy transformation. Governments will have to be resolute in maintaining budgets for long-run investments.

10.2 Where the jobs will be

Some of the long-run changes in labour demand will be shaped by the socio-ecological transitions currently underway. Projections of population and of labour supply and demand are inevitably subject to considerable uncertainty, but the work reported in chapter 2 provides a valuable starting point for analysing what EU policies will have to accommodate.

For policy-makers, a dilemma is how far to go in building what is expected from transitions into the aims and instruments of different processes of governance. At the EU level, these processes function on at least four different time scales:

- Annually, comprising the cycle around the European semester and the country-specific recommendations.

- The five-year mandates of the College of Commissioners and the European Parliament.

- The decennial time span of the principal economic development strategies – first Lisbon and now Europe 2020 – although subject to intermediate revisions.

- An indefinite perspective for the sustainable development strategy (SDS), even though it has shorter planning horizons.

The seven-year span of the EU budget, embodied in the Multi-annual Financial Framework, sits between the second and third, while more specific strategies for, for example, energy or environmental action overlap with the third and fourth.

An obvious point of departure is that the long-term transformations of the socio-ecological transition (SET) should emanate from the indefinite SDS, suggesting that it should set out key strategic orientations consistent with such transformations. Such an approach would establish thematic priorities at the EU level, which could then be required elements of all other initiatives in much the same as the single market is in virtually all economic policy initiatives today.

10.2.1 Scenarios

The assumptions and relationships behind the projections presented in chapter 2 for the 'friendly' and 'tough' scenarios highlight many of the areas in which timely and appropriate policy action can be expected to make a significant difference to outcomes. While the numbers attached to the projections have to be interpreted with considerable caution, not least because they assume that there will not be a substantial policy response, the differences between the scenarios show what is at stake.

A decline in EU labour supply is projected under both the 'friendly' and 'tough' scenarios, with only a handful of exceptions among the member states. Under the 'tough' scenario, the decrease, not surprisingly, is larger. Although overall population is expected to continue rising, the explanation is its age profile. This carries the obvious policy implication that a concentration on skills and on the employment rate will be required to offset the head count loss in maintaining the output from labour. Upward pressure on wages is probable and would be expected to widen the gap between skilled and unskilled. The intriguing finding that the increase in wages is likely to offset at least part of the negative effect on the income tax base from a lower number of taxpayers is important for policy. It implies that fears for the sustainability of welfare systems may be unjustified. However, if global competition results in a downward pressure on wages, these relatively favourable interpretations may not be realisable.

Common features of the two scenarios include:

- More heavily constrained public finances will constrain spending on social investment and could reduce employment in non-market services.

- Private services sectors will be where the greatest job creation takes place.

- A sizeable increase in employment in construction is explained partly by investment in renovating housing, linked to energy savings.

- In the decade prior to the crisis, the tradables sectors (using the definition put forward in chapter 3) shed just under four million jobs in the EU, while jobs in non-tradables grew by 27 million, one third in the non-market services and two thirds in the various private services and construction sectors considered to be non-tradable.

- Job losses in tradables have been observed in most member states, whereas all saw job creation in non-tradables.

There is a clear distinction between high- and low-skilled occupations. Jobs have consistently been lost in low-skilled occupations in the tradables sector, but high-skilled workers fare better. Low-skilled workers are better protected in the non-tradables sector, but are more at risk than in the past. It is in the highly skilled occupations in non-tradables that the main net job creation occurs, especially after 2020 when the pre-crisis trend is restored. These projections are based solely on the qualifications of workers rather than the tasks they undertake, and other evidence suggests that non-routine tasks in low-skilled occupations may have better prospects, as will the highly skilled working in areas requiring application of knowledge.

Policy issues that arise include the likelihood of under-utilisation of skills, and the difficult question of how much investment in human capital can be justified and what form the investment should take. There is an apparent paradox that although high-skilled non-tradables is the major source of employment growth, the unemployment rate in this area could increase. The projections use a broad-brush approach, which cannot readily signal whether it is better to favour lifelong learning or perseverance with the more intensive efforts to increase tertiary education. But if the issue is examined purely from the perspective of employability (as opposed to other, entirely reasonable, rationales for education such as social or cultural aims), there is likely to be an awkward debate about how much to invest in building up human capital that is then under-used.

Overall, the 'tough' scenario signals the magnitude of the challenges policy-makers have to face by 2030 if decidedly negative trends are to be arrested. The dangers of self-reinforcing processes are acute. A shrinking labour supply lowers growth potential and, by accentuating the squeeze on public finances, would mean that by 2030 total public consumption is over 15% lower than in the 'friendly' scenario. This reduction substantially reduces the scope for employment creation in publicly funded care services, which would detract from the response to ageing of the population.

10.2.2 Key messages for policy-makers

At the EU level

- The contrast between the 'friendly' and 'tough' scenarios offers clues to the domains in which appropriate policy action can render the 'friendly' more likely than the 'tough'. However, the many subtle links between effects have to be taken into account.

- While there is a place for common EU policies, differentiated labour supply policies will be needed, although with the shared objective of ensuring that the number of economically active persons is maximised. This implies that, in formulating future strategies and coordination mechanisms, the EU will have to be less top-down in its guidelines, targets and recommendations.

- Given the uncertain timing of different effects, a strategic approach will require timely interventions based on the identification of milestones.

At the national level

- Policies towards labour supply will have to take account of the different determinants highlighted in the NEUJOBS analyses.

- The effect of the interplay between labour supply and growth on wages can be expected to have substantial, if not always predictable, distributive consequences that will need to be reflected in tax systems.

- Because of decreased public consumption, foreseen to be more pronounced in the 'tough' scenario because of lower public revenues (despite some respite from rises in wages that would increase the yield in some member states – such as Germany – from income taxes), there are likely to be fewer public jobs, including in the social services of general interest.

- To the extent that private provision replaces public provision of certain social services, there will be equity challenges for governments to confront, as well as whether or not the jobs are created.

10.3 Energy policy in anticipation of a socio-ecological transition

From a policy perspective, the awkward reality of meeting the challenges of climate change and the exhaustion of resources such as fossil fuels is that it is very difficult to reconcile the certainty that something will have to be done, at some stage, with the knowledge that it is a something that today's leaders can neglect or postpone indefinitely without really incurring a political cost. Moreover, as the analysis in chapter 2 makes clear, the uncertainty about the timing of a socio-ecological transition raises a number of questions about the sequencing of the transition and the incidence over time of different sorts of impacts.

Clearly, fossil fuel use will not stop overnight; indeed, the advent of fracking and the switch from oil towards gas to satisfy various forms of energy demand is itself a transition of some consequence and may possibly be a socio-ecological transition in its own right. Equally, the increasingly toxic atmospheric conditions in emerging economies (notably China, now the world's biggest emitter of CO_2) will provide an impetus towards acceleration of the search for alternatives to fossil fuels. For the EU, which has tried to take a lead in curbing greenhouse gas (GHG) emissions, these dilemmas are accentuated by often contrary attitudes and actions in other parts of the world, and a narrative that suggests that if the EU unilaterally raises energy prices or embarks on a huge investment effort it will inflict competitive damage on itself in global markets.

There are intriguing and complex views in the SET literature summarised in chapter 4 on the nature of work and on how a transition from fossil fuels will affect jobs. Even the basic question of whether energy substitutes for labour or facilitates its more intensive use (as occurred in the coal regime, but not in the oil regime) cannot be convincingly resolved. However, there can be little doubt, based on historical analysis, that a socio-ecological transition will have a profoundly disruptive effect on established patterns of work and life. In this regard, much of the current debate around 'green' jobs, usually discussed in relation to the possible emergence in the short term of new sectors of activity associated with environmental policies, is tangential to the probable long-run consequences.

In Figure 4.5 of chapter 4, the authors set out what they describe as an "admittedly highly speculative" set of predictions about what a transition away from fossil fuels will entail, especially for employment. A parallel speculation on what these predictions might imply for policy is warranted, focusing especially on what would be a decisive break with the past rather than the extension of an existing trend.

Starting with the changes in the energy market, a switch to renewables and the increase in the share of electricity in final demand are, in many respects, two sides of the same coin. They will require a large investment effort, both to construct the production facilities and to develop the associated distribution facilities. It follows that there is likely to be an extended period of increased demand for construction and related jobs – one definition of 'green' jobs. However, the Fischer-Kowalski and Haas analysis, though by no means dismissive of such green jobs, points to more profound changes. They argue that the higher energy prices that they judge to be inevitable could reverse the substitution of human energy by mechanical energy, leading to more jobs requiring physical input.

Higher energy prices have a number of other likely implications. A first is income distribution, which may be adversely affected by a trend that is likely to aggravate fuel poverty. Energy demand is relatively income inelastic, so that higher prices will consume a bigger share of the budgets of poor households. There are obvious policy options in subsidies and tax policies. In Europe, fuel for motor vehicles is highly taxed (in contrast to, notably, North America) and there are more piecemeal arrangements for lead-in tariffs or other forms of cross-subsidy for renewables. Electric cars already receive favourable tax treatment, as do low emission vehicles in several member states, but as Fischer-Kowalski and Haas emphasise, there may be a countervailing need to increase taxes on resources to allow for reduced taxes on labour.

If, as they argue, there is wage convergence between the poorer and richer parts of the world, there may be some return of activities previously outsourced to low-wage countries, and perhaps a greater priority to recycling and repair, rather than the throw-away consumer society of the recent decades. Given an ageing population, there will also be a need for what they describe as "empathy'" jobs in the care sector. There are, however, striking imponderables in the analysis around the future trend of other private services and the likely impact of new bio-technologies and next-generation ICT.

Hao and van Ark, in an intriguing investigation of the knowledge economy that is expected to grow relatively in coming decades, find that energy intensity is lower when there is higher investment in the intangibles (such as design, software within ICT, branding or organisational innovation).[8] By contrast, higher investment in physical capital is associated with an increase in the energy intensity of the economy. While not entirely surprising, since the 'softer' investments rely on brain-power rather than physical power, a policy implication is that the very definition of investment as gross fixed capital investment needs rethinking. Alongside the continuing shift towards services that tend, in any case, to be less energy intensive, these findings suggest – but as the authors stress, do not prove – that the shift to the knowledge economy is part of a changing pattern of energy use. They also reiterate a point raised in chapter 3 of this book, namely that the changing global value chain, in which more of the energy-intensive stages of production are undertaken by emerging economies, means that the energy demand is diverted rather than reduced.

But there is also a macroeconomic dimension to energy provision that could affect jobs. The dramatic increase in domestic gas production in the US is not only having significant geo-political effects, but has also resulted in lower prices, which, in turn, feed into effects on competitiveness. Although there is disagreement about whether the calculations take sufficient account of indirect energy costs (and the resulting emissions), burning gas is thermally more efficient,[9] as can be seen from Table 10.1. It is, therefore, plausible that the fossil fuel era will be substantially extended, even if the long-term logic remains that it must end. Already, there are indications that the European policy response is both to try to emulate the US in developing fracking and to water down ambitions for energy transformation targets for the 2030 horizon.

Table 10.1 Carbon dioxide emissions per kilowatt/hour of electricity generated (grams/KwH), average 2008-10

	Coal and peat	Oil	Natural gas	TOTAL
World	971	779	450	573
EU27, of which:	920	709	361	442
Highest	*1266 (BE)*	*1100 (CZ)*	*435 (FR)*	*1059 (EE)*
Lowest	*658 (DK)*	*456 (FI)*	*211 (SE)*	*22 (SE)*
US	907	709	405	528

Source: International Energy Agency (2012).

10.3.1 The evolving EU policy position

The Climate Change White Paper launched on 22 January 2014 exposes some of the tensions at the heart of policy-making on climate change and energy-use transformation.[10] Two significant proposals are to end the insistence on GHG reductions from the transport sector after 2020 and to move from national targets for GHG to a single EU-wide target.

Transport has been subject to the fuel quality directive, which would have favoured supposedly cleaner options such as biofuels. Some environmental NGOs argue that biofuels are of dubious value because they have a damaging effect on CO_2 absorption (not to mention bio-diversity) through clearance of rain forests or other habitats to provide land for the fuel crops. Even so, the danger is that what could be a significant industry will be undermined by uncertainty about the EU's future policy stance. According to Epure, the trade association of the renewable ethanol industry, the industry currently supports 70,000 jobs (including indirect jobs), a figure that could grow to 200,000 by 2020, many of which are in poorer rural areas. If EU policy undermines incentives for producers, these jobs could be at risk. As explained by its Secretary General, Rob Vierhout:[11]

> The Commission has failed in its first test to provide a clear signal to investors that there will be a clear policy framework for sustainable biofuels in Europe after 2020. This proposal is short-sighted; the only winner will be the fossil fuel industry.

While such claims always have to be looked at with care to separate fact from sectoral interests, the wider policy question is how policy should deal with the undoubted tensions. Much of the drive for fracking is to tap into a fuel source that, while manifestly still emitting GHG, does so on a lower scale and will be conducive to improved European competitiveness because it is a less costly alternative.

As the rapid increase in US gas production from fracking shows, any long-range policy position is affected by the unexpected, including the sudden German rejection of nuclear power after Fukushima. In this vein, a NEUJOBS report by Behrens et al. draws attention to the sheer uncertainty around two of the main potential influences on the EU energy market, nuclear generation of electricity and the prospects for carbon capture and storage.[12] Nevertheless, they are clear that reducing GHG emissions by 20% by 2020 and by up to 80% by 2050 is feasible "using currently known technologies". This is a finding with important policy consequences, because it puts the onus on policy-makers to consider whether the (often difficult) policy choices needed should be made, but debunks suggestions that they are unrealistic.

A frequently heard message from business is that regulatory and policy certainty is essential to justify some of the very long-range investment projects that will be required. They also emphasise that cutting demand from energy uses for which the limits of decarbonisation are close to being reached is essential for the overall targets to be attainable. From a policy perspective, incentives will have to be aligned appropriately by finding price mechanisms that stimulate savings and regulatory interventions – whether in the form of standards or controls – that deter energy-intensive processes.

Behrens et al. also note pronounced differences between eastern and western Europe that invite policy responses. Some are already in the pipeline through the amendments to the regulations for Cohesion Policy, but as with other instruments of governance (including the possibility of a contractual approach between the member-state and the EU level), the case for creative forms of conditionality will strengthen.

10.3.2 Key messages for policy-makers

At the EU level

- A switch away from fossil fuels will eventually happen and will have profound ramifications for consumption, production, employment and many facets of the organisation of society.

- However, the timing of different stages of the transition is unpredictable and the scope for policy actors to steer the process is uncertain, not least because some effects will happen irrespective of policy input. In the Rumsfeld lexicon, it is an 'unknown known', yet also one for which many elements are reasonably well known and for which many of the consequences can be anticipated.

- Long-term energy transformations should be central to a revamped Sustainable Development Strategy, applicable over an indefinite time horizon, which should set out key strategic orientations consistent with such transformations.

- Such an approach would establish thematic priorities at the EU level, which could then become required transversal elements of all other policy initiatives, in much the same as the single market is in virtually every economic policy initiative today.

- Although a paradigm shift is probably occurring, it will be slow and subject to uncertainty about what will result. A key inference from the 'tough' scenario is that it restricts the options for the EU, with only the sustainability transformation option offering favourable outcomes.

At the national level

- Policy decisions will have to be made concerning both the mitigation of, and adaptation to, the effects of climate change and energy, as well as the balance between the two approaches and the sequencing of policy responses.

- New distributive challenges will derive from rising energy prices and from the need to invest in ecologically sustainable forms of transport and housing, but will need to be mediated at national level.

- Regulatory certainty greatly increases the willingness of business to invest in long-term projects, including transformative ones.

10.4 Influences on the labour market

While some of the longer-term consequences of a socio-ecological transition are bound to be more speculative, there are other influences on the labour market that could have effects in the medium term. Even here, however, surprises cannot be discounted.

10.4.1 Workplace innovation

The information brought together in chapter 6 on workplace innovation suggests that wide ranging evolutionary changes are taking place, but also that there are great disparities among the member states for which relevant statistics can be found. Not surprisingly, it is the Nordic countries that are in the lead in many of the innovations and, in a disappointingly familiar dichotomy, the southern European countries that show the lowest propensity for workplace innovation.

Two distinct, but connected policy issues arise. The first is how, assuming the policy direction taken by the lead countries is a desirable one, to ensure greater diffusion of the practices in question to the laggards. The second is whether there are particular workplace innovations that ought to be given priority, for example in the targets and policy packages associated with EU strategies (notably Europe 2020 or the Euro Plus Pact). The particularly skewed picture for teleworking reveals a nine-fold difference between the countries with the lowest rates (Italy and Bulgaria) and Denmark, where 36% of workers telecommute at least some of the time. Slovenia and the Baltic countries stand out as exceptions. As a practice with considerable potential to curb transport-associated energy use, the finding that the overall EU rate of telecommuting was just 12% in 2010 raises an intriguing policy question of whether it is a trend that may accelerate or one that will fail to do so. The research reveals a further twist to this puzzle, namely why, despite the advances in enabling technologies, there was so little change in the decade from 2000 to 2010.

Workplace innovation can contribute both to job satisfaction and, thus, to job quality from the perspective of the worker, as well as to productivity, making it also attractive to employers. However, it is not all one-way traffic, as some workplace innovations place added pressures on workers, adding to stress or insecurity. Telecommuting, for instance, has been found to increase hours worked, disrupting the work-life balance.

The public sector in many countries is a laggard, yet as public administrations come under ever-increasing pressure to deliver better value for money, there are opportunities for it to lead. In many countries today, shortcomings in public administration are being identified as more than just profligacy, suggesting that more intense reform of management practices may be demanded. Moreover, the public sector has the ability to experiment. An example of a well-conceived means of doing so is the TEKES programme in Finland, described in chapter 6.

What are the regulatory barriers to workplace innovation and are they being addressed? Some forms of regulation could make it harder to adopt more innovative approaches, especially if there is a strongly entrenched view on issues such as hours of work. The phrase 'atypical' is commonly used to describe labour contracts or working arrangements that depart from a national norm, whether it is the standard working week, holiday and sick pay entitlement, or some other aspect of working conditions. It has to be recalled, however, that such standards are themselves the result of complex settlements and that breaking away from them will be contentious. Policy-makers therefore have to reconcile a difficult tension between innovation and damaging disruption when contemplating changes to labour market regulation.

10.4.2 Labour market institutions

Among the crucial objectives that an ideal set-up of labour market institution should ensure are good matching between labour supply and demand, resilience in maintaining employment levels (especially in periods of weak aggregate demand), the capacity to accommodate new entrants, protecting wage income, and inclusiveness. However, in assessing the policy impact of competing configurations of the different facets of labour market governance, it quickly becomes evident that some of the more simplistic readings of the link from particular arrangements to outcomes are poorly conceptualised.

For example, mismatches occur for a variety of reasons and are not always amenable to solutions for migrants; similarly, the unemployment rate, whether in total or for target groups in the labour force, is not the only relevant test of whether the institutional mix has the right aims in a system in transition. These aims are, in part, captured in measures such as EPL (employment protection legislation related to preserving employment), the replacement rate of unemployment benefit, and job promoting and activation policies, but a deeper understanding is required to steer policy in the right directions. The material presented in chapter 9 focuses on the workings of the institutional arrangements and looks at the various dimensions separately, not their interrelationships. To this extent, it is not orientated towards outcomes, although this is an obvious policy concern. Among the policy conclusions that can be inferred from the evidence reviewed, the following are noteworthy:

- There is a general downward trend in EPL, although Poland is an exception, but this raises questions of whether it matters.

- The nature of EPL is critical and is not necessarily captured by single measures. There are large variations in the extent to which protection is afforded to temporary as opposed to permanent workers.

- Unemployment replacement rates vary hugely, differing by a factor of four for single workers, but have tended to be quite stable over time – arguably reflecting the long-run social settlements in each member state.

- Trends in labour market policy spending are varied, with some of those spending most seeing a decline during the 2000s. This has to be seen in the context of unemployment and labour market turnover rates, as well as (more recently) the pressures on public finances.

- The lack of evidence of a convergence towards a single model is hardly surprising and it may be a chimera to expect it. Even within the CEE, where most systems are insurance-based, they are characterised by extensive national differences that make a simple categorisation implausible.

There is some support for the proposition that tougher EPL is inimical to innovation, although there is a need to consider what the mechanisms are, and not just rely on aggregate correlation. More detailed findings suggest that EPL is at most a second-order factor in relation to innovation and thus that a crude policy prescription of easing rigidities in the labour market is unlikely to be fruitful. Nevertheless, there is some evidence that the wrong sorts of labour market institutions deter innovation; this may not be very surprising, but even negative policy implications have value in identifying what to avoid.

To the extent that replacement rates and EPL are substitutes, a policy issue arises around which is the preferable route. This concerns social risk management and recalls the policy debates of the early 2000s about the 'costs of non-social policy' in which it was argued that simplistic cuts in social provisions would often have damaging indirect consequences that negated the presumed benefits. Questions for policy-makers include whether the evolution of the flexicurity model takes sufficient note of these considerations and whether the policy prescriptions advanced at the EU level suit the exigencies and institutional mix of different member states.

10.4.3 Job quality

Job quality has been a persistent, though often rather oblique component of successive iterations of EU employment strategies since coming to prominence at the Essen European Council in 1994. It has been both a horizontal objective and one that has been the subject of specific guidelines or policy measures. A consistent finding is that where it is job quantity or quality, the former tends to win.

Yet as Kovács argues in chapter 5, labour law does not directly involve itself in job quality. What the research stresses is the often slow pace of change and the fact that it is path-dependent. Reforming governments from one end of the political spectrum may make far-reaching changes, but if they are succeeded by an opposition from the other end of the spectrum, the inclination may be more to mitigate the reforms at the margins, rather than reverse them.

There is considerable ambiguity around what is meant by job quality, with a range of expressions employed almost as synonyms in many member states. This ambiguity has two opposed implications for policy. On the one hand, it allows a fair degree of interpretation to be introduced, enabling policy-makers to tailor policy measures as well as the terms used in national debates to respect national sensitivities. On the other, it can mean that an ostensibly common EU policy or approach to employment principles can be undermined, although it may be that even if this happens, it does not matter much. Where language can matter is when it pushes policy-making systematically in one direction rather than another, as may be the case in the balance between flexibility and security, as suggested in chapter 5.

Some forms of flexibility do confer greater rather than lesser security on the individual, for example by fitting better with the needs of the employer. Choices around working conditions, acquisition of skills or opportunities for self-fulfilment are means by which security for the individual is enhanced in what can appear to be 'flexibilisation'. Security can, in these circumstances, enhance work-life balance.

10.4.4 Key messages for policy-makers

At the EU level

- The EU level can fulfil a vital cognitive role by identifying and diffusing good practices and facilitating the refinement of innovative or experimental policy approaches.

- In its governance processes, notably the annual cycle around the European semester and the country-specific recommendations, the Commission and the Council should give more emphasis to medium- and long-run objectives for labour market institutions, including by proposing milestones for their evolution.

- Workplace innovation has the potential to unlock latent productivity and can also contribute by raising employment rates, but has sometimes been inhibited by concerns about 'atypical' work, which should be allayed.

- The narrative around terms such as job quality has to be carefully framed to enlist support from social partners and other stakeholders.

At the national level

- Careful recalibration of the regulation of the labour market can ensure that it supports rather than inhibits business and public sector innovation, but the choices have to reflect the distinctive institutions and preferences of member states.

- The public sector, both directly as an employer and indirectly (notably through its procurement function), can establish standards and promote workplace innovation.

- Tax systems and ancillary policies such as transport can be used to encourage new working arrangements.

10.5 Skills demand

The varied nature of jobs thought of as low-skilled raises a range of policy issues. Some such jobs are quite demanding in the sense of requiring a range of non-cognitive skills, a finding that has a bearing on what education systems can or should offer. As a result of polarising tendencies in the labour market, more qualified candidates often compete with those with only lower qualifications, increasing the likelihood of mismatch, while possibly also having an adverse effect on social mobility. One issue raised was that this requires attention to be paid to the performance of educational systems, possibly including monitoring them as part of the scorecards used for the macroeconomic imbalances procedure. National differences include yawning gaps in basic ICT skills and capabilities.

The EU lags behind the US in productivity, arguably because of inadequate innovation or and slow integration of ICT.[13] While the gap is a cause for concern, there are 'catch-up' opportunities in enhancing levels of productivity. However, the projections also point to a possible slowing of the creation of service sector jobs in the countries that are obliged to rein in debt (whether private or public) to the greatest extent, mainly in southern Europe. Indeed, under both scenarios, the share of the industrial sector in the economy is projected to rise. This trend may further limit the demand for lower-skilled workers who are already facing a loss of job opportunities from the pressures of globalisation in tradables sectors.

Particularly for the high-skilled, a major policy challenge will be to ensure that there is sufficient demand to accommodate the rising supply of skilled workers. At the same time, sufficiently far-sighted policies have to be put in place to anticipate new or growing demands for particular skills. A tricky question is whether existing categorisations based largely on qualification levels capture what is needed. As the results of a survey conducted by the OECD of adult skills, as part of its Programme for the International Assessment of Adult Competencies (PIAAC), show, there are "serious skills gaps in Europe's labour force", as a consequence of which future growth and competitiveness are at risk.[14] Among the more worrying of the PIAAC findings for the EU countries covered is the relatively high proportion of the EU workforce that is insufficiently equipped with the ICT skills needed to "match the needs of today's changing labour markets". The report notes that such skills are often the subject of continuing education and training, making the outcome more problematic. The diversity in performance among EU member states is highlighted.

While skills are prominent in the Europe 2020 strategy and can be expected to remain so as the new Commission takes office later in 2014, some of the insights from the NEUJOBS research point to a need for careful rethinking of how the skills agenda is taken forward. An obvious, if under-appreciated, policy issue is how to reconcile quantitative targets for skill enhancement with qualitative changes in the mix of skills.

10.5.1 Is education the answer?

The obvious policy solution to a skills deficit is to increase investment in education and to ensure that it is better targeted, although such targeting has to take account of demand. In this regard, Haita et al. find that "the skill-mix demand is very diverse across the countries analysed, implying that there is no universal 'European' demand and that domestic institutions and structures affect how demand for workers in the low- and medium-skilled segments of the labour market is formulated".[15] Even so, they observe that in service occupations employers look for what they refer to as non-cognitive social skills and personal characteristics, but that these requirements are often in addition to formal educational qualifications depending on the national context. To the authors' surprise, Danish employers place much less emphasis on formal education and cognitive skills than do Czech or Irish employers. Their explanation is that Danish employers especially value flexibility, and may have become used to a labour market in which 'flexicurity' principles have become well entrenched.

10.5.2 Key messages for policy-makers

At the EU level

- Despite the shortcomings of existing means of coordinating standards and qualifications across the EU, the objectives remain valid and should be a priority for EU policy.

- The skills gaps revealed by the PIAAC survey are disturbing for a European economy with ambitions to become increasingly specialised in knowledge-intensive activities.

- In the current climate of fiscal austerity, one policy option is the privatisation of some social services of general interest. NEUJOBS research suggests that a possible result of increased private provision of these services could be a downgrading of the skills demanded in the sector. If this happens, there are risks of a decline in the quality of services.

At the national level

- Although human capital enhancement is, rightly, recognised as essential for future competitiveness, there needs to be a national debate about the education model and the other goals of education systems, such as equality.

- Lifelong learning and an enhancement of the scale and quality of tertiary education have to be reinforced, especially in those member states exposed by the research findings as having deficiencies.

- The implications of a hollowing out of the middle of the skills distribution are likely to be profound and will require large-scale rethinking of the role of public policy in facilitating transitions to new occupations.

- A specific concern may be the emergence (and how to forestall it) of low skills equilibria in which employers only demand low skills in certain industries or localities and the resulting effects on worker flexibility and mobility.

10.6 The evolving welfare state

The social investment turn in welfare policies can be seen as a response to the threats to the financial sustainability of social protection systems that weigh too heavily on public finances, but also to the need to rebalance work and welfare in a way that is economically sustainable. In some respects, it is certainties rather than uncertainties that are driving welfare reform, especially demographic trends. Longevity and a reduced fertility rate reshape the age profile of the population, rendering pay-as-you-go arithmetic less sustainable. But there are also uncertainties surrounding, on the one hand, the outlook for altering the employment rates of hitherto under-employed segments of society, and the receptiveness of Europeans to immigration as a means of boosting the working-age population on the other.

10.6.1 Social investment

Social investment can be interpreted both as a means of identifying what should be prominent in the mix of policy measures and as a policy paradigm. The latter implies a rather different stance on what the welfare state's core philosophy is, moving it away from an emphasis on redistribution or insurance against various social risks towards investment in human and social capital. Within this philosophy, some measures, for example most active labour market policies, are readily identifiable as forms of investment, while some which might be classified as having other societal objectives can also be seen as investment; Esping-Andersen portrays family policies in this way.[16]

The analysis by Dräbing in chapter 6 posits three key differences between the social investment approach and what she calls 'passive welfare states', which can be interpreted from a policy standpoint. The first, a focus on societal development, has the clear policy message that dealing with fundamental challenges such as ageing of the population requires a mix of policies to increase productivity and employment rates, especially in segments of the population where economic activity is low. Policy intervention can facilitate this by countering bottlenecks or by rendering social protection systems more supportive of, for example, work-life balance. Second is a focus on human development and endowing individuals with greater capabilities to enable them to enhance their employability in a changing labour market. The third strand of social investment is a focus on diminishing long-term need for support from the welfare state instead of short-term mitigation of risks and needs. Here the policy challenge is to find ways of breaking cycles of deprivation or exclusion in such a way as to reduce the probability of poverty while improving life chances.

For welfare systems in flux and faced with spending constraints, these three facets of social investment link to a range of potential policy orientations:

- Passive income support is not enough and needs to be complemented by active measures to foster connections to the labour market and social inclusion.

- The erosion of skills in periods of recession or weak demand needs to be prevented.

- Welfare systems must be adaptable to new social risks.

New sources of risk or pressure on the welfare state include the interplay between changing household structures and the role of the family in countering social problems.

The trend identified by Dräbing is towards increased expenditure on what she calls capacitating welfare spending relative to compensating outlays. However, she also cites evidence that a change is occurring within the two categories: Sweden, for example has increased spending on childcare services. These findings highlight the fact that change in welfare states is the norm.

The investment focus can be seen as consistent with the contention that employment is the best route out of poverty, with human capital as the key variable. In its idealised form, as explained by Taylor-Gooby, the social investment approach to welfare can bring together economic and social objectives in a self-reinforcing manner.[17] However, social investment is a political as well as a policy challenge, according to Vandenbroucke, Hemerijck and Palier.[18] In calling for a 'social investment pact', they argue that effective social investment for the long term needs to be accompanied by short-term fiscal consolidation, stressing the importance of finding solutions for the unskilled who have the fewest employment opportunities. While not denying the importance of wage moderation and policies to boost competitiveness, they advocate a more complete policy approach that is centred on boosting human capital and social inclusion. In this regard, it is important to recognise the key role that the corporate sector can play in supporting training systems. Some of the largest companies in Europe play a vital role in this respect through their support for apprenticeships.

One phenomenon is that although there some broad changes are taking place, such as the increase in childcare provision, countries differ markedly in whether or not this is at the expense of existing benefits (notably family benefits). Active labour market policy (ALMP) outlays are subject to huge disparities, as shown by the expenditure data assembled by Dräbing, but public funding is only part of the equation and looking only at spending as a proportion of GDP is likely to mean the complementary contribution of appropriate incentives and supportive structures is missed. In policy terms this is tricky terrain, because it can be hard to draw boundaries between solidarity and self-help or between entitlements and responsibilities.

A direct causal link between a social investment approach and 'better' socioeconomic outcomes would be hard to prove, and the analysis in chapter 8 makes no such claim. It is, however, worth reflecting on how a social investment paradigm can become a basis for success. The policy approach encompasses more than just the adoption of specific policies that have 'investment' rather than 'passive support' characteristics, because it also relies on the building of trust and of other appropriate social and institutional features. In some of the Nordic countries, the foundations of contemporary social investment were constructed many decades ago – consider the Rehn-Meidner model in Sweden – and have become defining and, importantly, broadly accepted elements of national societies. They are far from static, and can evolve quite radically if reforming governments come to power or if particular features of the system lose support.

10.6.2 Whatever happened to flexicurity?

In 2007, following publication of a Commission communication, the European Council endorsed the four strands of the flexicurity model as a basis for the development of national systems. These were:

- Promoting greater flexibility in labour market regulation, notably by easing overly restrictive employment protection legislation
- Encouraging human capital development, including through life-long learning
- Adoption of active labour market policies
- Reform of social protection systems

Having been adopted in the 'good times' of 2007 when the focus of labour market policy was on boosting employment rates through activation and enhancing the quality of work, doubts rapidly surfaced about whether flexicurity had any relevance in a world in which unemployment had again become the principal challenge. In short, could flexicurity, as Tangian expressed it, cope with "bad weather"?[19] Trade union representatives have long felt uneasy over flexicurity, often portraying it as a Trojan horse for the deregulation of labour markets.[20] The security dimension of the concept was originally portrayed as being about protecting the worker rather than the job, but for the unions this conception challenged established norms about resisting redundancies or the closure of workplaces.

A qualified answer is offered in work by Mandl and Celikel-Esser, who find enough evidence to show that flexicurity principles have continued to be prominent in the policies that have been developed since the onset of recession, and they conclude that "there is room for flexicurity in economically difficult times".[21] They note, however, that in most of the measures identified as forms of flexicurity, "the concept as such only implicitly deals with maintaining jobs". In practice, this has meant extensive resort to measures that favour internal flexibility within companies and other employing organisations, rather than firing, and it is worth asking whether this finding points to a paradigm shift that can be attributed to the flexicurity model.

It is, in any case, misleading to think of flexicurity as a stable model, and better instead to view it as a set of ideas on how to govern labour market relationships. Thus, in Denmark, there have been many developments in the policies introduced nearly 20 years ago, yet at a procedural level there can be little doubt that the commitment to flexicurity is undiminished. Among the ten Integrated Guidelines for the Europe 2020 Strategy, number 7 can be interpreted as being a rather powerful restatement of flexicurity goals and the wording of the guidelines continues to stress wider social ambitions and not just the dismantling of labour market regulation. Similarly, the tone of the country-specific recommendations addressed to many member states reflects flexicurity aims.

10.6.3 Key messages for policy-makers

At the EU level

- Social investment as a paradigm is expected to be at the core of an EU-wide policy approach to the future of the welfare state (Hemerijck, 2012), but will require further conceptual and practical development.

- Similarly, although flexicurity remains central to the policy model, it will require some updating to take account of the changing labour market of the next 15 years, especially in offering terms and conditions of employment that are flexible from the perspective of the worker.

- Two of the areas in which such development is most needed are devising policies for social integration of immigrants that reflect 'investment' principles, and finding ways to ensure sufficient returns to social investments in segments of the labour market with low employment rates. The EU level is the appropriate one to develop shared strategies for these tasks.

- The EU level can also take the lead in identifying and diffusing innovations in public administration that can diminish dependency on welfare support.

At the national level

- Social investment can mean different things in different national contexts, but the central importance of its 'investment' message has to be stressed and made operational in each member state.

- For the social transitions, likely actions include raising the retirement age, activating groups in the working-age population with low participation rates and rethinking health and care services, but these actions call for differentiated responses, which also reflect national labour market and demographic circumstances.

- Family and work-life balance policies need to evolve to accommodate the changing demographic profiles, with new approaches needed to care for the elderly so as to reconcile increased participation with care obligations.

- Tax and spending systems will need recalibration to ensure that appropriate incentives are in place, both to encourage individuals to invest in themselves and to overcome obstacles to activation.

- Although public funding concerns are an unavoidable factor in reforms of social protection systems, it will be important not to confuse cuts in spending with value for money in making some of the hard choices. In particular, governments have to be prepared to 'spend to gain' where there is evidence that short-term costs can generate long-term savings or much better outcomes.

10.7 Policy implications: Reconciling long-run goals with today's agenda

Achieving long-run transformations when the bulk of the policy incentives are short term will never be easy, and is a fundamental source of uncertainty from a political economy perspective. Such changes need leadership and policy consistency, as well as targeted investment. Although it is unsurprising that the immediacy of crisis management has dominated the policy agenda since 2007, an ensuing question is whether there have been damaging consequences for the EU's longer-term goals.

At the national level one of the more intractable challenges is breaking down resistance to change in such a way as to make implementation credible. Some member states are now at a precarious point where the need for far-reaching reform (not least in the labour market) is acknowledged and pressing, but they lack the political consensus or administrative capability to generate a momentum for change. Fears of a lost generation or of an upsurge in 'hysteresis' cannot easily be dismissed, and the long-term transitions that were set in motion just a few years ago risk being overtaken by short-term priorities. The

NEUJOBS research findings in this book shed light on these issues and identify a number of policy options.

10.7.1 Have long-run sustainability objectives been sidelined?

As recently as 2006, when the EU's Sustainable Development Strategy was re-launched, the social and environmental dimensions of long-run sustainability appeared to have become defining features of the model of economic development espoused by the EU. Moreover, it is prominent as a treaty goal: Article 2 of the Lisbon Treaty sets out the fundamental goals of the Union, and sub-article 3 states that it "shall work for the sustainable development of Europe based on balanced economic growth and price stability, a highly competitive social market economy, aiming at full employment and social progress, and a high level of protection and improvement of the quality of the environment". The fact that sustainable development is first in this list of socio-economic goals suggests that it is the encompassing one.

- Policy message: Long-run transitions are achieved less by a handful of dramatic changes than by an accumulation of smaller steps. For the transition to occur, what matters is the direction set by policy-makers, even if they often have to compromise on the timing or scope of specific measures.

How should sustainability be interpreted for policy purposes when considering the long-run transitions investigated by the NEUJOBS project? The environmental dimension of sustainability is perhaps the most readily understood by the public and politicians alike, because it is easy to explain how a sustainable environment could be threatened by pollution or how emissions affect climate change.

- Policy message: How a socio-ecological transition will unfold and the policy changes needed to make progress have to be convincingly articulated, even if achieving progress is politically tricky and likely to be slow.

Social sustainability is more elusive and often more complex to explain in policy terms. It is associated with watchwords such as opportunity and mobility, as well as the issues that are usually at the forefront of European discourse, notably cohesion, equality, poverty reduction and job quality. Equally, there are risks that, through the combination of external drivers of the sort examined in the NEUJOBS project and ill-judged policies, the social environment might degrade. Such degradation could be shaped by shifts in "a large number of factors, including customs and traditions, culture, spirituality, interpersonal relations and living conditions".[22] What the evidence presented in earlier chapters shows is that there are both direct effects of policy interventions in specific fields, for example in affecting social goals such as work-life balance or equality, and also cumulative and indirect effects from the range of relevant policies.

- Policy message: The interconnections between initiatives in areas such as work-life balance, skill enhancement and social inclusion are often poorly understood, but understanding them is vital for a comprehensive response.

10.7.2 Governance at the EU and national levels

On the face of it, the Europe 2020 slogan of smart, sustainable and inclusive growth implies that sustainability remains central to the EU policy agenda. However, as Diebold observes pointedly: "The EU's sustainability programs are currently paper tigers which have little influence on the course of current political decision-making".[23] She argues that the ambitions in the EU sustainable development strategy – social as well as environmental – were well conceived, but have simply been overtaken by events.

- Policy message: In its governance processes, notably the annual cycle around the European semester and the country-specific recommendations, the Commission and the Council should give more emphasis to medium- and long-run objectives for labour market institutions, including the setting of milestones for their evolution.

The EU lacks clout in many policy areas germane to the skills and societal transitions discussed in this book and it remains the case in the EU that most policies are predominantly reserved for national (or lower tier) policy-makers. Since the late 1990s, when the European Employment Strategy was launched, mutual learning has been one way out of this dilemma, under the umbrella of the open method of coordination (OMC), a mode of governance that has been more criticised than applauded.

- Policy message: The cognitive, deliberative and steering impacts of the OMC should not be too glibly dismissed and, with some fresh approaches, can be a valuable policy tool.

Inevitable disputes over burden-sharing – among member states or between the EU and other parts of the world, as well as between generations, different interests or types of households – are bound to compound the difficulties. These and other political economy factors need to be taken into account when ambitious policy goals are established, because (as has been shown repeatedly in the struggle to resolve the euro crisis) it is typically easier to say "no" than "yes" when the latter means you might have to pay upfront.

- Policy message: Socio-ecological transition is a common concern, so that it is vital to stress the collective costs and benefits of policy action and to recognise that collective long-term gains will often exceed short-term cost savings. An implication is that policy-makers should consider a collective discount rate for assessing such long-term gains.

Being 'pro-green' has become part of the brand identity of the EU, so that even though the EU's performance in promoting ecological sustainability may fall short of its aspirations, it is still a potent legitimating narrative.[24] Yet the apparent backsliding on climate change targets, together with the new, harsher realities of the post-crisis context, make it hard to claim that it can become the defining narrative for the EU in the period to 2025. Similarly, in relation to societal change, established features of the European social model have been openly challenged, rendering it less persuasive as a defining policy orientation. However, many of the underlying SET trends are inexorable and have to feed into evolving European norms for a sustainable future.

- Policy message: Many of the policy choices implicit in the NEUJOBS transitions will be disruptive and costly for some stakeholders, even though they are likely to be unavoidable. Governments and leaders will have to consider how to defend such choices and to adopt appropriate communication strategies for this purpose.

Overall, although there is a discernible shift towards social investment affecting some of the policy areas on which NEUJOBS focuses, the diversity across Europe is striking. A resulting policy question is whether this matters and, if so, what should be done over a ten to fifteen year horizon to recast welfare states. There are EU level and national level answers to this question. For the EU level, social policy presents the dilemma that its formal competence is limited by the Treaty and nearly all the levers of policy are at the national (or in some cases, sub-national) level, so that its scope for intervention is heavily circumscribed.

- Policy message: Social investment as a paradigm is expected to be at the core of an EU-wide policy approach to the future of the welfare state, but will require further conceptual and practical development.

- Policy message: As shown by the negative collective effects of procrastination in dealing with various effects of the crisis, closer policy coordination is required, leading to an uncomfortable tension between tiers of government. Policies that foster trust and social cohesion can contribute to a more effective social investment mode.

Moreover, the agenda focusing on skills and flexicurity remains a significant part of the policy mix emanating at the EU level and embodied in the semester and Europe 2020 processes, as well as in the macroeconomic adjustment packages for member states receiving financial assistance. At times, too, the EU level can help in a somewhat Machiavellian sense by being blamed, allowing governments that struggle to overcome the objections of vested interests to play the 'Brussels demands' card. Part of the story should be about identifying good practice, but the scope for the EU level to promote experimentation should also be acknowledged. Innovative policies can emerge from local initiatives, which then require adaptation to work elsewhere. The EU level can be the source of funding for this purpose, but also has to accept that experiments can fail, so that some tolerance of unsuccessful policies has to be countenanced, rather than condemned as 'bad' spending.

- Policy message: In spite of the criticisms sometimes levelled at soft modes of coordination in the EU, it is a governance mode that will remain important in diffusing good practice. However, more should be done to make what is discussed and analysed at the EU level relevant at the operational level in member states.

A socio-ecological transition needs targets and indicators for monitoring progress, but also has to rethink what is being measured. The Stiglitz Commission made the emphatic point that "it has long been clear that GDP is an inadequate metric to gauge well-being over time particularly in its economic, environmental, and social dimensions, some aspects of which are often referred to as *sustainability*".[25] One of the key distinctions that the Stiglitz Commission stresses is between current well-being and whether that well-being can be sustained over time.

- Policy message: Fresh thought is required on the indicators and milestones used to monitor long-term transitions.

10.7.3 Dealing with the political challenges

For some of the countries examined in the NEUJOBS research, achieving transformations consistent with the long-run transitions at the heart of the project will be a daunting challenge. Where they lag behind on skills or on boosting the share of renewables in energy supply, there is plainly no overnight fix, nor is there an easy solution to paying for the necessary investments. A political challenge for those governments that have low social investment is to examine what they forgo by not changing and thus to revisit the bases of their welfare states. But governments also need to be alert to some of the direct and indirect consequences of SET, some of which are distributive while others are allocative in nature. Among the many policy issues that emerge from earlier chapters are:

- How to offset potential competitive vulnerabilities to rising energy prices or to more binding restrictions on resource use for businesses.

- Fuel poverty and its effects on inequality could be a significant policy issue: there is a strong regressive effect from rising fuel prices insofar as they constitute unavoidable expenditure.

- How to re-orientate the Cohesion Policy to reflect the adverse effects of territorial polarisation in its diverse forms.

- Inter-country and intra country considerations linked to polarisation, such as young/old, dynamic/static and dependent/not, although there may be win-win outcomes for regions able to seize the opportunities for new activities.

- Why has ICT not (or not yet) been a countervailing force?

- How to balance and distribute labour demand and supply in an era where there are systematic (and polarising) influences on worker location.

- What relationship should SET have to the reform of welfare provisions?

In some member states – Italy being a good example – the combination of slow growth, over-stretched public finances and an extended list of structural flaws does not augur well for a shift of gear, but could be partly offset in two ways. First, because public policy will have to do more with fewer resources, careful sequencing of policy measures will be essential. While some structural changes incur unavoidable upfront costs for the public finances (pension reform being a prime example), many of the more acute problems require legislative or cultural changes or a new approach to public management. An early emphasis on such measures, though politically difficult, could be highly cost effective.

A second orientation would be to favour policy interventions able to contribute to two (or better still, more) policy objectives. For example, substituting (so-called 'Pigouvian') environmental taxes for taxes on labour eases the pressure on labour costs and helps to deter polluting behaviour. The advantages of such 'double dividend' policies may be self-evident, but they are rarely emphasised and often only hinted at obliquely in strategy documents.

- A key policy conclusion is the unsurprising, but still important, one that the relationship between labour market institutions and the behaviour of stakeholders is complex, implying that simplistic policies (whether neo-liberal or the contrary) are likely to be unhelpful. There is also a strong risk of either unintended consequences or outcomes that satisfy one set of goals or normative considerations at the expense of another. The reform agenda therefore needs to be sensitive to such tensions.

Another crucial policy conclusion is that a roadmap is vital and that the EU level of governance has a particular responsibility to stand as far as possible above the fray in this regard. Strategies such as Europe 2020, or those geared towards sustainable development or recasting energy policy, can, in principle, fulfil the required governance function. But they can only make a telling contribution if they are pursued robustly, seen as politically salient and shown to make a difference to citizens. Too often, however, the EU's well-intentioned policy interventions fall short of meeting these criteria. This highlights the fundamental political challenge facing the EU and its institutions in responding to all of the NEUJOBS transitions: it has to show not just that it has viable answers, but that it is a relevant actor in pursuing them. As Hall reminds us, enabling major transformations requires an alignment of interests, creativity and political impetus, so that '"it should not surprise us that a new paradigm has not yet emerged. Such processes take time."[26] There is time, but what emerges from much of the research reported in this book is that the clock is ticking and that timely policy interventions are needed.

Bibliography

Auer, P. (2010), "What's in a name? The rise (and fall?) of flexicurity", *Journal of Industrial Relations* 52, pp. 371-386.

Begg, I. (2013), "Are better defined rules enough? An assessment of the post-crisis reforms of the governance of EMU", *Transfer*, Vol. 19, No. 1, pp. 49-62.

Belke, A. (2013), "Towards a genuine economic and monetary union: comments on a roadmap", *Politics and Governance,* Vol. 1, No. 1, pp. 48-65.

Behrens, A., C. Coulie and J. Teusch (2013), "The potential evolution of the European energy system until 2020 and 2050", NEUJOBS State of the Art Report No. D11.1 (www.neujobs.eu).

European Commission (2012), "A Blueprint for a Deep and Genuine Economic and Monetary Union: Launching a European Debate", COM(2012) 777 final, 28 November, Brussels.

_____ (2013a), "Labour market Developments in Europe 2013", *European Economy* 6/2013, Brussels.

_____ (2013b), *Survey of Adult Skills (PIAAC): Implications for Education and Training Policies in Europe*, Brussels: European Commission.

_____ **(2014),** "A policy framework for climate and energy in the period from 2020 to 2030", COM(2014) 015 final, 22 January, Brussels.

Crouch, C. (2008), "What will follow the demise of privatised Keynesianism?", *Political Quarterly,* Vol. 80, No. S1, pp. 476-487.

Darvas, Z. and S. Merler (2013), "The European Central Bank in the Age of Banking Union", Bruegel Policy Contribution No. 2013/13, Bruegel, Brussels.

Dervis, K. et al. (2013), *Greek Myths and Reality*, Washington, DC: Brookings and ELIAMEP (www.brookings.edu/research/papers/2013/08/06-greece-recovery-dervis).

Diebold, C. (2013), "Europe's sustainability strategy – a casualty of the euro crisis or an ambitious restart?", Bertelsmann Stiftung Policy Brief No. 2013/06, Gütersloh, Germany.

Esping-Andersen, G. (2009), *The Incomplete Revolution: Adapting to Women's New Roles*, Cambridge: Polity.

Hall, P.A. (ed.) (1989), *The Political Power of Economic Ideas*, Princeton, NJ: Princeton University Press.

_____ (1993), "Policy Paradigms, Social Learning and the State: The Case of Economic Policy-making in Britain", *Comparative Politics*, Vol. 25, No. 3, pp. 275-296.

_____ (2013), "Brother can you paradigm?", *Governance*, Vol. 26, No .2, pp. 189-192.

Haita, C., L. Kurecova, M. Beblavý and A.-E. Thum (2013), "Demand for low- and medium-skilled workers across Europe: Between formal qualifications and non-cognitive skills", NEUJOBS Working Paper No. 4.3.3 (www.neujobs.eu).

Hao, J.X. and B. van Ark (2013), "Intangible investment and the intensity of energy use", NEUJOBS Working Paper No. 3.4 (www.neujobs.eu).

Hemerijck, A. (2012), *Changing Welfare States*, Oxford: Oxford University Press.

Hooghe, L. and G. Marks (2001), *Multi-level Governance and European Integration*, Lanham, MD: Rowman and Littlefield.

International Energy Agency (2012), *CO_2 Emissions from Fuel Combustion (Highlights) 2012 Edition*, Paris: IEA.

Jorgensen, H. (2011), "Danish 'flexicurity' in crisis – or just stress-tested by the crisis?", Friedrich Ebert Stiftung International Policy Analysis, Bonn.

Koster, F., J. McQuinn, I. Siedschlag and O. van Vliet (2011), "Labour market models in the EU", NEUJOBS Special Report No. 1 (www.neujobs.eu).

Lenschow, A. and C. Sprungk (2010), "The myth of a green Europe", *Journal of Common Market Studies*, Vol. 48, No. 1, pp. 133-154.

Lisbon Council (2013), *The 2013 Euro Plus Monitor: From Pain to Gain*, Brussels: Lisbon Council.

Mandl, I. and F. Celikel-Esser (2012), "The Second Phase of Flexicurity: An Analysis of Practices and Policies in the Member States", Foundation for the Improvement of Living and Working Conditions, Dublin.

Pawlowski, A. (2008), "How many dimensions does sustainable development have?", *Sustainable Development*, Vol. 16, No. 2, pp. 81–90.

Stiglitz, J., A. Sen and J.-P. Fitoussi (2009), *Report by the Commission on the Measurement of Economic Performance and Social Progress*, Commission on the Measurement of Economic Performance and Social Progress.

Tangian, A. (2010), "Not for bad weather: Flexicurity challenged by the crisis", Policy Brief No. 03/2010, European Trade Union Institute, Brussels.

Taylor-Gooby, P. (2008), "The new welfare state settlement in Europe", *European Societies*, Vol. 10, No. 1, pp. 3-24.

Tros, F. (2012), "Flexicurity in Europe: Can it survive a double crisis?", paper presented at the ILERA World Congress, International Labour and Employment Relations Association, Philadelphia, PA, 2-5 July.

van Ark, B., M. O'Mahony and M. Timmer (2008), "The productivity Gap between Europe and the United States: Trends and Causes", *Journal of Economic Perspectives*, Vol. 22, No. 1, pp. 25-44.

Vandenbroucke, F., A. Hemerijck and B. Palier (2011), "The EU needs a social investment pact", Opinion Paper No. 5/2011, Observatoire Social Européen, Brussels.

Notes

[1] European Commission (2013a).

[2] Begg (2013); Belke (2013).

[3] Dervis et al. (2013).

[4] European Commission (2012).

[5] Lisbon Council (2013).

[6] Hall (1993).

[7] Hall (2013, p. 191).

[8] Hao and van Ark (2013).

[9] International Energy Agency (2012).

[10] European Commission (2014).

[11] Press release, 23 January 2013 (http://www.epure.org/).

[12] Behrens et al. (2013).

[13] van Ark et al. (2008).

[14] European Commission (2013b).

[15] Haita et al. (2013).

[16] Esping-Andersen (2009).

[17] Taylor-Gooby (2008).

[18] Vandenbroucke et al. (2011).

[19] Tangian (2010).

[20] Auer (2010).

[21] Mandl and Celikel-Esser (2012, p. 73).

[22] Pawlowski (2008, p. 83).

[23] Diebold (2013, p. 5).

[24] Lenschow and Sprungk (2010).

[25] Stiglitz et al. (2009, p. 8).

[26] Hall (2013, p. 192).

LIST OF ABBREVIATIONS

ALMP   active labour market policy
BMR   basic metabolic rate
CCS   carbon capture and storage
CEDEFOP   European Centre for the Development of Vocational Training
CEE   central and eastern Europe
ED   excess difference
EPL   employment protection legislation
EROI   energy return on energy investment
ETR   ecological tax reform
ETUC   European Trade Union Confederation
GDP   gross domestic product
GHG   greenhouse gases
HR   human resources
ICT   information and communication technology
ILO   International Labour Organization
ISCED   International Standard Classification of Education
ISCO   International Classification of Occupation
LMP   labour market policy
NIDI   Netherlands Interdisciplinary Demographic Institute
OECD   Organisation for Economic Co-operation and Development
OMC   open method of coordination
PEC   primary energy consumption
PISA   (OECD) Programme for International Student Assessment
SER   standard employment relationship
SET   socio-ecological transition
SDS   sustainable development strategy
SOCX   Social Expenditure Database
SSC   social security contribution
STEM   science, technology, engineering and mathematics
UNEP   United Nations Environment Programme
UNESCO   United Nations Educational, Scientific and Cultural Organization
URR   unemployment replacement rate
WPI   workplace innovation

ABOUT THE EDITORS

Miroslav Beblavý is the Coordinator of NEUJOBS and a Senior Research Fellow at CEPS (since 2009). He is also a Member of the Slovak Parliament (since 2010) and Associate Professor of Public Policy at the Comenius University in Bratislava, Slovakia. Between 2002 and 2006, he was the State Secretary of the Ministry of Labour, Social Affairs and Family in Slovakia. His areas of interest include employment and social policy, education policy, fiscal policy, governance and corruption.

Ilaria Maselli is a researcher in the Economic and Social Welfare Policies unit of the Centre for European Policy Studies (CEPS). Her main area of expertise is the analysis of labour markets, in particular in their interaction with education and technological change. She is also a visiting researcher at the Gokhale Institute of Politics and Economics in Pune, India.

Marcela Veselková is a Senior Research Fellow at Slovak Governance Institute and an Assistant Professor at the Faculty of Social and Economic Sciences, Comenius University in Bratislava. Within NEUJOBS project, she conducted research in the area of educational and social policies, skills formation and job quality.

INDEX